Success!

Gorton D. Harrad

Successful Writers and How They Work

LARSTON D. FARRAR

with some of the World's

Outstanding Professional Authors

Introduces you to

Successful
Writers
and how they work

HAWTHORN BOOKS, INC. PUBLISHERS · NEW YORK

FIRST EDITION

September 1959

Acknowledgments

The Writers Who Helped Me

IN PREPARING to write this book, I contacted writers in various fields, and I take pleasure in listing here those who cooperated with me. I have added some data identifying each as "successful" so you may judge for yourself whether or not they have a right to talk about writing and to discuss their own areas.

There is no implication that these are the only successful writers in the world, the *most* successful, or that any of them has been commissioned by fate to give us the last word about how to work to become successful. But I believe you will agree that they do represent a good cross-section of successful writers at work today and that their thoughts are well worth consideration.

Here are those who helped me to help you:

ALDEN HATCH, biographer of the world's great, including Woodrow Wilson, Franklin Roosevelt, President Eisenhower and Pope Pius XII.

RICHARD GEHMAN, contributing editor of *Cosmopolitan,* fiction writer and author of a recent book on article writing.

NORMAN VINCENT PEALE, newspaper and magazine columnist, author of *The Power of Positive Thinking* and other best-sellers.

HAROLD HELFER, short story and free-lance article writer for publications ranging from *Grit* to *Esquire.*

WILL OURSLER, whose articles are known to millions of readers of *This Week,* and many of whose books have been best-sellers.

HARRY EDWARD NEAL, retired Secret Service agent, story and article writer, and author of *Writing and Selling Fact and Fiction.*

LESTER VELIE, roving editor of *Reader's Digest,* whose articles also have been featured in many magazines.

FRANCES and RICHARD LOCKRIDGE, inveterate writers of detective tales, whose "Mr. and Mrs. North" has become one of the decade's most widely-known television series.

EDISON MARSHALL, known to millions for such best-sellers as *Yankee Pasha, The Vikings,* etc.

DORA ALBERT, magazine article writer.

O. A. BATTISTA, magazine and book writer.

FRED KERNER, author of books, a television series and now editor of Crest Books and Premier Books.

ROBERT PAYNE, author of *The Gold of Troy* and many other books, considered one of the most prolific writers in America.

ABIGAIL VAN BUREN, author of the popular "Dear Abby," daily advice-to-the-lovelorn in hundreds of newspapers.

ROGER BURLINGAME, former magazine editor and author of many books of non-fiction, biography and Americana.

PINKY HERMAN, columnist for *Motion Picture Herald,* and author of scores of hit songs including *It's a Wonderful, Wonderful Feelin'* and *It Must Be Luv.*

HUGH ROSS WILLIAMSON, British playwright, novelist and essayist and formerly editor of *The Bookman,* London.

A. C. SPECTORSKY, associate publisher of *Playboy* author of *The Exurbanites,* and anthologist of many books including *The College Years, The Book of the Sea,* etc.

ERSKINE CALDWELL, author of *God's Little Acre, Tobacco Road,* and the biggest selling author of fiction in the world's soft cover market.

RICHARD L. NEUBERGER, United States Senator (Democrat) from Oregon, and the only free-lance writer ever elected to such office. His articles have appeared in *The Saturday Evening Post, The Nation,* and *Reader's Digest.*

EMIL ZUBRYN, who forsook the United States for Mexico after having been executive of a newspaper syndicate in New York and has since written extensively for the leading magazines.

SLOAN WILSON, author of *The Man in the Gray Flannel Suit* and other books and articles.

EVAN HUNTER, author of the successful novels, *The Blackboard Jungle* and *Strangers When We Meet,* which sold to the movies for hundreds of thousands of dollars (before taxes).

GEORGES SIMENON, author of more than 200 novels, the basis of many motion pictures.

BEN SMITH, story and article writer, author of *Renegade Rider, Trouble at Breakdam,* and other westerns.

BLAKE CLARK, roving editor of *Reader's Digest,* author of scores of magazine articles.

JESSE STUART, novelist, teacher, author of more than 500 published short stories, and poet laureate of Kentucky.

THOMAS P. KELLEY, of Toronto, Canada, author of many books and magazine articles.

SCOTT YOUNG, of Toronto, Canada, writer of juveniles and short stories.

DEANE and DAVID HELLER, whose articles cover travel, history, personalities, sports, etc., in most of the big and many of the smaller magazines.

JOSEPH N. BELL, article writer.

KENNETH S. GINIGER, writer and editor, whose anthologies have sold hundreds of thousands of copies.

JOHN GASSNER, play anthologist and author, Sterling Professor of Playwriting and Dramatic Literature at Yale University.

SAUL K. PADOVER, historian and editor of the complete works of Thomas Jefferson.

FREDERIC A. BIRMINGHAM, formerly editor of *Esquire* and author of *The Writer's Craft.*

LEWIS BROAD, British newspaper editor and biographer of Oscar Wilde, Anthony Eden and Winston Churchill.

While I have labeled these authors as "successful writers," many of them disclaim the appellation.

It is my belief that you will be interested in the variety of their viewpoints, the differences in their writing habits, and the unanimity of their opinions on many subjects impinging upon the writer and his work.

The diversity of opinion on various aspects of writing, of course, is no more marked among these professionals than is true in other walks of life. If architects, for instance, did not disagree, we would have only one kind of building.

If you are interested in writing, or just interested in reading *about* writers, I think you will find it worth your while to encounter the views of these various individuals who have written earnestly and without inhibitions what they feel about the subjects on which I queried them.

To My Mother and Father

Mr. and Mrs. Sam Cross Farrar

I wish to thank all those friends—literary or not—who contributed to this book, directly or indirectly. I am particularly indebted to the successful writers—successful in my judgment—who gave freely of their time and views to help me. I accept their counsel gratefully, and in behalf of all the people who read this book and may be impelled to become better writers because of it.

*When you sell a man a book you don't sell him
just twelve ounces of paper and ink and glue—
you sell him a whole new life.*

—CHRISTOPHER MORLEY

Contents

Introduction

Books are not absolutely dead things, but do contain a potency of life in them to be as active as that soul was whose progeny they are; nay they do preserve as in a vial the purest efficacy and extraction of that living intellect that bred them.

—MILTON

IN THE introduction to my first book on writing—*How to Make $18,000 a Year Free-Lance Writing,** published in March, 1957, I pointed out that although I had been a working writer for many years, I was not a literary person. Up to that time, I had never been to a literary tea, or even a cocktail party for writers.

Since publication of that book—plus a couple of others—things have changed. I was invited to join the Authors' Club of London, and accepted the invitation. I have also become a member of The Authors' League of America and the Armed Forces Writer's League, whose motto is "Write America Right." I feel more like a literary person, too, because I have attended several cocktail parties for authors, have lectured to a writing group at 55 Irving Place, New York City, where O. Henry once lived (this is a restaurant now), have visited Walden Pond, associated with both Ralph

* Hawthorn Books.

Waldo Emerson and Henry Thoreau and I once actually carried a handkerchief in my right sleeve for a whole day without losing it.

It has been amazing, in some ways, for me to discover just how much an author—in contrast to a mere journeyman writer—is recognized in this enlightened civilization. Since my first book on writing was published, I have had repeated printed messages from the Pauline Bloom Workshop in Brooklyn to take its step-by-step course in writing. I have been offered a 40 per cent discount if I want to sign up for literary studies with The Simplified Training Course. The director of this course told me in a special mimeographed message that *I* could be a successful writer! (Exclamation point is his.) He assured me that he had the formula, the know-how of teaching, and an almost infallible method of direct, practical professional training at a remarkably low tuition cost.

I have been invited to join The National Writers' Club, in Denver, Colorado, which would give me the privilege of free criticism of any one of my unpublished manuscripts. Twin-Hit Tunes Recording Company and Music Publishing Company, in Daytona Beach, Florida, have notified me that *I*, too, can be a successful songwriter! (Exclamation point is theirs.) This company told me that I could be "the envy of friends and neighbors," if I would just work with them, at a small fee, to get my lyrics set to music. I assure you, however, that none of this attention has turned my head. In spite of these blandishments I am still firmly in control of my purse.

It has been a source of no little gratification to receive invitations from various subsidy publishers who have told me that I can have all my future books printed just as fast as I write them—for their standard rates of payment! One company told me that, as a published author, it wouldn't cost me a cent more to do business with them than it would for an author who had not been published.

Although I did not take advantage of these many offers, I nevertheless feel an inward thrill that I should be so recognized. It is a little like a copy boy who has been given his first opportunity to write obituaries. At that point he knows he surely is on his way up.

With this recognition has come a feeling that I am better qualified to write this new book—for writers and those who are toying with the idea of writing someday (when the mood overcomes them)—than I was when I started my book on the commercial aspect of writing.

In preparing this new book, I have been in touch with a number of very fine writers. In some instances, this contact was face-to-face; in others, it was on the telephone. In many instances, due to the fact that many of the most successful writers are wanderers, it was by correspondence that I contacted them. I have dined with Blake Clark at the University Club; eaten breakfast at the Sheraton-Park with Fred Kerner; visited Walter Lippmann in his beautiful home on Woodley Road; conversed in the gold-leafed ante room of the Capitol with Senator Richard Neuberger and dined with David and Deane Heller. I have visited with Mr. and Mrs. Thomas P. Kelley in Toronto, Canada. I have even had a drink with Governor Foster Furcolo, the literate and popular Governor of Massachusetts, who, like Neuberger, is both a successful writer and politician.

In every instance, I have tried to find—for you—the Great Secret: Why are *they* successful, while you and I are relatively unknown, unsung and unpaid? I wish that I could give the secret to you in one sentence—or rather, *sell* it to you—for I would save myself much work and save you the trouble of having to read 100,000 words to get this secret. Unfortunately for both of us, this message cannot be condensed. If there is a secret which successful writers possess, and the rest of us do not—I sincerely hope that it becomes apparent in the following pages. I have examined writers both extensively and intensively, much as a laboratory technician, striving to find the secret of a cure for a specific infection, researches first in one direction and then in another, attempting to collate *all* his material. The scientist realizes that when he knows enough about all phases of any physical subject, he can unravel almost any secret relating to it. I cannot claim that I have uncovered *the* Great Secret of successful writers. I can only say that, somewhere in the knowledge I have tried to collect for you, *you* will perhaps find this secret. If you can then put it into one sentence, one paragraph, or one page, I will rejoice with you.

Francis Bacon said, "Some books are to be tasted, others to be swallowed, and some few to be chewed and digested." It is my hope that you will want to chew and digest this one and will treasure it in years to come.

LARSTON D. FARRAR

Fairfax, Virginia

Successful Writers and How They Work

I

The Writer—
A Man Apart

Of all those arts in which the wise excel,
nature's chief masterpiece is writing well.
— JOHN SHEFFIELD

WHY are *you* reading this book? The answer, of course, is because you are interested in writing and writers. But why are you interested in writers? The answer is individual, but I believe there are some general factors about yourself that you might ponder.

Your interest in writing—and writers—*could* be attributed to a superior intelligence. If this is true, and you actually are more intelligent than many other individuals, it is only fair to warn you that this could lead to danger for you. Intelligent people are more curious than others; this curiosity leads them to *think*. Sometimes, it causes them to look around them and see abuses that need correction. Seeing these abuses, these intelligent people take stands on issues. Everyone knows that taking a stand, on any issue, at any time, entails a certain amount of risk.

It seems odd to say it, but the truth is, it is dangerous in many circles, even today, to know too much. So you should be forewarned (hence, forearmed), in case you suspect you are a bit more perspicacious than the fellow on the next stool at the hamburger joint. I must warn you that many tests made by psychologists and educators here and abroad have shown that those individuals who reveal an interest in writing usually are among the most intelligent, alert, and sensitive of the people among whom they live. Note carefully that I use the word "usually," for this gives you an out. It *is* possible for people with normal intelligence to be curious about writers. I don't want to accuse you of anything that might spoil your feeling of togetherness with your fellowmen. It is not my intention to be divisive.

Frankly, your interest in writing—and writers—may be just curiosity, and nothing more. Perhaps you are like those people who follow a fire engine that roars by. You are attracted by the excitement and by the flames that shoot toward the sky. You hear of a writer, or of a book about writers, and, like the people who go around the day after the fire to see the blackened ruins, you want to read about what has happened to people who have stuck their necks out.

It is entirely possible that you are interested in writers merely because, as anyone knows who reads the newspapers, writers make news. They attract publicity. True, not *all* writers get publicity, and a lot of them get much less than they want, or feel they deserve. But enough writers do get in the papers often enough to impress upon the average man the fact that some writers are extremely clever, some are lucky, others are courageous, and that most of them are active members of the human race, interested in everything, from spurring a revolution in Cuba to encouraging more Americans to play Scrabble.

It is possible that you are interested in writers because you are tired of reading about togetherness and sweetness and light. If so, you have come to the right counter.

Just think for a moment of writers who have been on the front pages in recent years, and you will understand why writers are considered to be men apart.

There was Henry L. Mencken, in the last years of his life, appearing in Washington before the U. S. Post Office Department, to help defend the right of *Esquire* to go through the mails.

Arthur Miller, the playwright-husband of curvaceous Marilyn Monroe, was freed, amid big headlines, of contempt of Congress charges resulting from his refusal to inform against men whom he was alleged to have known as Communists many years before.

Boris Pasternak, the Soviet author of *Doctor Zhivago*, a novel which painted a grimly true picture of Russia today, was forced to retract his acceptance of the Nobel Prize for literature and hounded unmercifully by the Soviet press and party functionaries.

Harry L. Golden, of Charlotte, N. C., author of the best-selling, *Only In America*, was revealed to have been an ex-convict. He served a term in a federal penitentiary many years ago after being convicted of mail fraud.

Captain John D. Bulkley, who earned more than $200,000 as a result of writing about his heroic exploits in World War II, revealed that he had given every penny of it to charity.

Milovan Djilas, former vice president of Yugoslavia and author of *The New Class*, was sentenced to seven years in prison for having depicted Communism as a system in which the masses are exploited by the bureaucratic upper class.

The Reverend Martin Luther King, Negro integration leader of Montgomery, Ala., was stabbed and critically wounded (he recovered) by a woman in New York City while he was in a department store autographing copies of his new book, *Stride Toward Freedom.*

The mass of clippings before me also reveals that writers have been in the news for every kind of activity possible to name or imagine in this society: one is suing his wife for divorce, another has decided to renounce one religious faith and embrace another; a third has just married one of Hollywood's most glamorous starlets; another has decided to float on a raft across the Indian Ocean, and

another is trying to go on an atomic submarine under the North and
South Poles in the same year, and, if possible, also ship on the first
man-carrying rocket to the moon.

A great prophet, talking to his closest followers, once said: "Ye
are men set apart." I believe that writers, most of them perhaps
not consciously or having planned it that way, eventually realize
that these words apply to them with peculiar poignancy. For writers, blessed (or cursed) with some perception, and possessed, for
good or evil with curiosity and a sense of responsibility, *are* men
set apart.

Many of the world's great writers have recognized this fact, but
none expressed it more succinctly than Thomas Carlyle, who wrote
that "literary men are . . . a perpetual priesthood."

Since the earliest days of the traveling troubadours, who sang of
many things, and the roving raconteurs, who told stories which
they made up to amuse the open-mouthed peasants in medieval
towns, storytellers have been known as men of great experience
and great wisdom, and no little courage. Their wisdom was a com-
pendium of experience, mingled with curiosity about strange-
sounding places and far-off people. Their courage was manifest
because it took more than ordinary spunk to leave people whom
they knew, and could trust to some extent, and go into new and
strange communities.

These travelers were the newsmen of their day, spreading
choice morsels of gossip that the more staid members of any community could not possibly learn because they had chosen to remain
in one place. The troubadours, besides carrying news, obviously
had a desire to *help* others—to laugh, to be saved, or to buy medicine. This caused these roving story-tellers to study people more
closely in the various towns they visited. They learned that the
people in one area would laugh at one kind of joke, while the people in another would stare blankly upon hearing it.

With the coming of the printing press, the writers became more scholarly. Besides being able to travel, they were among the best read men of their time. It was because they had read more than anyone else, and felt a responsibility to interpret what they had learned, either through fact or fiction, that these writers became leaders of movements in all the "civilized" countries. Sometimes they were religious writers; at other times they were political philosophers. In virtually every instance, the writers whose names still come down to us today are those who wrote with a purpose, even if, as in the case of Shakespeare, the purpose was only to hold a mirror to mankind so that mankind might look at its own face and laugh, or cry, or rail against its fate.

Every person has his own reasons, either those he understands or those he merely *feels,* for admiring writers or for wanting to be a writer. Therefore, every person knows—in his own heart and mind—whether or not he really deserves to be called a writer.

In the field of writing, as in many an occupation or profession, it appears that many are called, but few are chosen. The number of would-be writers is incalculable. Rather than decreasing, as time passes and as other forms of interest and amusement come onto the stage of life, the interest in writing, and experiencing the thrill of being in print or on the radio or television, constantly seems to be increasing.

There are many reasons why more and more intelligent people, or courageous people, want to be writers. One of the principal reasons is that writers, living or dead, have made a terrific impress on the world.

If you think that being imprisoned, as Djilas has been, is a twentieth century innovation for authors, you aren't up on your history. One of the earliest Jewish historians (he was the only one to make mention of Jesus, outside of the Gospels) was Flavius Josephus, who in 66 A.D. was in charge of Jewish forces fighting in Galilee against the Romans. When the Romans overthrew the rebellion, he was imprisoned. He won his freedom after three years by proph-

esying correctly, that Vespasian would become Emperor. Josephus
was present with Vespasian's son, Titus, at the siege of Jerusalem,
70 A.D., and when the city fell, he went to Rome and spent the
remainder of his life writing.

And if you believe that being in the news because of an interest
in social and political affairs is a novelty for writers, consider,
briefly, some of the experiences of the successful writers of other
centuries.

François-Marie Arouet, better known as Voltaire, dominated the
eighteenth century, in many respects, living through three quarters of it (he died in 1778 at the age of 83). He was in and out of
more than one bastille during his adventurous life. He tried every
form of literature, and excelled in all of it. Yet, he is most famous
as a satirical analyst of the society in which he lived and moved.

Voltaire made news virtually all of his life, after he reached
young manhood. He became so arrogant, early in life, that he was
whipped by six of the Duke of Rohan's lackeys, and imprisoned.
His letter of protest to the government ran as follows:

"I affirm humbly that I have been murderously attacked by the
brave Chevalier de Rohan, supported by six thugs, behind whom
he boldly took his stand. I have constantly sought since then to
repair, not my honor but his. The task has been too difficult."

As a result of this fracas, Voltaire was exiled to England for three
years. From that time, he became the interpreter of British culture
to his own French compatriots, and it is safe to say that he became
the chief political reformer of this period, through his vigorous
writings. When he returned to France, one of his first books was
burned and Voltaire himself barely stayed out of the bastille.

He took refuge in the court of Frederick the Great, of Prussia.
Voltaire had gained a huge fortune by clever speculation, and he
was able to establish himself at Ferney, just inside the border of
France from Switzerland, to which he might escape, if necessary.
During his lifetime, he produced upwards of seventy volumes of

literature, developing the philosophical tale to the peak of perfection. He was one of the greatest champions of liberty who ever lived.

On the hearse which carried his body to the Pantheon in Paris, where it finally was buried (after having rested inappropriately in an old convent), there were these words: "Poet, philosopher, historian, he gave wings to the human intelligence; he prepared us for freedom."

George Gordon, Lord Byron, was one of the great emancipators of the early nineteenth century. Born lame, his condition accentuated by infantile paralysis and his own riotous living, he was the son of a libertine. He inherited his title and estate when he was eleven, entered Cambridge when he was seventeen, by which time he had had many loves.

He took part in more than enough activities to satiate a normal man. He traveled in Europe and Asia Minor, swam the Hellespont, made love indiscriminately, contracted malaria and wrote unceasingly. At twenty-three he took his seat in the House of Lords.

At twenty-four, he was famous. Although he had a clubfoot and spindly legs, he was said to be unusually attractive to women, with features both delicate and sensual and a pallid brow that apparently made him irresistible. Lady Caroline Lamb, wife of the future Lord Melbourne, masqueraded as a boy to visit his rooms. When he became tired of her, she tried to commit suicide at a ball. Lady Oxford, who was twice his age, became enamoured of him, and then Lady Frances Webster. When he met his half-sister, Augusta, who had married her cousin, a Colonel Leigh, the mutual attraction was immediate. He finally married pretty Anne Isabella Milbanke, but a short time after a daughter was born, "Annabella" returned to her family, demanding a separation and charging Byron with incest with his half-sister.

Lord Byron, railing at the hypocrisies of society, left England, never to return. In 1816, he joined Shelley, Mary Godwin, and her stepsister, Claire Clairmont, who became another Byron mistress and bore him a daughter. Oddly enough, the period of his greatest debauchery coincided with the period of his most creative achievements in writing *The Prisoner of Chillon, Maid of Athens,* and other poems known to countless millions. *The Prisoner of Chillon,* in fact, was written in honor of a Swiss patriot, François de Bonnivard, who had been imprisoned for his political beliefs.

Byron joined an incipient revolutionary group in Italy, and, when nothing became of this movement, he gave money, advice, and himself, to a Greek liberation group. Eager to give his life, if possible, in the cause of human freedom, he died when he was only thirty-six, in 1824, having been denied his last great hope, that of finding "a soldier's grave."

Because of his brilliant ability with words, and his bitter and capacious invective, he became the symbol of political and intellectual liberalism in his day.

Thomas Paine, the English political writer and radical pamphleteer, gave the world *Common Sense, The American Crisis, The Rights of Man,* and *The Age of Reason.* He held official positions and worked for the American colonies during the Revolution, but later fell out of favor in this country. Banished from England as a traitor because of his aid to the Colonies, he participated in the French Revolution and once again both gained and lost favor. He was imprisoned during the Reign of Terror, going back to the United States when the situation permitted. He died in this country, in poverty, and was refused burial because of his religious rationalism.

Victor Hugo, French poet, dramatist and novelist, was exiled in 1851 for violent opposition to Napoleon III. When he returned to Paris finally in 1870, he was hailed as a prophet and hero. He wrote fifty volumes, including many masterpieces.

Thomas Jefferson wrote the Declaration of Independence, which was edited in a minor way by Benjamin Franklin and John Adams, and, in a few passages, by Congress. He said it was "intended to be an expression of the American mind." Like Lincoln's Gettysburg Address, it seems destined to win an immortal place in the literature of mankind.

Ben Jonson, after killing a man in hand-to-hand combat in the Low Countries' war against Spain, later killed a fellow actor in London in a duel, and narrowly escaped hanging. In the prologue to *Every Man Out of His Humour*, his first play produced in 1598, Jonson made it plain that his satire was designed for a useful purpose in helping to correct social evils.

Oscar Wilde was called "the spoiled child of society" until he was forty years old. At forty-four, he died, a derelict, in France. Oscar Fingal O'Flahertie Wills Wilde was born October 16, 1856, in Dublin, Ireland, the son of a distinguished Irish surgeon. He was educated at Trinity College, Dublin, and at Magdalen College, Oxford, where he won the Newdigate Prize for poetry at twenty-one. He was a celebrity as an undergraduate, wearing long hair and a languishing look, oddly cut, carefully cobwebby clothes. *Punch*, England's famous humorous weekly, never tired of caricaturing him and his velveteen breeches.

When he was twenty-six, he made a spectacular lecture tour through the United States. He told the customs office that he had "nothing to declare except my genius," and that he was disappointed by the Atlantic Ocean.

He married at twenty-eight. But he remarked in a short while that "women spoil every romance by trying to make it last forever." He began dallying in other directions. He wrote the novel, *The Picture of Dorian Gray*, during this period.

When he was forty, Wilde was accused of undue intimacy with the Marquis of Queensberry's son, Lord Alfred Douglas. Advised to bring suit for libel against the Marquis, he lost the suit and, in turn, was tried for statutory offenses under the criminal law. He was found guilty and served two years at hard labor.

After his release Wilde changed his name, moved to France, and drank himself to death. He died of cerebral meningitis, November 30, 1900. He was buried according to the rites of the Roman Catholic Church in the cemetery of Bagneux, on the outskirts of Paris. Lord Alfred Douglas was chief mourner.

François Rabelais, whose writings dominated the sixteenth century, began his youthful activities as a novice in a Franciscan monastery and in due time became a priest. When he published *Pantagruel*, it promptly was censored by the theological faculty of the University of Paris. He later wrote *Gargantua*. It is said that out of simple everyday life Rabelais shaped "a perfect picture of rural manners," and one of the world's masterpieces of rollicking satire. He was saved from more persecution only because of his close friendship with high Cardinals of the church.

Samuel Langhorne Clemens adopting his pen name of "Mark Twain" when he mentally revolted against the lawlessness of Virginia City, Nevada, while working on the *Enterprise* there, risked his life to show up the corruption in that infamous and lawless town, and, except for what seemed to be the hand of fate (coupled with his own ability to think quickly), he might well have died in a duel for his crusading zeal. His prospective opponent in the duel saw a bird's eye shot by another man (whom he mistook for Mark Twain), and decided not to go through with it.

Walt Whitman said of *Leaves of Grass* that "I expected hell, and I got it." Reviewers wrote that Whitman was a criminal monster. One said that he was "as unacquainted with art as a hog is with mathematics." Another wrote that he should be publicly flogged.

Only Ralph Waldo Emerson—who was universally respected in American literary circles at that time—would stand by Whitman.

Even today, far from enjoying peace and security, either in the United States, in the Soviet Union, or in satellite countries, writers who have the courage of their convictions continually make news because what they write runs contrary to the prejudices of those who may read their novels or essays. Yet writers continue to explore the frontiers, and, as a result, they continue to be considered men apart.

If it seems from all this that every writer, whether he knows it or not, is at heart at least partly a reformer, then who am I to deny the evidence? Not too long ago, the motion picture actor, Clark Gable, speaking to the press in Washington declared that he planned to buy only light material for his new production company. He wanted, he said, no part of any novels written with a purpose, and he wasn't interested in those espousing causes.

Well, it is entirely possible that Mr. Gable—and Hollywood generally—can find light novels, and those ostensibly written without a cause in the mind of the writer. I seriously doubt it, however, for my studies of writers—both the ones history has adjudged as "great," and a great number still living who have not yet been judged by history—indicate that all writers who expend enough of their energy to get published *do* have a cause in mind. What about *War and Peace, The Brothers Karamazov, God's Little Acre*? Were these, as top pictures of recent years, written by men who believed in something or were they written merely to amuse the populace?

I believe it can be demonstrated that a writer—a writer of quality —has in him the element of a *reformer*, although it frequently is tempered with a sense of humor and the realization that all change comes with time. It is not necessarily simultaneous with the publication of an article exposing an evil, or a book designed to put the glaring spotlight of a writers' pitiless attack on a particular segment of society.

Clarence Buddington Kelland, who is in love with the *status quo*, reflects his love for the Republican Party, free enterprise and the American Way in virtually everything he writes. So do many other writers who feel that rocking the economic or political boat is a dangerous pastime.

There are many other writers who feel just the opposite. They think that the way to keep the world happy is to keep it moving toward something they think is better than what we have. They reflect their philosophy in everything they write. Either way, the writers very definitely write with a "cause" in mind, Mr. Gable to the contrary.

It is not generally realized, but Kenneth Roberts, who is best known perhaps for his *Northwest Passage,* gained his early fame for campaigning against the billboard evil through the pages of *The Saturday Evening Post.* This was in the mid-twenties, when, be it noted, the evils of excessive roadside advertising were more blatant and less controlled than today. If progress has been made toward eradicating unsightly roadside advertising signs, a share of the credit for fighting against this social evil must be given to Mr. Roberts, who had more than mere entertainment in mind when he wrote his articles. *The Post,* of course, which has always competed with outdoor advertising, was motivated less by "reformism," since its financial stake was obvious.

A writer who himself denied that he ever wrote for any "cause" —Samuel Hopkins Adams, a grand old man of American litera- ture—nevertheless did that very thing. Perhaps few persons, rela- tive to the vast population, thought that a series of articles in the old *Collier's National Weekly Magazine,* by Samuel Hopkins Adams, then just becoming a formidable figure in American jour- nalism, would be partly responsible for the later passage of the Federal Pure Food and Drug Act. Time revealed that Mr. Adams was more powerful in leading the people—and the politicians who were following them—than any other single writer of that period. The grain dealers and others who feel the heavy hand of federal regulation, due to the Food and Drug Act, still refer to Mr. Adams as "that crank reformer—Adams," although he later became known as one of the most conservative men in American literature.

Surely, you will say, there are more reasons why writers are men apart than because some of them are men of convictions and others feel a call to reform things. You are right. Many men have convictions, and never write anything worth publishing. Others have "causes," and also never become writers. What are the other factors that seem to set writers apart?

One important reason why writers are men apart is that they are, to some extent, the *decision makers* of our society. Merely to sit down and to write seriously, entailing as it does a person's complete attention, is a decision. When a person carries it out, he has overcome the first great hurdle in becoming a writer. From the moment he starts to write until he pauses to rest, he must make decisions at every step. He must determine what to call his article, story, poem, or essay. He has to make a decision as to what to feature, i.e., what to tell his prospective readers first, what to tell them next, and next and next. Each *word* represents a decision, because there are synonyms for virtually every word used by a writer. Instead of writing "throw a rock," he can write "hurl a stone," or "toss a pebble."

By the time a writer has written, and has seen published, enough of his work to earn the appellation of "successful writer," you can be sure that he has learned *how to make decisions.* In learning how to make decisions—even bad ones—the writer, if he stays at it long enough to be called "successful" by an appreciable number of people, learns many other things, both about himself, about society, and about phases of life around him.

Thus, he becomes a knowledgeable person, which I think is another characteristic that makes writers men apart. There are many knowledgeable persons in our society, and I would be the last to claim that the writers are the only ones. But the fact remains that, relative to the 176,000,000 Americans, some 50,000,000 would qualify as youths, children, or babies, or too old to keep up with what's doing. They could not be termed "knowledgeable," in the sense I mean the term. Among the remaining 126,000,000 Americans, only some 8,000,000 are college graduates. It is possible, in this complex society, for a person to be "knowledgeable" without having graduated from college, but it isn't very likely that a person without a well-rounded college education will become knowledgeable in many facets of life.

Among the 8,000,000 college graduates are many specialists. They labor long hours—far more than the usual eight hours each day—over their specialties. I know physicians who practice all day and study medical techniques most evenings merely to keep up with their own fields. They are among the first to admit that they are not "knowledgeable" about many diverse areas of this society. Some physicians have only a nodding acquaintance with political affairs. To many of them, the theatre, and all the people in it, are as strange as the ways of the Hottentots may be to someone who has never been to Africa.

But writers—if they are to be successful—must be knowledgeable in many areas of life. Even if the writers specialize in writing about medicine, science, politics, or other subjects, they still must maintain a nodding acquaintance with developments in all major fields, otherwise, they might be caught lacking when, at times, some development in an adjacent field impinges upon their own field. Of course, a writer learns early that the world is a unit, with many, diverse parts, and that he must know something about developments in all possible fields. In learning of these developments, he becomes knowledgeable.

Another reason why I believe writers are men apart is because they usually are *idea men*. Virtually every advance in human knowledge and welfare has come more because of ideas, than because of chance. Since the Renaissance, virtually every good idea has come from writers, in science, finance, literature, or morality. Consider the great political movements toward popular government, and you will realize that, except for dedicated writers, freedom for the vast masses of the people never would have been possible. Or consider the spread of religion in the Western

World. Protestant, Catholic and Jewish writers—many of them with best-selling songs, poems, books, or books or sermons—have inspired millions to accept their faith, or to hold a higher appreciation for the things of the spirit.

This perhaps best explains why writers are considered such special people. They are men with new ideas—frequently *inspiring* ideas. They not only go to the trouble to learn what *is* happening, but many offer new interpretations and give hope to new people coming onto the scene. The writer must be motivated by good goals—at least, they must be good, in his judgment—to pay the price in discipline and energy for turning out material to help people to think better, to live better, or to take a firmer hold on their right to life, liberty and the pursuit of happiness.

Writers have always let their minds wander into new and uncharted fields, where they might find new paths for the human race to follow. Everyone knows that science-fiction writers, years ago, foresaw the invention of the atom bomb and the development of space travel by rockets. It is not so well known, or recognized, that fiction writers have been ahead of modern science writers, in envisaging what the world would become. Jules Verne was one writer who saw beyond the narrow confines of his own day. He predicted developments that came many decades after his death.

Writers give us new words and new expressions, and new *thoughts*.

Horace wrote: "Men ever had, and ever will have, leave to coin new words well suited to the age. Words are like leaves, some wither every year, and every year a young race succeeds . . . A word, once sent abroad, flies irrevocably."

The process of thinking—really thinking and not just memorizing or idly speculating about someone else's thoughts—is *work*. It may come, at times, in a flash of inspiration. But a new thought mostly comes, like Thomas A. Edison's inventions, out of a great deal of just plain work. Edison made more than 44,000 experiments with various kinds of materials before he discovered just what would be needed to go into the filament of a light bulb to keep it glowing brightly.

Although Robert Southey's prose fills forty volumes and his collected verse, together with the explanatory notes, fills ten volumes, he is remembered for only one poem, "The Battle of Blenheim," the most satirical poem on war ever written.

The son of an unsuccessful merchant, Southey was born August 12, 1774, in Bristol, England. He entered Westminster School when he was 14, and was expelled for writing an article against flogging, a common (and highly regarded) practice. The humiliation aggravated Southey's spirit of protest. When he was nineteen he wrote a revolutionary epic poem, "Joan of Arc." When he was twenty he espoused the cause of the French Revolution, becoming a leader of the "pantisocrats."

Two decades later, he had lost his revolutionary ardor. He had not only his own family to support, but Coleridge's. He became a regular contributor to *The Quarterly Review,* the most prominent Tory publication in England. He was offered the Poet Laureateship upon the death of Henry James Pye, who, it was said, had attained the honor by rescuing the wig of George II while His Majesty was hunting one day. (Lord Byron said that Pye was "prominently respectable in everything but his poetry.") Sir Walter Scott, who had been proposed for the honor, refused it and recommended Southey, who accepted it. Byron, full of republican ardor, attacked Southey and his principles.

Southey spent his time in a library of some 15,000 volumes. Wordsworth remarked that Southey away from his books seemed to be out of his element. Honors and troubles descended on him simultaneously. He recovered from the loss of several children when he suffered a new affliction.

"I have been parted from my wife by something worse than death," he wrote. "Forty years she has been the life of my life, and

I have left her this day in a lunatic asylum." Three years later, she died. Two years afterwards, Southey married again. His own mind began to fail. He died at seventy, March 21, 1843. There is a bust to his memory in the Poets' Corner, Westminster Abbey.

The best writers of any generation are the *leaders* of that generation. If the writers fail, or if they are thwarted in expressing themselves, then the civilization fails to achieve what it might have achieved.

It is because of his decisions, and because of his ideas, the writer runs afoul of the *mores* of his civilization and the prejudices of the people more often than men in any other profession.

"John Oliver Hobbes" (Mrs. P. M. T. Craigie), who died in 1906, put her finger on the difference between writers who simply write to entertain, and those of quality who write to be heard, when she said:

"A false success made by the good humor of outside influences is always peaceful; a real success made by the qualities of the thing itself is always a declaration of war."

There are a great many writers who blend easily into the society in which they live and die. Seldom is there any controversy surrounding them, for they live, as it were, as a part of show business. They are people of soft spirits, or of little or no spirit, who have learned to wield soft words that appeal to other soft spirits, of whom there are many in every society in every generation.

But the writers whose name you see on the front pages frequently are controversial figures. This was true of Charles Darwin, and it was true of Robert G. Ingersoll, and it was true of Billy Mitchell, of Heywood Broun, of Henry L. Mencken, and of Drew Pearson. It is true even of a man like Norman Vincent Peale.

The *ideas* of the idea men—the successful writers—of course have been as limitless as the universe itself. Writers show, in their variety, that they recognize life's limitless challenges, and this, too, sets them apart.

Is a writer, as a radio disc jockey once asked me, "just an introvert entertainer"? It is true that many, perhaps most, of the people in show business consider that writers *are* a part of show business, and that the editorial field is just a branch of their business. There *is* an element of show business in writing and, to a certain extent, all of us, writers and non-writers alike, are desirous of playing parts on the stage where we might be more famous, or more influential.

But a writer, in my humble judgment, is more than just another performer, whose purpose is to divert or amuse the populace. He must have a purpose greater than that of just amusing the people. He must teach the people. Even more than that, he must stimulate the people to action, spur them to work for goals which the writer believes are constructive.

The writer is a mixture of Paul Revere, warning the people; Abraham Lincoln, prodding the people to think; Carl Sandburg, enlightening the people about new phases of human existence which they may have felt, but had never seen expressed until he expressed them.

A few writers in every generation strive to capture new frontiers. A writer is like an explorer. He knows—from the books on the shelves at the library—what wildernesses have been conquered and put to use by mankind. In spite of the fact that all these millions of books have been written—and it seems every phase of human activity has been examined, catalogued and made available to the public—the writer believes there is still a wilderness to be conquered. He strives to push out a little farther, in his imagination, or to dig a little deeper in his research. He wants to tell man more about man, and man's world, or to tell the old story in a new way.

Francis Bacon said that "reading maketh a full man, conference a ready man, and writing an exact man."

It is this exactness that often infuriates individuals about whom something may be written. You can write, "I believe all politicians are crooks" all day long, and no politician will get angry with you.

They might even smile at you. If, however, you tell of the pecula-
tions of one political leader, he will hate you. He may even try to
destroy you. This is the danger every honest writer faces whenever
he strives to fulfill the highest functions of a writer.

Writers, in essence, are men who hold up mirrors mercilessly before society. Sometimes, society does not like what it sees. It strives,
as history has shown, first to destroy the book, and, failing that, to
destroy the writer.

Victor Kravchenko, a Russian diplomat who defected from the
Soviet, wrote a best-selling book entitled, *I Chose Freedom*. The
Russians never forgot it. After World War II, libel suits were
brought in France against him and his publishers, in an attempt to
destroy his influence. Mr. Kravchenko risked his life and his reputation by going to Paris to fight for his words. After a terrific see-
saw battle, he won in an open court of law in France.

Every era of mankind, since the first Stone Age man began to
carve out crude symbols on the walls of caves, has had its writers.
Not all writers have been lionized in their periods, although every
era seems to have had *some* writers who were. Voltaire seemed to
rule the social roost, wherever he might be residing. His fame went
before him.

Many of the successful writers of America today are not called
upon to be heroes, in the way Pasternak or Djilas has been challenged. Yet, in a true sense, American writers every day prove that
they have the courage of their convictions and are not ashamed to
tell exactly what is taking place around them.

Not too long ago, Blake Clark wrote a piece about Indian claims
legislation that had been passed by Congress, making possible new
and omnivorous financial demands upon the United States Treas-
ury. This story made headlines on the front pages of newspapers
in many parts of the United States, and Mr. Clark was roundly
denounced by, among others, Indian claims lawyers, Congressmen,
bureaucrats, and, of course, tribal spokesmen.

It takes courage to be exact—or specific—in showing up what might antagonize one group, or several groups, in society. Such writing inevitably results in petitions from pressure groups to the magazine. It can conceivably bring bodily harm to the writer, if the members of the affected group are stirred up so, that less-responsible members may become infuriated and resentful.

A writer, in fact, runs a risk of bodily injury, and even death, whenever he is courageously exact in exposing influences harmful to society. A newspaper editor in Illinois, who had been engaged in exposing a gangster element in her town, disappeared several years ago under mysterious circumstances and is presumed to have been killed. A Texas editor wrote a slashing editorial one day about an evil situation in his city; the next day he was shot in cold blood by the man he had exposed.

Not every writer, of course, can wear a red badge of courage. There are many who, either out of fear or because they do not think the stake is high enough, temper their words to avoid a showdown. There are others who specialize in types of writing that could not possibly be offensive to any groups or individuals—such as scientific writers, those who write sermons and innocuous stories and essays about harmless subjects. However, even these writers cannot be sure that they will not, inadvertently, offend.

Words are more powerful than most of us consider. A few simple words can make a man's life Heaven, or Hell. If words, written down, are the right words and are aimed at the right target and with the right amount of power, they can blast their way into men's hearts and minds and cause all kinds of upheavals—personal, economic, political and social.

Many thoughtless persons view the work of writers as inconsequential, or of little or no effect. But history does not bear them out. If you want to know where a society is heading, politically, socially or morally, study the writings of the principal authors of that time.

If you drive through the country, after midnight, you will see that home after home is dark. In each house, the occupants are asleep, taking their rest from the world.

If you pass through a city, you may see a light in one window, perhaps, high in a skyscraper. This may be a writer, working far into the night, and into the early morning, striving to come to grips with a subject that, he feels, will make a mark on those who may read it, in a poem, an article, a story, or a book.

Out in the countryside, you may see a light in a den in a house on a hill. This, too, may be a writer, striving in the solitude of the sleeping world to express some thought, on paper, that will influence and help or amuse and enlighten the people of the work-aday world of tomorrow.

A writer, even a poor writer who isn't very successful, has a more intense life than almost anyone else in the society.

Not long ago, a writer-friend, down in the dumps, came to me. Everything was going wrong—and everything has a way of going wrong, at times, in writing. He was barely making a living. His material was always bouncing back.

"Remember, other people have problems, too, even the rich ones," I said, trying to be helpful.

"Oh yeah? What banker has problems?"

"Don't you consider that, even with your bad breaks, you get more out of life than a banker?" I said to him. "Just consider what a dreary time you would have spending your time foreclosing on people, or threatening them with financial disaster. Or just take a close look at the next credit manager of a department store you see and decide if you want to be like *him*. Or consider the jerk who runs the collection agency down the street. He's got furrows in his brow, and he isn't thirty years old yet."

He grinned. He knew I was right. He would never have changed places with any one.

II

Who *Is* a
Successful Writer?

*I consider an author's literary reputation
to be alive only while his name will insure
a good price for his copy from the bookseller's.*

—OLIVER GOLDSMITH

IT may seem pedantic to devote a chapter to the question of who
is a successful writer. This problem of determining success—in
writing or in life—has long bothered me. It is essential that we get
some idea of what success is before getting you steamed up about
becoming a successful writer.

Looking around you at the world today, who would *you* consider
to be a successful writer?

Do you consider the unidentified person who wrote an Oscar-
winning movie in 1956, but did not come forward to get his Oscar,
a successful writer? This writer was one of the famous "Hollywood
10" who were called up before the House Committee on Un-Ameri-
can Activities and refused to answer its questions. This particular
writer went to jail, and, after serving his term, began to write movies under another name. It was embarrassing to his production company—which had "fired" him under his real name—to have it known

publicly that the same man had sold them a script under his new
name. So he never received the prized Oscar. Yet, the question
remains: Is he, or is he not, a successful writer? Put it another way.
Would you consider that *you* were a successful writer if you could
sit down and knock out a movie script and collect $100,000 for it
under any name, even if you couldn't collect the Oscar you won?

Or take another writer whose name is a household word. A
former President, several years ago wrote a book. It sold for $6.50
a copy and was what is known in the trade as a "flopperoo." The
other day, an item in a Washington newspaper noted that this book
was seen for sale at a secondhand book store for twenty-nine cents.
He received hundreds of thousands of dollars for the book. Yet, is
he a successful writer?

Would you say a writer is successful whose books have sold in
the millions? Charles Sheldon wrote a book, *In His Steps,* which
just might be the most widely-read book, outside the Bible, ever
printed in the United States. Yet, he failed to copyright it, and it
was printed by numerous publishers. Circulation ran into the millions, but he collected hardly a widow's mite for his work. Was he
a successful writer?

Or perhaps to you the mere writing of books makes a man a
successful writer. If so, I can give you—on the q.t.—the names of
several authors I know who have books on their library shelves that
they have written. The books, unfortunately, never sold even a
thousand copies each, but the writers seem to get a great satisfaction out of showing their "literary works" to their friends. But is a
man who cannot write a book that will sell, a successful writer?

Many writers are recognized, feted, or rewarded lavishly with
fame and money in their lifetime. To name only a few, there were
Voltaire, Sir Walter Scott, Oscar Wilde, Mark Twain, Ralph Waldo
Emerson, and, today, men and women like Grace Metalious, Robert
Penn Warren, John O'Hara, and hundreds of others.

But those people who have written books that did not sell, or those who may write anything that seems to meet a ready audience *today*, can take heart from the lessons of history, if their desire is for lasting fame. They can remember that Walt Whitman was pummeled by the critics of his own time and summarily dismissed by his chief in the Department of Interior, where Whitman was a minor clerk. This bureaucrat, who had been a Methodist preacher, discovered evidences of "immorality" in *Children of Adam*. William Douglas O'Connor, an Abolitionist author, wrote a pamphlet in defense of Whitman, coining the phrase "the Good Gray Poet," which lived on. However, Whitman was never given the adulation he deserved in his own lifetime.

Or consider Herman Melville, who wrote *Moby Dick, Typee,* and other noted works. Scorned by the critics and neglected by the people, he spent his last forty years in what one writer termed "unhappy spasms of creation and ill health."

Melville once wrote: "If, at my death my executors (or more properly, my creditors) find any precious manuscripts in my desk, then I prospectively ascribe all the honor and glory to whaling; for a whaleship was my Yale and Harvard." He jumped ship on two occasions, and lived in Tahiti and among South Sea cannibals. An infected leg forced his return to what he called "snivelization."

Yet, today's critics put him with Emerson and Whitman in the triumvirate of great American literary lights.

Then there was George Meredith, the British novelist and poet, who wrote continually—one edition alone of his works ran to thirty-nine volumes. He did not really come into the public eye until forty years after the publication of his first books. Fortunately, he lived long enough to learn of his "success." When he was seventy-seven, he received the Order of Merit, not often given to men of letters in England, and enjoyed his fame until his death four years later.

During her lifetime, Emily Dickinson, who lived all her fifty-six years virtually as a recluse in her parents' home in Amherst, Mass., had only four poems printed, and they were published "by stealth," without either her knowledge or permission. On her death, of Bright's disease, her relatives unearthed more than 1,000 of her poems, crammed away in bureaus and closets for decades.

Lewis Carroll—whose real name was Charles Lutwidge Dodgson —lectured on mathematics at Oxford for twenty-six years. Under his real name, he published treatises such as *The Formulae of Plane Trigonometry,* and *A Syllabus of Algebraical Geometry.* Under his pen name—which he never acknowledged in his life—he was the author of *Alice's Adventures in Wonderland.* When the good Queen Victoria read and liked *Alice's* she sent a messenger to Mr. Dodgson saying that the royal eye would like to see more of his work. Forthwith, he presented to the Queen *An Elementary Treatise on Determinants.* There is no record that she ever asked him for anything else.

Although he had been commended for his writing at Oxford as an undergraduate, it was not until thirty years after his death that the extraordinary poetry of Gerard Manley Hopkins was published. When he was twenty-three, he became a Roman Catholic and burned all his earlier literary work. He left the manuscripts he turned out while a priest and professor to a friend, Robert Bridges, who was later poet laureate of England.

In spite of the popularity of his songs, in his own day, including "My Old Kentucky Home," Stephen Collins Foster died in poverty in New York City. He was only thirty-eight. He had written more than 130 ballads and countless dance tunes. At thirteen, he had composed a song that won wide circulation.

Three quarters of a century after his death, Stephen Foster was considered one of our nation's great folk song composers. A postage stamp was issued in his honor, and his bronze portrait bust was unveiled in the Hall of Fame for Great Americans.

Ernest Dowson, whose name is familiar to most high school children as a British poet, died at thirty-two. Coming from an eminent family, he went to Queen's College, Oxford, but left without

completing his studies. He then went to London, where he joined
the Rhymers' Club. He alternated between periods of deep religious
observance and dissipation.

He wrote a poem to a pretty but dumb waitress, the daughter
of a restaurant keeper. He loved her idealistically, not physically,
but she was both puzzled and indignant. She ran off with a waiter.
Dowson, feeling that his life was ruined, began to drink deliberately, and lived in squalor.

Just before he died, he went to France, became a convert to the
Roman Catholic Church and died on February 23, 1900. Still, many
a modern writer would like to have even Dowson's niche in the
Hall of Fame in modern English Literature.

So—who is a successful writer?—It is not a simple question.
Would *you*, for example, want to swap places with some of the
men you undoubtedly would classify as successful writers?

Take Boris Pasternak, in exile in his own cottage outside Moscow.
Would you swap places with him, and take the brickbats close at
hand while the bouquets are all far away?

Or Milovan Djilas, the former vice president of Yugoslavia, now
languishing in jail for a long term, and lucky even to be alive? Do
you consider him a successful writer? His book impressed the Western world. But, would *you* pay the price he paid to be a success?

Or consider people closer to home. Would you say that Kathleen
Windsor, who is known as Mrs. Paul Porter in Washington, D. C.,
is a successful writer? She wrote *Forever Amber*, which made her
rich, but none of her subsequent books has created any widespread
attention. Is she a successful writer? No one disputes that she is a
rich one.

Is the fellow in the cubby-hole office downtown who is running
a mail-order advertising service and making $25,000 to $50,000 a
year writing sales letters, a successful writer? Does his career represent the acme of success to you?

Is Supreme Court Justice William O. Douglas, whose books invariably create lots of talk but seldom seem to create big sales, a successful writer? If so, then perhaps you had better start to be a writer by studying to be a lawyer. Erle Stanley Gardner, author of the "Perry Mason" books (and TV series), did just that.

Trying to define "success" has bothered men for centuries and it is not now likely that you and I will be able to pin down this will-o-the-wisp. But we may get a better idea of it by thinking about it. Let's see what some of the brilliant writers of other times have said about success.

Sir John Suckling described it as "a rare paint, which hides all the ugliness."

Alexandre Dumas, who first made that hoary observation—"Nothing succeeds like success," pointed out that all human wisdom is summed up in two words —"wait and hope."

Disraeli declared that "The secret of success is constancy to purpose."

And Browning wrote: "A minute's success pays the failure of years."

Emily Dickinson, with rare good judgment, pointed out that "success is counted sweetest by those who ne'er succeed." John C. Collins later paraphrased her statement like this: "The secret of success in life is known only to those who have *not* succeeded."

Alexander Smith said: "In the wide arena of the world, failure and success are not accidents, as we so frequently suppose, but the strictest justice. If you do your fair day's work, you are certain to get your fair days' wage—in praise or pudding, whichever happens to suit your taste."

"If this life be not a real fight, in which something is eternally gained for the universe by success, it is no better than a game of private theatricals from which one may withdraw at will," said William James. "But it *feels* like a real fight."

Nietzsche, the great German writer, declared that "nothing ever succeeds which exuberant spirits have not helped to produce."

But to Walter Pater, success was something entirely different.

"To burn always with this hard, gem-like flame, to maintain this ecstacy, is success in life," he said.

Robert Contine Cunninghame-Graham took a decidedly pessimistic view.

"Success, which touches nothing that it does not vulgarize, should be its own reward . . ." he said. "The odium of success is hard enough to bear, without the added ignominy of popular applause."

Rudyard Kipling declared: "A man may be festooned with the whole haberdashery of success, and go to his grave a castaway."

Frank Moore Colby asserted: "In public we say the race is to the strongest; in private we know that a lopsided man runs the fastest along the little side-hills of success."

W. Somerset Maugham once said: "You must not pursue success, but fly from it."

Allan Seeger declared: "Success in life means doing that thing than which nothing else conceivable seems more noble or satisfying or remunerative . . ."

"He has achieved success who has lived well, laughed often and loved much," asserted Bessie Anderson (Mrs. Arthur J.) Stanley.

It is not easy, you see, actually to define *what* a successful writer is, just as it apparently is not easy to find out *who* is a successful writer.

Writing is an intensive occupation, it is also an extensive one. There are short story writers, poets, novelists, article writers, fashion writers, columnists, dietician writers, givers of advice-to-the-lovelorn, advertising writers, radio and television writers, news writers, technical writers, scientific writers, political ghost-writers, and press agents—to name just a few *kinds* of writers in this vital field of endeavor.

But I believe it is easier to define *what* is a successful writer—or least, to define what I believe a successful writer to be—than to tell you *who is* a successful writer. That is because "success" is an entirely subjective concept.

If I were to write and sell an article to *Forbes Magazine of Busi-*

ness, let us say, I would think no more of mentioning it to the man at the liquor store down the street than would a lumber retailer think of conversing about a quick order of two-by-fours he had just sold to someone to repair a barn. Selling a business article, to me, is just about as ordinary as cutting another person's hair is to a barber.

I have known individuals who have been trying to write for money for some time who tell me breathlessly about a sale to a business magazine. Their whole manner changed as a result of this sale. They obviously considered themselves on the high-road to success.

"I never knew how it felt before to be a *successful* writer," a young lady told me, after she had sold one article to a popular magazine, for which she was paid $150. And who was I, or you, or anyone else, to dispute that in her own mind, she *was* a successful writer?

It may surprise you, but my research has revealed relatively few living men who consider themselves "successful writers." I contacted *hundreds* of writers—all of whom *I* considered to be successful, because they had written either best-selling books, or, through many superior quality articles or stories, had made a fair amount of money out of writing. Many of them, in fact, were surprised that I referred to them as successful writers.

"You're talking to the wrong fellow," one writer told me seriously. "I've written a few things that have sold to the so-called better magazines, but I don't consider myself a successful writer by any means."

I received back from writers, scores of letters many telling that they felt I had made a mistake in including them in my list of successful writers.

"In fact, I haven't written anything for years," wrote an author who has a dozen movie credits to his name and is reputed to be worth a million dollars. "I don't see how I can be considered among the successful writers of this period."

Another, a personal friend, wrote: "I'll be glad to help you, but I honestly believe you have made a mistake in believing I am successful. I merely make a fair living, doing the kind of work I want to do."

One noted writer wrote that I was being arbitrary in choosing a certain number of writers to whom to direct my questionnaire. His idea was that I should ask the 100 "best editors" to choose the most successful writers, and then contact the writers chosen. I realize this might be a good idea, but I told him that someone would first have to choose the 100 "best editors," and that, too, would be a subjective choice, since each of us would choose different lists of the 100 best editors, or the 100 best anything else.

All success is purely relative, and what each of us considers a success is subjective. One man feels that if he can get through the month, pay for his expenses, and not have to go to a loan shark, he has had a good month. Another man, counting his dividends, might feel that if he averages less than $5,000 in a month, he is a failure.

A woman who once attended a writing class, of which I was the teacher, had a ready response when I asked someone to volunteer a definition of a successful writer.

"That's easy," she said quickly. "A successful writer is anyone who has ever sold to *The Saturday Evening Post*."

"Do you mean a fact article or a fiction story?" I asked quickly.

I hastened to point out to her the absurdity of her statement, without slurring the *Satevepost*, of course. There are hundreds, if not thousands, of successful writers, in my judgment, or at least, nationally-known writers who have made plenty of money in the writing field without ever selling a line to any one magazine. They have specialized in movie scripts, or in writing plays, or political speeches, or books for children.

Unfortunately, many of us equate success in the writing field with a contribution to this or that magazine. Many successful writers—both rich and famous—would laugh if you told them they would have to sell an article to *Harper's Magazine,* let us say, to be considered a success.

I plead guilty to being arbitrary, in contacting the writers whom I consider to be successful. Each of us has a right to choose his own idols. I am the first to admit that the men whose articles and stories I like might not be the same who write the articles and stories you like to read.

By what standards do *you* judge a successful writer? Your standards are not necessarily binding on a Mohammedan, or on a citizen of Soviet Russia, or a Frenchman. A Catholic might have his favorite writers, and it is possible that his views might be colored by his religion. The same, of course, might be true of a Protestant, or of a Jew, or of any other person of any religious faith. In the same way, some men might admire a certain writer because they know he is an Elk, or a Rotarian.

Your definition of a successful writer undoubtedly would be different from mine. But since I happen to be writing this, I'll give you my definition, so that you can argue with it, or agree.

A successful writer, I think, is a person who has achieved more than local or regional impact by virtue of his literary efforts and is earning enough from those efforts alone to meet his economic obligations without feeling too pinched for money. This successful writer also is a person—man or woman—who is widely read, both in the classics and in modern literature—and feels in his heart that his best work is yet to be done. He (or she) is not discouraged that what he has done is not his best, because he still has hope of life and a future, and is working vigorously, striving to increase his literary ability in every way possible. He might feel that he *has* achieved more than the average writer, but that he not yet has achieved what *he,* himself, feels is the best that is in him. So a successful writer, to me, is not a "has been." He is a "will be."

The writer's age has nothing to do with it. He is not resting on his laurels, but is competing actively *now.* A young woman such as

Françoise Sagan might fit this description of a successful writer, or an elder like Somerset Maugham, who still writes each day. The writer who has achieved greatly, but has stopped writing, is not, in my judgment, a "successful" writer today. He may have been yesterday, or at some other time, but for one reason or another he has withdrawn from today's battles.

As I have noted, *my* definition of a successful writer may not be yours. Many people have much lower goals and standards than I have. Many have much higher.

The writers to whom I directed my questions defined a "successful writer" in various ways, as follows:

Alden Hatch: A successful writer is anyone who can make enough money to live on.

Harold Helfer: Success is something every man has to evaluate for himself. Merely making money and gaining some sort of prestige isn't always enough. My own view is that success means that a writer is able to do the kind of writing that is closest to his heart.

Will Oursler: A successful writer is one who achieves what he seeks to achieve through his writing, whether it be money, fame or the great American novel.

Norman Vincent Peale: Successful writing, today or in any era, consists essentially in being able to communicate effectively with other people via the printed word.

Richard Gehman: I think a successful writer is one who earns a living at his trade and also derives a certain amount of satisfaction from it. It seems to me that the vast majority of writers these days, especially magazine writers, are struggling along on incomes disproportionate to the amount of public service and entertainment they provide.

Harry Edward Neal: I think the answer . . . must depend upon the main reason that motivates one to write at all. The man or woman who writes only to please himself or herself, perhaps making no effort to be published, succeeds so long as he or she writes. The

writer who seeks literary fame is not as likely to find it in writing
for magazines as he is in writing books, for magazine readers as a
rule pay little or no attention to authors' names. If this fame-seeker
does write books, he may discover that fame is as vaporous as fog
and as difficult to grasp, but I believe that if he perseveres and
maintains his self-confidence, looking upon rejections or worst-
sellers as mere stepping stones, he will eventually achieve enough
renown to be "successful." I agree with the late and wise Samuel
Johnson, who said that "No man but a blockhead ever wrote except
for money." Accordingly, the writer who writes primarily to earn
money must measure his own success in terms of his literary cash
receipts and his desired standard of living.

Richard and Frances Lockridge: There are a dozen answers. A
successful professional writer is, obviously, one who makes a living
at it. But most good—and successful—poets don't, of course, make
their livings by poetry.

Edison Marshall: A successful writer these days is precisely what
a successful writer was 100 years ago—a writer who is widely and
respectfully read.

Dora Albert: A successful writer, in my opinion, must first of all
be a successful human being. That means that he must have mental
health—get along well with himself, with others, and integrate himself into his community. In addition, unless he writes purely for
scholarly reasons, he should earn some money doing a type of writing he likes. That gives him a sense of achievement.

O. A. Battista: I frequently give a talk entitled, "How To Be A
Successful Writer In Twenty Easy Years." In a nutshell, this is my
formula for becoming a successful writer—when you do not possess any outstandingly unique journalistic talents, as is the case
with me. Twenty years of dogged persistence at writing for the
love of it, instead of only for the cash of it, will bring almost anybody an additional twenty years of writing for the love of it *and*

the cash of it. A successful writer is anybody who can—eventually
—sell at least *half* of what he writes.

Fred Kerner: In this highly competitive day and age, when writing is no longer a pastime or a part-time activity, I would think that
a successful writer is one who can earn a living at his craft. And I
say craft advisedly—for while the wielding of words *is* an art, the
creation of commercial writing is a craft. I would think that in the
classification of "successful writer," you could list any top newspaperman who is holding down a byline job with any major newspaper or news agency. These men and women are the most work-aday of all writers, and from my own experience, I know that a top
newsman can turn out anywhere up to 10,000 words of well-crafted
copy in any given day. Success, then, while it may be judged artistically—and in the final analysis it *must* be judged artistically—is
still essentially the ability to earn a living at the typewriter.

Pinky Herman: The word "successful" covers a lot of territory.
I have written many songs which did *not* make the Hit Parade.
Yet I felt that they was successful . . . songs like, *The Bible My
Mother Left Me,* which did not earn a lot of royalties, but which I
feel was inspirational. Another was, *My Fav'rite Initials Are U.S.A.,*
which gave me lots of pleasure to have written with Andy Kirk and
Arthur Terket. There are many kinds of "success" in the literary
field, believe me.

Roger Burlingame: A successful writer is a writer who makes
money.

Robert Payne: Melville was a supremely unsuccessful novelist in
his own time, but a supremely successful one in our own. I remember reading that all Faulkner's books were out of print in 1940. He
was not then "successful," though most, and perhaps all of his important work was already written. I think a good writer should go
on the assumption that success is a bitch.

Hugh Ross Williamson: My definition of "success" is to be able to be yourself without any compromises except those that are dictated by courtesy and—in the proper sense—charity. Hence, "a successful writer" is to me, one who can be that in print, irrespective of sales or financial rewards.

A. C. Spectorsky: I think the answer to the question requires that each writer or would-be writer must ask himself what he hopes to attain as a writer. Does he want financial independence, freedom from a job, or a sense of creative fulfillment, fame, appreciation, approbation, group membership in those circles which follow the arts, etc.? Once he has determined his own particular reason . . . he can evaluate the degree to which he has attained this goal. . . . I think, for example, that a shy and diffident person might realize that his desire to be a writer is motivated less by creative urge than by a feeling that this is the only way in which he can communicate with his fellow man. I deem this to be a perfectly legitimate reason for striving to be a writer, and I think that the self-understanding such a man might realize by asking himself the question candidly could go a long way toward helping him to direct his own activities.

Senator Richard L. Neuberger: A successful writer is a person who can support himself and his dependents with his pen alone.

Emil Zubryn: I'd say a successful writer is a free-lancer who is *entirely* dependent on his income from writing.

Sloan Wilson: The answer of course depends on how the asker defines "success." Some mean money, some mean good reviews. I would say a successful writer is one who says what he wants to say and is read either by multitudes or by a few whom he respects, and makes enough money to give full time to his writing. That's from the writer's point of view, of course. From a more general point of view, a successful writer is anyone who adds anything useful or beautiful to the store of world literature.

Erskine Caldwell: A writer is successful if seventy-five per cent of his work is published.

Evan Hunter: A successful writer today, as judged by everyone but the writer himself, is a person whose books are on the best seller list and whose books make a lot of money. To the writer, a successful writer is a person who, through his own experience and observation, manages to bring meaning and illumination to a small segment of this very puzzling thing called life.

Ben Smith: A successful writer always has been and always will be one thing: a writer who is being *read.* Being published is a step in that direction, being accepted by the reading public is the rest of the story. Neither phase can succeed without the other. The amount of money a writer makes is only an indirect barometer of his success, because his financial return is too closely geared to the state of the culture he is living in. In France, good writers starve simply because, according to the French, it's art for art's sake. America . . . The United States . . . has the best ratio of return for time spent in this crazy business. Perhaps success can be summed up in the words of Charles Morgan writing in the *Yale Review:* ". . . the greatest tribute that a writer can earn is not that we keep our eyes fast upon his page, forgetting all else, but that, sometimes, without knowing that we have ceased to read, we allow his book to rest and look out over it with newly opened eyes."

Jesse Stuart: A successful writer is one who writes, in his day and time, something that will live after he is dead and dust. Money hasn't everything to do with successful writing.

Blake Clark: A successful writer is a person who has written enough to believe on the basis of sales and achievement, that he is growing to master his craft. The more a writer masters, the more he wants to master, and in this sense, not one of us ever becomes successful—to himself. Yet, with accomplishment, i. e., publication and readership, a writer does get peace of mind, in the highest sense. The sense of fulfillment is as great, if not greater, for a writer who has built a satisfying article as it is for an architect who has built a satisfying building.

Thomas P. Kelley: A successful writer these days is one who can make money out of it. If he can bank a few bucks, he's a genius.

Scott Young: I think a successful writer is one who is writing what he believes to be the best he is capable of, and is making a living doing that.

Deane and David Heller: A successful writer, in our opinion, is one who can make a living at it. There might be other definitions. One who wrote for satisfaction, even if he never sold, might be successful in a sense, if he developed the skill of self-expression to a higher degree than he possessed before he began to write.

Saul K. Padover: There are two general ways of measuring success: (a) money and recognition; (b) self-satisfaction. I should say that a successful writer is one who *feels* that he has done his best, this feeling being reinforced by publication and critical approval.

John Gassner: I cannot answer this question without saying that nowadays a successful writer is also apt to be a successful editor and teacher or lecturer.

Kenneth S. Giniger: A successful writer is one who has reached his own personal objectives in writing, whether those objectives be literary acclaim, financial rewards, the pleasure of seeing his work in print, or any combination of the three.

Georges Simenon: What kind of a success? Where? It can mean being on the best-seller list once every year and it can be to stay for centuries in textbooks all over the world. To be praised by very few or to be read by the people at large. To be or not to be proud of oneself.

Joseph N. Bell: A successful writer is the same as a successful man in any business. He has attained a sense of fulfillment. Money *is* important, of course, but it is not the *prime* goal.

Frederic A. Birmingham: A successful writer is one who eats regularly.

Lewis Broad: If a man makes much money out of his achievements and a name for himself with the public—then he is *ipso facto* successful. There is the second judgment to which every writer, in common with all other craftsmen, must submit to himself—that of his own ideals.

As to the first, my claim must rest on my chief work, the biography of Sir Winston Churchill. This has been published in the principal European languages, Russian excluded. With its publication in the United States in the fine Hawthorn Books edition, sales are now beyond a quarter of a million. With my biographies of Oscar Wilde and Sir Anthony Eden, my books must now be aggregating a sale of over 400,000 copies. It was never within my dreams that my work would ever become known to so wide a public.

My literary conscience is not to be beguiled by such delusive results. I regret to find, when I look back on my past writing, that so frequently there are offending passages that fall below the standard I have come to set myself. This is to write about the great figures of history in a way that the best story-tellers wrote of the heroes of old. . . . It is a laborious matter, not to be achieved without much writing and rewriting . . . I would not, therefore, set myself as a model for the writer seeking the road to quick success. . . .

Putting your finger on "success"—in the literary field—is as difficult as trying to hold a little mercury between your thumb and your fingers. Success is as beautiful—and as transient—as a giant moth that may flutter at the night-window for a moment, or a half-hour, and then be seen no more.

There really is *no* one condition, state of being, or dollar figure that can be proclaimed the *one* successful pinnacle for a writer. Men we call "successful" themselves recognize this fact.

Not long ago, a Naval officer who has sold many fact articles to magazines came to me with a fiction book manuscript. He asked my opinion of it, and I told him. It was not a saleable story, although, as I pointed out to him, this merely represented my own opinion and should not be taken as holy writ.

As I thought of him, and how much he had given to this book

manuscript, I realized the dissatisfaction—with his previous accomplishments—that he felt. This, I believe, is part of the process of becoming a successful writer, or a successful person, regardless of your interests or your abilities in life. The first step to improving your present position—in writing, or in any other phase of human activity—is the realization that you are not now as proficient as you feel capable of becoming. If there is a road to take to become successful—in life generally or in writing specifically—it is the road of dissatisfaction with your own abilities and accomplishments. By cultivating this feeling of dissatisfaction with yourself, you will examine your work with a more jaundiced eye, will strive to improve it both in little ways and in big ways. Then, whether or not you ever are numbered among the successful writers by others, you will realize, at least in your own mind, that you are making some progress toward becoming a better writer.

Is successful writing a column on new medical discoveries each month in *Cosmopolitan* by Lawrence Galton, a poem by Ogden Nash, a novel by Evan Hunter, a catchy new slogan which occurs to the president of an advertising executive as he speeds home on a commuter's train, or a society column in the local newspaper? Yes, all of this, and any of it, *is* successful writing, if the writer *feels* that he has created something new that will entertain, amuse, inform, or change the world as he knows it.

Who is a successful writer? Is it Winston Churchill, finishing off his memoirs, Maurice Zolotow interviewing a glamorous movie star, Betty Crocker discovering a new menu, Abigail Van Buren thinking of a clever response to some reader who is trying to stump her on a marital snafu, Ernest Lehman working on a new movie script, or a new cub reporter working over his two-paragraph story of the Rotary Club meeting? *All* of these are successful writers, if they feel that they are making some progress toward increasing their ability to write in such a way as to increase their impact upon readers today and those who will be reading a generation, or a century, or a thousand years from now. No one arbitrarily can tell who *is* a successful writer, and who is not. We can only, as the Apostle Paul says, "see through a glass, darkly," for writing is as much a thing of the spirit as praying, or loving, or hating.

III

The Biggest
Stumbling Block

*Fool! said my Muse to me, look in thy
heart and write.*

—SIR PHILIP SIDNEY, in
Astrophel and Stella

THERE is one stumbling block that stands between most of us and
the goal of "successful writer" so many of us yearn to reach. It is
that we hesitate to pay the price—in work and in thought—to perfect our literary skill to the mastery of one phase, or several phases,
of communications.

What is the biggest stumbling block that prevents *you* from becoming a successful writer? If there were only one answer to that
question—for all the would-be, and partially successful, writers of
the world—and I knew it, I could get rich quick by putting the
answer on a record and selling it.

But there is no *one* answer. Every person has his own stumbling
block, or blocks, usually found in the person himself. If *you* are
not producing the kind of material that you know you are capable
of producing, do not point the finger of blame at conditions, time,
circumstances, or any external factor. If you say you are a house-
wife, and have several children for whom to care each day, then I

can say this may *seem* to be a good reason, but it cannot be the deciding factor. Why can I say this? Because there *are* housewives, with small children, who *do* produce literary material every day. A lot of it is good material, as some editors of big magazines can testify.

If you are poor and say that you cannot produce because of the poverty of your surroundings, examples can be given to refute your statement that poverty is the deterrent factor.

"The writer doesn't need economic freedom," William Faulkner said in *WRITERS AT WORK*. "All he needs is a pencil and some paper. I've never known anything good in writing to come from having accepted any free gift of money. The good writer never applies to a foundation. He's too busy writing something. If he isn't first rate he fools himself by saying he hasn't got time or economic freedom. Good art can come out of thieves, bootleggers, or horse swipes. People really are afraid to find out just how much hardship and poverty they can stand. They are afraid to find out how tough they are. Nothing can destroy the good writer. The only thing that can alter the good writer is death. Good ones don't have time to bother with success or getting rich. Success is feminine and like a women; if you cringe before her, she will override you. So the way to treat her is to show her the back of your hand. Then maybe she will do the crawling."

Mark Twain at one time was bankrupt and $90,000 in debt—and that was a time when $90,000 was almost what a million would be today. He nevertheless put his mind to work and produced some of his most important stories.

Chidiock Tichborne, the sixteenth century British poet, awaiting execution in the Tower of London, having been convicted of being in a plot to kill the good Queen, wrote to his wife, Agnes, the night before he was executed on September 20, 1586. His letter enclosed three stanzas beginning: "My prime of youth is but a frost of cares."

He was twenty-eight. The poem, "On The Eve of His Execution," has lived more than 350 years.

Christopher Marlowe wrote his four great plays—*Tamburlaine The Great, The Tragical History of Doctor Faustus, The Jew Of Malta,* and *Edward The Second*—in a six year period in which, for the most part, he hovered on the edge of poverty. He was killed at twenty-nine in a brawl in a cheap tavern over whether he or a drinking companion would pay the bill.

John Milton, who had "retired" at twenty-four, in order to achieve "by the help of Heaven, an immortality of fame," was blind by the time he wrote *Paradise Lost* (copyright for which he sold for 10 pounds, through necessity) and his own daughters, Anne and Mary, by his first wife, hated him because they had to read aloud to him. When Mary, for instance, learned of his third marriage, when he was fifty-four, she remarked that a wedding was no news, but if she "could hear of his death, that would be something."

The examples of writers who *produced,* in spite of external obstacles are endless. Your relative poverty is not the reason you are not writing.

If you think that your youth—or age—may have something to do with your inability to write material that will sell, let me assure you, that you are barking up the wrong tree. While age—youth or senility—may be a factor, it certainly is *not* the deciding factor. There are youthful writers on every hand, just as there have been for centuries.

By the time Sir Thomas Wyatt received his Master of Arts degree from St. John's College, Cambridge, at seventeen, his undergraduate verses were being widely quoted. Francis Beaumont, an infant prodigy of the early seventeenth century, had written two tragedies by the time he was twelve, and before he was out of his early twenties, his plays were being produced in London. John Milton produced poems when he was ten, and, although his father wanted his son to be a clergyman, he thenceforth brought him up "deliberately to be a man of genius" in literature.

When only ten, Abraham Cowley, another seventeenth century poet whose work still delights millions, wrote an epical romance, and at eleven he composed a more "mature" epic. His first volume of poems was published when he was fifteen. At thirteen, Matthew Prior translated Horace and Ovid into English verse, and at ten, Alexander Pope planned his lifetime of study in detail, beginning that year by translating Greek and Latin. He wrote *Solitude*, still one of his most celebrated poems, when he was twelve years old. By the time he was seventeen, the literary masters of the early eighteenth century were forced to admit him to their company. Incidentally, Pope wrote in his *Essay on Criticism* that:

> *"True ease in writing comes from art, not chance*
> *As those move easiest who have learned to dance . . ."*

In our own time, we can seldom read the book review page any more without learning of some teen-ager who has just sold his, or her, first novel. Françoise Sagan, the French novelist, wrote and sold her first novel, *Bonjour Tristesse,* in her teens, and Pamela Moore, who wrote *Chocolates For Breakfast*, is still in her teens. As a publisher remarked recently: "Nowadays young girls are writing books which, a generation ago, they wouldn't have been allowed to read."

Apparently, these young people learned early—by reading and thinking, without hampering restrictions, prejudiced parents, or other thwarting factors—how to write that which is satisfying to a large number of persons. Like the little eleven-year-old boys who are master physicists, or the youths in your neighborhood who can repair your automobile (although you may know nothing about motors), many young people apparently have a natural aptitude for writing and their genius flowers if the atmosphere in which they live and work allows them to produce.

Old age, on the other hand, is certainly no excuse for *not* writing. W. Somerset Maugham, in his eighties; Ernest Hemingway, in his sixties; William Faulkner, in his sixties, and many other writers, ancient and modern, have proved by example that although the hand may be feeble, the mind need not become less sharp. George Bernard Shaw turned out some of his greatest works in his physical dotage, and Winston Churchill, although palsied, is still at work on his memoirs.

The locale is often mentioned by would-be writers as their hampering factor. Men in the Army say that if they were not hampered by military restrictions, they would do the literary work they want to do. Marion Hargrove, who wrote, *See Here, Private Hargrove,* did so while taking basic training in a World War II Army camp. It became a best-seller.

People in New York City say that if they had a nice home in the suburbs, they could turn out the kind of literary material they want to. People in the country say that if they were in the hustle-bustle of New York City, they would be inspired to do the right kind of literary work. Everybody who is *not* a successful writer imagines that there is something outside himself that is preventing him from doing his best work. The evidence—*all* the evidence—indicates that this is one reason why these would-bes, or might-bes, never do become proficient. They will not focus their gaze on their own shortcomings, i. e., their literary and intellectual shortcomings, and as a result, they never correct the factors that militate against them.

Not long ago, I talked with a man of sixty-five who is trying to write books, and who, in my judgment shows great promise. I asked him why he had not started writing sooner in life—what *his* stumbling block was. It was obvious to me, from what I had seen of his work, that he had a great imagination and was quite facile in the use of English.

"My biggest stumbling block was lack of real ambition to be a writer," he replied. "I always have had fun with words—working cross word puzzles, cryptograms, and the like—and I have been an avid reader. But I was in the retail business, making a lot of money and enjoying life. I saw no *need* to be a writer. The older I became, the more I saw the need to express myself through creative writing, and the greater became my yearning to do it. Now, at sixty-five, I am determined to leave a few manuscripts on this earth before I depart, even if not one of them is ever printed. I feel that my biggest stumbling block—in becoming a successful writer—has been the profit I made as a retail store owner."

The research I have done among writers who became successful strongly indicates that more men become writers—and successful writers—because they can't do anything else, and be happy doing it. Yet, they do want to live comfortably—so they are forced, by circumstances, to learn the various things to do, and the various things not to do, to become at least passably successful. In other words, becoming successful as a writer means overcoming an economic handicap, and because there is a handicap to be overcome, the writer strives with greater vigor to make his mark.

I am thinking now of a writer whose earnings top $50,000 a year. In conversations, I have learned that his father was a school teacher. The family lived on the edge of poverty, but, because his father was an educated person, this future writer was made aware of how many wealthier persons lived, both in the town in which he was reared and in the broad world outside that town. He resolved to make money as a writer in his spare time, although following in his father's footsteps as a teacher.

He began to write early, letting his father criticize the material. When he was graduated from the university, this future writer obtained a post teaching English at an overseas university. There, he contributed reviews to the local newspaper. He also began to do research about the colorful and historic town in which he found himself. He wrote a book about it. The book was no great success, but a magazine wanted to reprint a portion of it and paid him well. He continued to write for the local newspaper and to teach and to send off material to this magazine. Finally, he was earning more money by his "extra" writing than he was by teaching, so he resigned his post at the university, moved to this country, and launched his career as a writer. Today he is among the most successful, in fame and wealth. The period covered was some 25 years —between the time he became an English teacher and the time he could feel, that he was a "successful writer."

What was his biggest stumbling block? "It was always myself," he told me recently. "If I had just raised my horizons and had started aiming higher as soon as I left college, I feel sure that I would have learned more quickly the ins and outs of commercial writing today. I can't blame anyone except myself that it took me decades to attain what others attain in a few years."

Another point that becomes obvious is that the stumbling blocks are more mental than actual and physical.

"'I feel keenly, now than I am selling to the top markets regularly and have both a book under my belt and a movie coming up, that my own *inability to think big* was the biggest stumbling block in my path," a successful writer told me. "It is inside a person—his capabilities, his desires, his ambitions, his will to do. If his capabilities are big, but he lacks the confidence that he can do big things, then his capabilities are wasted, until he gains the necessary confidence. *Desire* has much to do with his achievements."

This brings up the question—does a writer work harder when he needs money, friends, recognition? What is it that drives men to pay the price, in loneliness, concentration and effort, to write articles, stories and books?

Here is the way a number of writers answered this question:

Alden Hatch: A writer works hardest when he needs money. He is apt to *lose* friends by working too hard.

Harold Helfer: Some people write better under pressure, others perhaps when they can be more relaxed. I don't think it would make much difference in my case. The urge to write is too great.

Will Oursler: Nobody knows when (or why) a writer works hardest. I think it is a matter of being in love with his work, plus a healthy desire to feed his family.

Norman Vincent Peale: There is nothing that can more imperiously drive a writer to sustained hard work than the challenge to get over a significant message.

Richard Gehman: I think writing, which is essentially communication of thoughts or information, is much better when it is done under tranquil conditions.

Harry Edward Neal: Yes, I think a writer works harder when he knows his writing will help fill a need—for money, friends, or other things. Probably his work is the better for it.

Frances and Richard Lockridge: A writer works hardest when he needs money.

Dora Albert: I don't think that being on the verge of starvation is necessarily inspirational. However, all writing probably is the result of a conscious or unconscious need. If a man needs friendship or companionship, then his writing is a compensation for frustration. However, I don't think frustration is a necessary pre-requisite for successful writing.

Fred Kerner: I imagine that a writer does work harder when he "needs," although, personally, I work harder when faced with a deadline. Again, I imagine this is due to my newspaper training. With deadlines staring you in the face the clock becomes your spur. For the average writer who makes writing a means of livelihood, certainly the need for money is going to be all-important. And, again, I do know people who have become writers because they felt that this would be a way for them to enlarge their social life.

Roger Burlingame: A writer works hardest under pressure.

Robert Payne: The need for money is a wonderful incentive to get the work completed. So is a deadline, especially the imaginary deadline which a writer sets for himself without the least intending to keep it. The temptation is to linger on the work, so enjoying it all the more.

Hugh Ross Williamson: There is considerable truth in Dr. Johnson's famous dictum: "Sir, no one but a blockhead ever wrote except for money."

Erskine Caldwell: A writer works harder when he wants to write.

Senator Richard L. Neuberger: I think a writer does his best when he derives a sense of creative achievement from the product of his efforts.

Emil Zubryn: I don't know. I've never been *impelled* to write for any of the reasons you mention. Money is not important to me, never has been, and is only a means to an end. I've done without it. I don't put any special significance to a byline to influence friends. . . . Maybe it is because I am an introvert and don't really need companionship—being more of a hermit than anything else.

Sloan Wilson: A writer usually works harder when he needs money, but he may not work better.

Evan Hunter: I think a writer works hardest, perhaps, when he needs money. But after he has the money—as I now do—there are other drives which push him into continuing as a writer. I imagine these drives are essentially neurotic ones, and vary from writer to writer. I couldn't even attempt to analyze them.

Ben Smith: No one works unless he needs money. I don't believe the ancient crappola that a true writer would write whether he made money or not. Me, if I had a million dollars I'd nominate this typewriter and a couple more I have lying around for ballast on the first moon rocket, and I'd spend the rest of my life going around the world (And then write the story, with pictures, for *True*).

Jesse Stuart: I write better when I feel depressed, or deeply stirred in joy or sadness.

Tom Kelley: No, I think that a writer is handicapped under stress.

Deane and David Heller: No . . . we've found that when you really need the income from writing, there's some sort of perversity which keeps your material from being up to par. Worries, money or otherwise, are distracting, and keep us from doing our best.

Saul K. Padover: A writer does work harder under pressure, whatever it may be.

John Gassner: Every incentive helps. Money is undoubtedly an incentive. So is the rage for fame. So is the need to compensate for shortcomings or the need to express (or "abreact") tensions and suffering ("We learn in suffering, what we teach in song," said Shelley, and Heinrich Heine wrote: *"Aus meinen grossen Schmerzen; Mach ich die kleinen Lieder."*).

Kenneth S. Giniger: I think that most writing is motivated by need—economic, social moral or psychological—and that the greater the need the more intensive the work of the writer.

Georges Simenon: It's awful not to need anything. But it's awful, too, to need too much.

If you are a beginning writer, or one who is advancing in the literary field, and want counsel, it appears from what I have learned, from the professionals, that there is just one way to overcome your biggest stumbling block: *Write.* Write anything—letters, advertisements, stories, articles, poetry, news stories, or whatever, but write.

Here is the advice which our panel of writers were good enough to volunteer for my use, as to what advice they would give other writers:

Alden Hatch: My advice to beginning writers is to be sure of another source of income. Always write about things you know at first hand. Try to find a good editor or agent who will teach you your craft; someone immediately in touch with the market, *not* from a cloistered campus. Let the pros tell you what to do. Don't be style-proud.

Harold Helfer: Read an awful lot. Another thing: Remember that a rejection slip is just one person's idea. Never give up on something you fully believe in.

Will Oursler: As much as possible, a writer should learn to pace himself properly, whether it is a story, an article, or a book. You may be able to win a quick victory with a one-round knockout, but you should be prepared to go the hard gruelling distance. This is particularly true on a book, when the last few chapters may find you groggy and battle-worn.

Above all, remember that you are in a field of communication. We write to be read and writing that is not read might just as well never have been written. Have something to communicate to somebody and make sure that you do put down what you have to say to whomever that somebody may be. If you reach but one nameless person, with but one line of what you write, you may change the course of the universe.

Norman Vincent Peale: To the beginner at the art of writing, I would commend the following precepts: (a) Be clear on what you want to say, and then find a simple and interesting way of saying it; (b) work at it hard. As I once heard it very aptly put by Felix Morley, "The only way you become a writer is by the consistent application of the seat of the pants to a chair."

Richard Gehman: I am afraid I can't wrap up my advice to beginning writers in a paragraph. I am having trouble wrapping it up in 1,000 words in my book. But I do think a young writer ought first to develop some skill with the language which is his tool, get a general education, either formal or informal, and, above all, practice. One of the principal difficulties a young writer has is overcoming his self-consciousness at the typewriter or at the pad and practice helps eliminate that handicap—usually. I think letter-writing is a good way for a youngster to practice—certainly it has helped me. Then, too, I advocate a certain amount of time wasting. Everything that happens to a writer, whether he is doing something constructive or not, is grist. I remember one of the lowest points of my life when I was 18, recently fired from a newspaper, and unable to get a job on another. I did nothing for about six months but loaf and resist my parents' entreaties to get some other kind of job. This "wasteful" period of my life, twelve years later, served very nicely as material for a short novel I sold to *The Ladies Home Journal.*

Harry Edward Neal: Probably more established writers have given more advice to beginning writers than have professional people in any other field! Undoubtedly the advice I offer has all been given before by writers who are better known and more experienced than I. However, here is what I would tell the beginner:

First, decide *why* you want to be a writer.

Write something at the same time every day, even if it's only a letter home or to the editor of your local newspaper.

You can always find an excuse for not writing (a leaky faucet that needs fixing, a car to be washed, laundry to be done, a floor to be waxed, a bridge game to be played, a lawn to be mowed, etc.). If you look for such excuses when it's time to write, don't try to be a writer. You'll never make it!

Don't expect to become a professional—repeat, professional—writer in a short time. Writing is an art, and to be a professional writer you must plan to study and work as earnestly as the piano student who aspires to the concert stage, enduring the drudgery of scales and practice, reconciling yourself to spending years in developing the techniques and skills which will lift you out of the amateur class and make you truly a professional with all of the attendant rewards.

Never be discouraged by rejection slips.

Don't judge your writing by the opinions or criticisms of family or non-writing friends. If you have faith in a story, let an editor decide whether it's good or bad. If you get it back, and if you still believe in it, never stop sending it out.

Learn to take and appreciate harsh and honest criticism of your writing from those who know what they're talking about.

Books and classes can teach you something about the techniques of writing, but only YOU can teach yourself to be a *writer*.

Above all, *write, write, write!*

Lester Velie: As for working habits—or tips to writers—Winston Churchill's physician once told me that the whole world is divided into "earlies" and "lates." The *earlies* are those who do their best work in the morning—the earlier the better. The *lates* are those who do their best work at night. Churchill, incidentally, is a *late*. It is best to roll with the punches in these matters and find out whether you are an *early* or a *late,* and adjust your writing habits accordingly.

Frances and Richard Lockridge: Approach writing as a craft, and learn the craft, by practice. Watch people and listen to them and try to decide what makes them tick. A reasonable attempt to acquire skill ought to convince any sufficiently bright person whether he has aptitude or had better try something else. Those who have more than aptitude will discover it, and to them advice would be an obvious impertinence.

Edison Marshall: I don't see how I can advise young writers. If they are writers—real writers—they need no advice. Their instincts will do the trick. If they just *want* to write, and have not the *impulse* to write, nobody can help them, including you. I mean, of course, creative writers, not syndicate and news writers, of whom I know nothing.

A real writer has no real companions. He likes people and occasionally he is liked by people, but friendships are too expensive, in time and energy, for a dedicated writer to maintain. He has to have enough money to live. Because of psychological factors (going back to my father's near-financial collapse when I was in my teens, when I didn't have a nickel to spend and no decent clothes), I abjured all association with young people. I learned the structure of the English language and was in the *Satevepost* at twenty-one, *Who's Who* at twenty-four, had accumulated a half million dollars at forty. I needed, or thought I needed, a great deal of money. I have given no thought, or very little, to money in the past twenty years. I know my case is not typical and probably of no use to young writers. I think the best sign of success is not my financial position, or the fact that I wrote *Benjamin Blake*, Guild selection, or *Yankee Pasha*, which sold more than 1,000,000 hardback copies in the United States alone, but that I have published a novel, a widely read novel, every year since I professed the novel (giving up serial writing) in 1940, and that at my age I still write with vigor and joy and except for my family and friends, I don't really give much of a damn about anything except writing, and my doings apart from writing must contribute directly or indirectly to my writing or I don't carry on with them. I don't know which is my best book. *Yankee Pasha* was the best tale, *The Vikings* the most imaginative (and made the best movie), *Great Smith* and *The Inevitable Hour* were the most literary, according to my vague idea of the meaning of that esoteric word. *Benjamin Blake* was my explosive breakthrough from the confinement of the magazine serial and still the favorite of many of my readers.

Abigail Van Buren: I don't mix up my career with my family, because my family is my career. Writing is my hobby. I don't rewrite and labor over anything. I find that my first idea is usually the best. I can't "expand" anything. I have something to say, and I say it . . . period. My husband is my "editor" and is the only one to see my work before it goes to the publisher.

Dora Albert: My advice to beginners would be: Try to get what you write published, even if it is only in a local newspaper. Don't be discouraged that a single editor has returned an article. When your articles appear in print, study the published article, to compare it with the carbon copy of the article you mailed. Notice the changes the editor has made, if any then try to decide why he made those changes. By doing this continually, you will learn how to edit your own copy more successfully.

O. A. Battista: Unless a person likes to write—even for no particularly obvious reason—I don't think he or she will ever become an outstandingly successful writer. I started pounding out novels at twelve years of age (I have six that I wrote between ages twelve and sixteen, gathering dust in my attic). Nobody could stop me. That is what I wanted to do.

Persistence, next to interest, is a writer's biggest asset. Make up your mind you are going to crack the big markets, study them, and then throw your work at them—in as neat and as professional a manner as possible. But never, never give up! Get discouraged once, and the chances are you will be done for.

Fred Kerner: I think that the advice I would give any beginning writer can be summed up in one word: "Write." . . . I think that everyone who wants to write ought to get a job on a newspaper and keep it for a number of years. Newspaper training teaches how and where to dig for the facts, it teaches the necessity for writing clearly and succinctly, it teaches you how to write quickly.

Pinky Herman: I'd say, "Run—do not walk—to the nearest exit out of the writing business." Particularly to an aspiring songwriter, I suggest that: First, he does not fall for those advertisements soliciting "poems, song lyrics, music-without words." In almost every case these ads are set up by song sharks to fleece amateur songwriters with empty promises which they cannot fulfill. Millions of Americans, each year, are taken in by these "sucker-bait ads." I would offer to these amateur songwriters this advice: If you have written either the words or the music of a song, try to enlist the aid of a local singer, orchestra leader, or music teacher, and ask to be introduced to someone—a new writer—like yourself, who could supply the necessary words or music to complete your song. Once that has been done, then the song can be taken personally to local singers. If the song is accepted by a singer or orchestra leader and creates local attention, then have the song recorded on a recording (acetate) which doesn't cost more than $4 or $5. This then can be used to demonstrate the song to a legitimate music publisher for a legitimate songwriters' contract. This method will cost the writer almost nothing except his time. Songs now well-known have been started in the very fashion I have outlined. Legitimate music publishers and American Music Societies deplore the "song rackets" that plague new and amateur songwriters in this field, and do everything they can to discourage, discredit, or stamp out the "song shark."

Roger Burlingame: I can wrap up advice to beginning writers in one word: write.

Robert Payne: Write as though you were fighting for your life, putting every ounce of your strength into it. Write as though you were the only writer. Write as though the universe had vanished, and you had to recreate it in your own mind. Above all, think of writing as an act of grace.

A. C. Spectorsky: I would give the beginner a non-writing assignment first. I would ask him to spend a good long day alone, asking himself over and over again whether he wants to be a writer or whether he wants to write. There are a great many people who would like to be writers; there are darn few people who want to write. Writing is extremely lonely, extremely exacting. It is impossible to goof off and get by—the way you can if you are on salary and happen to have a bad day. Nor can you fake it or bluff your way through it. I would tell the would-be writer who has decided that yes, he wants to write, that he can test the accuracy of his conclusion against the fact of whether he's done a lot of writing. If he's reached his majority and hasn't quite a volume of work already done, regardless of its quality, I'd question his real desire to write. Assuming a beginner really wants to write, I would make this suggestion to him: that he learn how to write a simple declarative sentence which says exactly what it means and means exactly what it says, before trying to get intricate, fancy, or stylistic. Apparently, judging by hundreds upon hundreds of manuscripts I've seen in the past twenty-five years, the simple declarative sentence is a very hard thing to master indeed. I would consider it essential.

Senator Richard L. Neuberger: My specific advice to writers is to write—just as I would tell an aspiring pianist to play the piano, or a golfer to play golf.

Emil Zubryn: If you want to write—then *write*, without benefit of schools, correspondence courses, books (no offense meant) or other gimmicks. In the talks I've had with pros, I have yet to meet one who *seriously* studied writing. You either have it in you—or you don't. And if you don't the best thing to do is to seek some other line of endeavor.

And the only other thing I can say is what the serious beginner already knows. If you want to succeed in the field, you must write, turn out the copy . . . also you must *believe* in yourself and what you write. When I believe in a piece, I don't give up. I've sold an article on its 42nd trip out!

Sloan Wilson: My advice is . . . if the process of writing isn't a pleasure, quit it. Money and fame come much easier and much surer in other fields. In sum, the only real reason for writing is the discovery that the satisfaction of self-expression is greater than the necessary pain of craftsmanship or art. As in other fields, money and fame go to those who seek them least.

. . . Honest writing isn't a business. It's an art which occasionally brings in a lot of money as a by-product. Many who call it a business know damn well it's an art, but are embarrassed to admit it. As a businessman, many a successful writer can thumb his nose at the world, but if he admits he's an artist, good or bad, he's wide open to attack.

Evan Hunter: I very rarely, in truth think about why I became a writer or how I write or why I write. I just write. On the other hand, I do have very definite goals and convictions . . .

I believe that most book publishers and magazine editors are *looking* for fresh young talent. If a writer is sincere about his work, if he isn't simply looking for quick fame and easy fortune, he will not go unnoticed. But if he is sincere, he will soon realize that writing is something more than an idle hobby and that there is a vast difference between penning a letter to Aunt Zenebia and being a writer.

Ben Smith: The best advice I could give a beginning writer is . . . don't, knowing full well that if he is destined to be a writer he will pay no attention to me at all. It's the toughest racket on earth . . . and the lowest paid. Competition is rough and there is very little fame. Most of your friends, when they finally are bludgeoned into realizing that the literary spark burns in your breast, will either say, "So what?" or wonder what excuse *they* can give for not getting out and earning an honest living.

To those who will eventually become writers, I'd say: First, bend every effort to mastering your craft. Don't read a story and think to yourself, "I can do better than that with the space bar tied down on my typewriter," because you're crazy as hell. Writing is a craft, friend, and a damned critical one and there is no place for the half-competent workman. Make every piece of work you turn out the BEST YOU CAN DO at that time. Never be satisfied with the level of your work. Make each story better than the last. How do you judge these things? That's where the sleeper is, my friend—there is no yardstick except the way you feel, and if you're a writer, you *feel,* and that's all there is to it.

When I began to write seriously, I was working on a cattle farm in Oklahoma. Naturally, I had no typewriter and no money. So I borrowed one, a folding Corona, that always threatened to snap off my arm. I had no ribbon for it and knew of no place within range where I could get one without cash. However, I had carbon paper. So I worked like this: I typed on the first page without being able to read what I was writing. Later, when I pulled the work from the typewriter, I could read the carbon and see where I was going. But I had all the time in the world and the makeshift did two important things that are helpful to me today. I learned to type, and I learned to make sure of what I put down *as I was writing it.* My subconscious has been bullied into playing ball with me.

Blake Clark: I believe that a would-be young writer should take on a big project, while still young, for any big project, once completed, proves many things *to* a writer, and about a writer and his ability. The fact that a writer can complete a book—that is satisfactory to one publisher—even if the book does not become a bestseller, indicates that he has the self-discipline to make a sustained effort. This is what is required in a writer all his life. . . . At the beginning of a writing career, unless you inherit money, you have to work day and night merely to keep going economically, and to make an indentation. A beginning writer must read omniverously. The most important single point I believe a young writer should learn is the importance of being specific. Instead of writing, for instance, that the room was "well-lighted," say that it was lighted by 10,000 candlepower from four over-hanging lamps, casting reflections. Stating time, place, examples—all are important to believability. Otherwise, the reader will not stick with it.

A person who starts to write for a living should go on the theory that it's hard—not disagreeable, not impossible, not without thrills, but still hard.

Jesse Stuart: If writing is part of a would-be writer's makeup, then he should stay with it through thick and thin. Never give up!

Thomas P. Kelley: Remember that you're going into a tough game, and the competition is rugged. An ace-in-the-hole sure helps.

Scott Young: Stick to writing, and do no jobs that are hard on the soul. In short, while learning, try to make a living at something you like, even if it is not as highly paid as what you *could* do. The more pay, the more work and other demands, the less time for writing. It is easy to put off being a writer—a million excuses, and any one will do. The difficulty of making a living and writing at the same time is the most common invalid excuse.

Deane and David Heller: Our advice to beginners would be: keep your output high, work like the devil, don't be discouraged, study the needs of editors carefully, and have faith in yourself in spite of discouraging rebuffs.

Above all, don't become engaged in fruitless arguments with editors. Either they like your material or they don't and if you make a nuisance out of yourself, you automatically kill any chance of success you might have.

Saul K. Padover: Write only if you feel strongly that you have something to say. Then you will get true, inner satisfaction, pride and self-respect. If you write only for money, that's OK, too, but then you are not really a creator but a businessman.

John Gassner: Look about you, look into yourself, observe a great deal, read a great deal, write constantly, revise constantly, *hear* what you write, write nothing or retain nothing that doesn't have some music of its own, some rhythm and cadence, though never write just willfully, and always try to make sense to the other fellow. Avoid mere self-indulgence.

Kenneth S. Giniger: The only advice anyone can give to beginning writers is that which Sinclair Lewis gave in his famous one word speech to a college journalism class: "Write!"

Georges Simenon: Read, read, read, then forget it. Live, live, live, don't forget it . . . and write, write, write . . .

Lester David: I think no would-be writer for a mass circulation magazine could possibly succeed unless he has, or can develop, an understanding of what *interests* people; not just some people, but *all* people, or as many as possible. He has to have a feeling for a mass audience. He has to know what scares people, what delights them, what worries them, and what they are yearning for. He has to be able to satisfy these yearnings, allay these fears, feed these delights.

Let me be specific. Time and again, young writers become all excited about a magazine article idea which has only specialized appeal. Perhaps it's a piece about wildflowers or an historical vignette or spear fishing. He sends it all over the place and can't understand why editors keep bouncing it back. Wild flowers simply delight him and he knows so many other people who are similarly delighted. Well, he drops the wild flower idea, and picks up a notion about a specific feature of the income tax law which has hurt his father's business considerably. This he considers a terrible, scandalous thing which ought to be eliminated, and he proceeds to bombard editors with a bit to do an expose. Again, he's rebuffed and again he mutters about the low mentality of editors who can't see a vicious situation when it's dangled before them.

Beginning writers are all too prone to miss the forest for the trees. What interests *them*, what is all-important to *them*, does not necessarily mean a heck of a lot to a reader in Joplin, Missouri.

This reader in Missouri—or anywhere else—is interested in reading about new and different ways to solve his own problems. He wants to know more about his family, his marriage, his sex life, his money, his religious life. He wants to know what makes him tick and how he can tick better. Reach this reader, dig for new and exciting discoveries and research studies about *people*.

Does this let out the article about wild flowers—the so-called "objective" piece? Not at all. There are quite a few specialized publications which want such articles. Even major magazines will seek out the special type of article. By and large I feel that the writer who writes about people, who helps them through his reporting of new discoveries and new attitudes, to find their way, has the greatest chance of professional success.

Lewis Broad: If writing is his line a writer will write on despite all discouragements, the lack of interest of family and friends, the devastation of rejection slips from editors. A born writer needs no help; his genius will discover itself. The less favoured writer should follow the model that most pleases him, or to sell his wares, should pick on the market that tempts him and imitate those who fill the columns in which he wishes to appear. . . .

Journalism is a road I would recommend to any would-be writer. News reporting calls for accuracy of the highest degree, brevity, simplicity and readability. These are the essentials of all writing—readability above all. Fancies and furbelows are at a discount in the newspaper. Far better be penny plain than two-pence coloured and ignored. After all, every author—we are all exhibitionists in words—wants to be read. There is no better training ground than journalism. I look in the writers' roll of fame and note the names of those who began in journalism, from Dr. Johnson to Bernard Shaw, taking in (it is an English list) Rudyard Kipling, Charles Dickens, G. K. Chesterton, James Barrie, Oscar Wilde, Arnold Bennett—I forbear from plaguing you further.

Frederic A. Birmingham: The best advice ever given to beginning writers, long before I agreed with it, was in one word: Write. . . . A writer learns the dangers lurking in the cliché, the improvements possible in a rewrite, and a horde of other straight-line habits . . . from writing itself, not from merely thinking about it.

Joseph N. Bell: Advice to beginning writers: Grow up. Become mentally mature before you waste your postage sending off material not based on hard thinking.

IV

What Successful
Writers Don't Do

Luck is infatuated with the efficient.
—OLD PERSIAN PROVERB

THIS book, as you can guess by now, is not going to be about the personal, intimate affairs of people who are successful writers. I don't intend to become a "keyhole journalist" this late in life. Yet, I believe you have a right to know the most intimate secrets that I could discover about the practices of writers, in relation to their work as writers. As I thought about the many hundreds of questions that would-be writers have asked me—a teacher of writing for some years—it seemed to me that I should learn, if possible, what successful writers succeed in *not* doing. If you and I can learn from the masters what *not* to do, at least we could save some time and wasted effort in learning what *to* do.

Remember, a writer, whether he is halfway successful or both rich and internationally famous, intrinsically has only a few assets, as a writer. They are: (1) his ability to get ideas and his ability to turn these ideas into words that make a salable book, story, article, song, or whatever; (2) his determination and ability to *sell* this book, story, article, song, or poem, to get the most out of it for the longest possible time. Obviously, the writers who are most success-

ful are those who have learned how to do these things. Just as
obviously, they have learned what *not* to do, in order to protect
themselves against defeat in every possible way.

First, I believe the successful writers whom I questioned have
learned *not* to talk about an idea on which they are working.

A successful writer saves himself much trouble, many heartaches,
and sometimes great disappointment with himself by *not* talking
about his ideas until he has finished writing them down.

"Fiction writing is a kind of magic, and I don't care to talk about
a novel I'm doing because if I communicate the magic spell, even
in an abbreviated form, it loses its force for me," Angus Wilson said.

Second, I believe the successful writers whom I have known do
not spend a great amount of time at meetings, in clubs, or striving
to be social lions. This is not due so much to the fact that writers
are introverts (some are, a lot are not) as it is to the demands the
writing profession makes upon all those successful men in it. A
writer may have to travel, or he may have to sacrifice his research
and writing time in other pursuits that do not seem to have much
to do with writing. Yet, everything that a successful writer does
must be geared to his daily output, whether he is turning out a
column for national syndication, or writing a book. There are just
so many days in a year, just so much time that a writer can spend
in research and writing. As far as possible, he husbands his mental
and physical resources, by not being too much of a social lion.
While he may discuss his profession with other writers over a
before-dinner drink, or attend a cocktail party occasionally, the
average successful writer does not show up as one of the audience
in very many writing seminars, or writing club meetings. While
many belong to clubs—such as the Overseas Press Club in New
York, the National Press Club in Washington, or similar social clubs
—they seldom, if ever, go to meetings at which someone lectures
about writing. The reason is that, when a successful writer is away
from his research and his typewriter, he does not want to waste

what "free" time he has listening to advice from people who, in his judgment, do not know as much about what he wants to do as a writer, as *he* knows. The successful writer recognizes the need for free-lance writers' clubs, on the part of those who need a social stimulation to continue. But the truly professional writer needs no stimulation to write beyond his own impelling urge, instilled in him from factors he may not be able to explain, or isolate.

Third, a successful writer does not consider *any* part of his work as unimportant, or relatively less important, than other parts. The more successful a writer—and the longer he remains a success—the more he realizes that *every* phase of his writing must meet and surpass a standard if he is to remain among the successes. A successful writer understands that the last paragraph of a story must be as accurate, and as well written, as the first paragraph, or the middle, or any other part. He knows that a misspelled word anywhere in the story—even if it goes by the editor's eye and is included in the final print copy—detracts from the net effect he wants to leave with his reader. Therefore, the successful writer *thinks* about every part of his story—his facts, his words, his spelling, the sentence structure, the paragraphs, and the total effect of the story.

I have heard many fledgling, or would-be, writers say: "Oh yes, I know that my plot is weak, but how is my story otherwise? Am I a good writer?" The answer is that everyone is a good writer, in a certain sense, if he can write a sentence as simple as "I am going to town." The successful writer does not look for compliments, or criticisms, from amateur sources. If there is a structural fault, or a glaring lack, in his book, article, story, or whatever, he wants the editor to tell him. Later, he will view the offerings of the current crop of critics, and will be affected by these criticisms in various ways, depending upon his temperament, his faith (or lack of it!) in the intelligence of the critics, and other factors. A successful writer realizes that while some professional friend might be able to help him on his article, story, or whatever, it is an imposition on this professional friend's time to bother the other writer. So you'll find very few professional writers carrying manuscripts around for opinions of the general public, writing teachers, or friends. The successful writer knows that the only thing to do with a completed manuscript, if he thinks it is ready to publish, is to send it to an editor who might buy it.

Fifth, a successful writer does *not* try to work mentally on more than one idea at a time. The mind, we know, is a marvelous thing, and every man's mind—if he has normal intelligence or better—can work subconsciously on a variety of problems. But in writing *a* story, *an* article, or whatever, a writer must direct his mind to a specific task, or, rather, a specific series of tasks, since each word, each sentence, each paragraph and each portion represents a new task.

It is my observation that those would-be writers whom I have known—and their number is legion—have failed mostly because of the fact that they would not pursue subjects *one at a time*. While talking about, or working on one idea, they would allow their minds to run off on tangents and get to thinking about another idea, or other ideas. As a result, *all* of their editorial work was futile, in that they never would energetically set their minds to working on one article, for one market, and finish this one idea before starting on another.

Each of us has a marvelous mind. But none of us, however brilliant, can add and subtract a set of figures at the same time. We'd strip our gears. As drivers, we cannot take two roads at once. The successful writer has learned that he cannot add and subtract at the same time, and that he can't take two highways in one car. He *directs* his thinking toward one idea, and continues until he has completed it. Having rid his mind of these thoughts, these challenges, these decisions, he finds it easier to direct it toward another specific task, and another, and another, as time passes.

It is possible for our minds to be working on an idea at all times, and we can change the direction of our thinking, as we please. But it is disastrous, to a writer, not to be able to focus his mind on one idea at a time. The reason some would-be writers continue to try the impossible is that they are both lazy and undisciplined. It is work to direct the mind, to *think*. They know, too, that such a process requires them to exercise self-discipline.

The really successful person learns to "shut out" the world, and all its random buffetings, and to concentrate on a specific poem, a specific article, or a specific book.

One successful writer expressed it this way: "I am an omnivorous reader, and I get ideas every time I read. The trick, I have found, if I am working on one idea, is to read with a purpose, or, if I am traveling, to think with a purpose, as I view the countryside.

"I make notes of other ideas that occur to me and then deliberately forget them, at least temporarily, while I continue to concentrate on the idea on which I am working currently. A man can strip his mental gears by trying to work on two ideas at the same time."

This is what other successful writers have told me. The disciplining of the mind, in some respects, to keep it on *one* subject—when thousands of subjects are presenting themselves—comes from disciplining the body. If you make yourself go to a library to look for material on a particular subject, you are heading your mind into the right channels. Or, if you outline a series of projects to do, in connection with your Big Idea, again, you channel your mind's thinking, while directing your body's actions.

Just to speculate idly about how you would like to write this or that article is, in a sense, both mentally frustrating and harmful to your spirit. This is day-dreaming, and successful writing is far removed from day-dreaming.

The writer is a *doer*. Writers may be brilliant conversationalists, at times. They may travel, and take part in civic activities. The reason why they are successful as writers is that they know how to concentrate, to cover an idea thoroughly, or work it up thoroughly, before fixing their attention on another project.

Sixth, a successful writer is one who is *not* discouraged by the little difficulties that constantly arise in this life to plague any person who strives to accomplish more than the "average." Perhaps this is the biggest reason why successful writers—or successful people—*are* successful. They have learned, with William Cullen Bryant, that "difficulty is the nurse of greatness—a harsh nurse, who rocks her foster children roughly but rocks them into strength . . . The mind, grappling with great aims and wrestling with mighty impediments, grows by a certain necessity to the stature of greatness."

I have known would-be writers, or might-be writers, who have wrecked whatever career they might have had by allowing themselves to be torn by the shoals of impatience, striving to do what no man can do, i.e., change the way other people act in their normal pursuits. The successful writer is not overwhelmed when someone loses one of his manuscripts. He takes it as part of the hazards of doing business in a cockeyed world. He realizes that, in this civilization, there are many square pegs in round holes, and that things go wrong all along the line . . . mailmen don't deliver some mail correctly, editors don't do their reading and reporting promptly, stenographers slip up and forget to put through a requisition, bookkeepers sit on checks and never think of the economic consequences to the writer, and so forth.

Yet, the successful writer—if he intends to continue to compete in the future—does not make a "federal case" out of seemingly unavoidable delays and slip-ups. I am one person who believes that everything is a big thing and everything is a little thing, depending upon who is viewing it, from what standpoint, where it takes place, and a million other factors. I am also one person who believes that most of the evils surrounding this civilization could be obviated if each of us would spend just a few minutes each day thinking of someone else's problem. This is a part of "figuring things out," so that we can make our peace with life. The successful writer is one who has either studied or experienced enough in this field to *understand* the problems inherent in every situation and, understanding it, to act reasonably from the other fellow's viewpoint.

A successful writer of my acquaintance told me recently of his experiences with a certain editor of a "large" magazine, notorious not only for poor pay, but for poor liaison with contributors. Although it advertises that it reports in two weeks, the reports are likely to be made in three months, if then.

"I received a letter from the editor of this magazine asking me to prepare an article," the writer related. "Although it is a low-pay market, I did the article promptly and sent it in. He sent me a letter saying he planned to use it. Six months later, not having heard from the editor, I queried him. He wrote me that he had lost the material!

"Instead of blowing my top, I wrote him a note telling him I had a carbon and would be glad to send it along. In three months, he wrote that he had found the piece, and was enclosing it, thinking I might want to bring it up to date before he used it. I made some changes—in line with the elapsed time and new developments—and sent it back. Eighteen months after I had sent this piece to the editor, I got a $75 check. But it still came in handy. I didn't get angry with him and give him a piece of my mind, for he is going to be in business at the same old stand in the future. I can't afford to kill my markets by being nasty to editors, no matter how much they may hurt me, inadvertently."

The successful writer does *not* cultivate his own impatience. He learns—in the process of working in the editorial field—that there are all kinds of editors, all kinds of editorial assistants, all kinds of situations that can hamper him and hurt him. Learning how to meet these difficulties—and still do his work day by day—is as much a part of becoming, and staying, a successful writer as the writing itself.

Seventh, successful writers do *not* spend their time, like Don Quixote, vainly trying to destroy windmills, to reform a magazine's outlook, or an editor's philosophy. Many an amateur writer takes it on himself to try to write a certain kind of material for a certain kind of magazine, and the material obviously is not designed for this specific magazine's audience.

Actually, the editor is not "resisting," when he turns down such material. He is merely exercising his ability, insofar as he has any, to ferret out the kind of material his particular audience wants, and to return to writers the kind that does not fit this audience's needs. The successful writer understands this, but the amateur, and some of those half-way between the amateur and the professional class, do not seem to understand it.

If a magazine is making money, appealing to a specific audience with a kind of message the audience likes, the editor is going to think a long time before he goes off onto any new avenues. He constantly is trying to find out how he can increase his existing readership by adding new readers, without losing his present audience. Therefore, the editor is in line for new ideas close to the mark. But to use an exaggerated example, a Republican magazine, edited for a Republican audience, is not likely to carry an article appealing to Democrats. Likewise, a magazine appealing to rich people is not apt to carry much material which casts doubt upon the efficacy of a lot of money. A magazine for bankers won't stay in business long if it comes out in favor of lower interest rates. The successful writer understands, is in touch with reality, and as long as he remains successful, he must remain in touch with reality.

Eighth, successful writers do *not* fritter away one of their greatest assets—time. They stick to their last. They are dedicated persons.

When a writer is not socializing, he is reading. When he is on a trip, he is reading, or interviewing, or sizing up whatever he has traveled to see. All is grist for his mill. Also he realizes the necessity of learning how best to use the time when he is fresh and feels up to working at his maximum.

I am acquainted with many people who want to be writers, or pretend to be "literary." Some consider they are writers because they gossip about other writers, or spend hours talking about books, or go to lectures or teas at which this or that writer will speak. These people are *not* successful—as writers—because they do not use their *time* to good effect.

Successful writers tell me that they budget their time carefully each day. They work—at the typewriter—a certain number of hours, but they consider their reading, interviewing, and observing, as part of their work, and they realize that a person's mind is like a spring—if it is not replenished constantly by a source of new ideas, the supply of good ideas dries up.

A writer learns that he must *live* to get good ideas, and that, when he is asleep, he is not experiencing. Therefore, he wants to use every minute he is awake, in some constructive way to increase his knowledge of his world and his ability to express his knowledge in a new and different way.

There are only 168 hours in a week. In questioning successful writers, I asked them if they thought it possible for a writer to become successful these days in his spare time.

"It is possible for a person to sell material occasionally," one writer told me. "But I can't see how anyone can expect to make his maximum indentation by working at it only once in a while, or intermittently. Writing in all fields is so demanding these days, I cannot believe it is possible for a writer to devote eight hours to other work and still be able to turn out material regularly that hits the spot."

To show where a 168-hour week goes, I asked a writer, who shall be unidentified, to keep his schedule for a while. We were both amazed at the demands made upon a writer's time, other than those of the typewriter.

This writer has a wife and two children. His wife helps him in his work by typing for him. His children are thirteen and ten, one in high school and one in grammar school. He belongs to a Protestant church and goes only occasionally. He is not a "joiner," otherwise.

Just *living*—and doing the things necessary to keep body and soul together, even if he had inexhaustible financing—takes a great deal of this writer's time. He has to sleep eight hours a night. That takes fifty-six hours out of his 168-hour week.

He has to eat three meals a day. That takes roughly three hours a day, or twenty-one hours a week. Just eating and sleeping takes seventy-seven hours out of his week.

He has to read the daily newspapers, magazines and some books each day. That takes roughly three hours a day, or another twenty-one hours a week. This makes ninety-eight hours without any production whatever.

He has to move about—to see the world he lives in, to interview people to get information, or to socialize, either with friends in their homes or in his own. This takes roughly twenty hours a week, leaving him, theoretically, fifty hours in which to produce.

But this writer is not only a writer. He is a *husband*, and a *father*. He has to spend some time with his children, other than at meals. He also has to keep tax records each day, both the money he takes in and the money he pays out that is deductible legitimately. He must go to the Parent-Teachers' Association meetings once a month, to a school affair once or twice a month, he must have the car inspected every six months, he must have the car repaired when it gets out of whack, he must spend time explaining what needs fixing to the plumber, and he has to answer mail from editors, friends, relatives and just plain curiosity seekers who write to him.

He also is a citizen. He has to vote. He has to make sure he is registered. He has to be sure that he has paid his local, his state and his federal taxes—on time. He has to attend an occasional meeting of his community association, merely to be sure that his property interest, in case he has property, is protected. He also must go to church, occasionally if not regularly.

All of these things take *time*. From the writer's standpoint—and from that of his earnings—the only productive part of all this will be in what he learns from his reading and observation and how much he can keep his mind working for him, on ideas and possible projects, while he is taking part in all this seemingly unproductive and uneconomic activity.

All of these extraneous school, church, civic, and other necessary activities take at least ten more hours a week from our hero's working schedule. He then has what seems to be forty hours left in which really to produce.

This breakdown of what a writer—whether he writes or not—must do merely to fulfill his basic obligations to his family and community indicates why it is not likely that very many persons who fill an eight-hour job—as a bookkeeper, plumber, clerk, or whatever —really turn out enough material in their "spare time" to become a successful writer.

Even a person who devotes *all* his time to writing—other than the time he is doing the things mentioned above—finds that he must ration the existing time at his disposal. Many writers *must* travel to do their best work. But travel is terribly costly in *time*, not to mention the money. A writer who spends two weeks away from his desk finds that it is piled high with letters when he returns. I estimate that a two-week trip away from my work requires about two weeks for me to catch up, and sometimes longer.

Ninth, successful writers do *not* spread themselves thin by trying to be other than what they are—*writers*. It is true that some men of great capacity can be great painters and great writers, and that a few can be great photographers and great writers, and that some can be great preachers and great writers.

But of some 200 successful writers whom I surveyed, only a handful has become famous in other fields. Most of them, I might add, disclaimed any ability even to make photographs, although most of them own cameras and take occasional snapshots.

Among those surveyed, one of the successful writers *was* a full-time minister. Yet, even in this case, he is not weighed down with administrative details, having sufficient assistants to take care of these matters. His interviews with parishioners he uses as grist for his writing mill. Another writer is becoming a painter of note, but he began to paint *after* he had become successful as a writer and he has never tried to use his paintings as a way of selling his editorial material. Painting, in other words, is a *hobby*.

For an editor to suggest to men like Blake Clark, Walter Lippmann, Georges Simenon, or Alden Hatch, that they make pictures, as well as send him copy, would be as inconceivable as for a patient in a hospital to demand that his surgeon give him a shave, or a shampoo, while performing an operation. The various jobs connected with editing a magazine demand the talents of many men—someone to design the book, someone to illustrate it, and someone to write it, among others. The writer's job is to stick to *writing*.

Tenth, successful writers do *not* waste their time, their emotions, and their thinking powers by being envious of other writers. I have been in the editorial field since 1935, when I sold my first story for $2. During that period, I have had occasion to work with some very fine men. At one time, when I was a copy boy on the old *Birmingham* (Ala.) *Post*, there were four men working in the city room who went on to fame and fortune in the writing field—Harold Helfer, Joel David Brown, William Bradford Huie, and Charles Edmundson. All, I believe, are competent and even brilliant writers. Bill Huie wrote *The Revolt of Mamie Stover*, and Joel David Brown ("J. D." or "Red," as we called him) has written two books that turned into big movies. Later, in other situations, I have been friends with writers like Eudora Welty, Margaret Mitchell, and others. Of all these writers, I do not know one who became successful nationally who was picayunish, or small-minded. Not a one of them sat around being jealous of the others, insofar as I could ever detect. Each one realized that whatever he could accomplish in life would be up to him, and must be done by *him,* not by belittling, undercutting, or low-rating other people.

In those years I have known many men who wanted to be writers, but never made the grade. Some today are holding down small jobs in small towns. In the years, in striving to encourage them or to help them to think in bigger terms, I have written to them. Only in rare instances have I ever received a reply. At the time I knew them, the principal occupation of these men would be commenting —mostly in a snide way—on the accomplishments of others in the city room where they worked. A lot of them seemed to think that every time they uttered a sentence tearing down someone else, it made them into bigger men. Yet, time has shown that just the opposite happened. Every word they uttered against the men who were doing things actually served to emphasize the midget minds of fault-finders and carpers. They have wasted their lives being envious of other men, for it is impossible for a person to produce anything good—in writing, or any other field—if his mind is taken up with envy, malice, jealousy and hatred of someone else who is doing his work as best he can.

There are small-minded men in every field who *seem* to be successful. I have met them in steel companies, in the Senate, and in the offices of publishers. But I can truthfully say that I have never met, and studied, a successful writer, or a man who might be destined to become successful as a writer, who is a small-minded, churlish person. You just can't devote the time you have to devote to writing, to become good enough at it to be successful, and divert your mind into hating and envying and gossiping adversely about people who *are* achieving in this field. A writer's talents and abilities are apparent. If he *has* the ability as a writer, and will exercise the initiative to use his talent, then I believe that nothing on earth can stand between him and success, granted that he retains his health. Impediments can be placed in his path by those who resent his success, but these impediments serve only to make him more determined and to exercise the various facets of his mind to overcome the obstacles. The people who specialize in placing such barriers certainly do not intend it, but they actually make a man into a bigger man, and a writer into a better writer, by placing obstacles in his path. If *you* want to be a successful writer, you can measure the rate of your development, and progress toward your goal, by the amount of time you do not spend being envious of others. The less time you give to thinking of other writers—in envy or malice—the more time you have to devote to your own work.

I haven't gone into the more obvious things that successful writers *don't* do, such as paying to have their books printed, or sending off money to writers' clubs for "criticisms," or wasting time answering obviously fraudulent ads trying to get them to subscribe to this or that course of writing. It is possible that some successful writers *have* taken these courses, but the ones to whom I have talked seem never to have wasted their time and money by sending their money to such promotional outfits. Successful writers I have known smile when you mention such courses. They point out that there is no "secret" to writing, but that there are techniques that must be learned in the process of writing and working in the writing field. Successful writers—who make their living from writing—want to get money *from* publishers, not send money *to* publishers. They never wasted their money with subsidy publishers of any kind, or on mail-order courses in writing. The successful writers are those who learned how to write by *writing*.

V

The Special
Problems of Writers

Literature—the most seductive, the most deceiving, the most dangerous of professions.

—JOHN MORLEY

EVERY profession has its special problems. Some are native to the profession and some of them are applicable to most callings. The knowledge of the special problems which writers encounter— that people in other trades, professions and businesses may *not* encounter—will help you to know more about our subject.

The importance of each of these special problems, of course, will vary from writer to writer. If a successful novelist takes a liking to a young fellow who wants to be a writer, and agrees to stand behind this young man and read every page of his copy and correct it, obviously this youngster doesn't run into a special problem that some other beginning novelist might encounter. In a broad sense, I believe that virtually *all* successful writers will run into all of the special problems, in one form or another, that I shall strive to make clear to you.

The fact that successful writers *are* writers—and not something else—makes it inevitable, in this or any society, that they have special problems. If you doubt that, then just think again about Djilas, Pasternak, and others who run afoul the prejudices of their society.

But even the most "accepted" writer in a society, if he is a writer, has special problems, other than those in which he runs the risk of being imprisoned, beheaded, or exiled. This is, as the philosophers would say, in the nature of things, for writers are engaged in a kind of work that is as strange and mysterious to most other people as the antics of a witch doctor are to those of us not members of the Witch Doctors' Union.

One of my sons, when he was just going into high school, used to come home from school and say: "We discussed writers in our English class today and most of the students were very curious about how you work. They seem to think there is something odd about anyone who is a writer. But I tell them you are not any more of a screwball than any of their fathers."

I would say that the biggest problem to a writer is *himself*. Successful writers recognize this. They know that to produce—and to produce well—they have to watch themselves carefully and discipline themselves constantly. There is just as much a tendency among successful writers to "put it off," "do it tomorrow," or "work when I feel better," as there is among the rankest amateurs. But the difference between the rank amateur and the professional is that the professional has learned how to handle himself, and the situation around him, to get himself mentally into shape so that he can face the machine and work. The most successful writers are men who have learned how to break a job up into pieces, and do it one piece at a time. Rather than putting an article off for a month, and trying to finish it in one day, a man like Blake Clark, for example, will write a page, or two pages, every day. After writing these pages, or two pages, he will collate them with the other pages he has written about the same subject. Then, the next day, he will write a page or two pages. When he feels like it, he will read over the whole thing and re-arrange. Then, day by day, he will add a little here, a little there, re-reading and re-writing as he goes. At the end of the time he has allotted, it will be done, and not with any special tearing of the hair. In quiet discipline, he keeps his mind focused on that one article all during his working period on it, and, of course, everything that he reads, every call he makes, every reference he tracks down, adds to the sum total of his knowledge about the subject. By the time he has done the research and the writing, day by day, little at a time, he has an article that bristles with authority and interest and authenticity.

Getting down to work each day is the most difficult task for each writer, apparently, regardless of his medium. Ernest Hemingway once told Thornton Wilder that he sharpened twenty pencils each day before he could get down to work. Willa Cather, according to Wilder, always read a passage from the Bible—not from piety, but to get in touch with fine prose. Wilder himself always takes long walks, then plunges into his work. Thomas Wolfe would roam the streets all night before he could get down to writing the next morning.

To be disciplined, the writer learns that he must make certain conditions outside himself conform to his pattern of work activities. If he is a writer who must have peace and quiet to think straight, then he arranges to have peace and quiet. If he is one who is unaffected by his surroundings, but has to be sure that he is physically up to par, then he does everything that is necessary to feel physically up to par. The writer finds out—by experience, usually—what conditions must be met for him to produce his best work, at his best pace. Unlike an amateur, who may leave such things to chance, the professional writer thinks about himself and his discipline and consciously directs his activities and his studies so that he will be impelled to do the work he wants to do.

The meditation, or gestatory period, is very important to many writers. Some have a short "gestatory" period. Georges Simenon, with his 400 novels, has a gestatory period of only two days. William Faulkner's may be six months. The meditation period is not wholly conscious, although some of it may be. Mostly, I think, the subconscious mind is at work. Sometimes the writer must "sweat it out." At other times, he may awaken one morning with the whole story in his head and feverishly must put it down.

"I never quite know when I'm not writing," says James Thurber. "Sometimes my wife comes up to me at a dinner party and says, 'Dammit, Thurber, stop writing.' She usually catches me in the middle of a paragraph. Or my daughter will look up from the dinner table and ask, 'Is he sick?' 'No,' my wife says. 'He's writing.' I have to do it that way on account of my eyes."

Nelson Algren finds his plots simply by writing page after page, night after night. "I always figured," he says, "the only way I could finish a book and get a plot was just to keep making it longer and longer until something happens."

Simenon, on the other hand, knows nothing about the events that will take place in his novels until he writes them. "Otherwise," he says, "it would not be interesting to me."

It is said that Charles Dickens wept when one of his characters died, or choked with laughter when one did something particularly funny. Most writers "get a kick" out of chancing on a situation, in their articles or books, where they have come up to a funny episode (of their own making) without realizing it until it has happened. And sometimes they are saddened when one of the characters, who showed promise, turns out to be a bad egg.

Truman Capote, who says he is physically incapable of writing anything he doesn't think he will be paid for, likes to know the end of a story before writing the first word of it. Indeed, he doesn't start writing until he has brooded over the story long enough to exhaust his emotional response to the material.

Successful writers, let's face it, mostly are pretty high-strung men and women. They may not seem so, but they are more *alive* than other people and they are more aware than their non-writing neighbors. If they were not more aware, more observant, more alive, they could not possibly observe the various facets of life they do observe so as to be able to write about these things in a way to get the material published.

Because they are "keyed up," particularly when writing, writers have a special problem in getting other people to understand this. If the other people with whom they are thrown into contact are writers, then, of course, they understand. But a writer usually does not marry a writer, and his children are not writers, and his friends usually are not writers. Seldom are his neighbors writers. Yet, all of these are people who conceivably might run afoul of him when he is busy at work. They represent a special problem to him. Writers meet this problem in various ways. Many writers keep special dens in their homes or apartments where, when they tell the family they are going to be working, they cannot be disturbed. I have known writers, faced with the problem of a book deadline, who would rent a hotel room and work in lonely solitude until they had finished the chore. Some writers have a cabin on a hilltop.

Just how each meets this problem, of course, is individual, for some successful writers are professors, living on cloistered campuses in large homes; others have a wife and children, crowded into an apartment in New York; some have large homes in the suburbs, or mansions in the country. But whenever you hear of a successful writer, you know that, through careful planning, he has learned how best to overcome, for himself, the problem of other people and the interruptions that they can cause to his work schedule. The more successful a writer becomes, the less the chances of interruptions, for he can hire secretaries, get a bigger house, and insulate himself against the irritations that bother those who are less well-heeled.

A typical successful writer can be hampered in his work by people in many ways. People call him up. If he is at all curious, he wants to take the calls. They write him letters. If he is courteous, he feels he must respond. Even the things the people put in the letters divert him from thinking of the projects on which he is working. Friends call on him to do special writing chores (without thinking of offering him a fee, of course), and clubs invite him to speak (naturally, at no charge!). The demands are constant and time-consuming. But he must learn to handle these demands in a way that will not lose him friends.

A writer—let's face it—lives in more than one world, and possibly, in the case of many writers, several worlds. Shakespeare's mind, undoubtedly, was crowded with characters from all kinds of worlds, and so are the minds of thousands of writers now living. For the characters which a writer "creates" are not really creations, they are inhabitants of the writer's mind. In the delineation of these characters—mentally—the writer lives with them, and they become alive and as vivid to him as they do to his readers, at the time they are reading about the characters and their activities. Facing the problems of one world—the real world of which he is a part—is hard enough on a writer. But when he has to face the problems facing his characters in half a dozen other worlds, it becomes burdensome. Is it any wonder that so many writers, as we know from history, are unable to stay in touch with reality? I could list a dozen who ended their days in mental institutions.

The writer, by letting his mind run in many channels, develops a sharper social consciousness than other people. He becomes aware of the little ways that he can hurt other people, and he learns that a little hurt, at a certain stage in a man's life, a child's life, or anyone's life, conceivably might be the most crucial event in that person's life. At the same time a writer builds a new set of morals. Sometimes, his personal morals may deteriorate because he is putting his mind to his higher set of social, economic, political, or other morals. It is not for me to judge the personal morals of writers, or of those notorious drunks and roués, living and dead, who have become successful as writers. But whether we excuse them or not, we have to understand *why* writers frequently do break down, entirely, in their personal moral lives. I believe the biggest reason is that they are living in more than one world and that they develop a keener social conscience than the average tradesman. These conflicts cause them to take refuge in other pleasures that are, at least momentarily, soothing.

Whatever the reasons, it is a fact that his *different* set of morals is a problem to every successful writer. He learns to weigh his words and to guard his actions, for there are so many people who are waiting—and willing!—to misinterpret his every sentence, and his every action. One of the writer's principal problems is "squaring" the world with the way he thinks the world ought to be. If the writer has not run up against this problem—and all of those to whom I have talked *have* encountered it—he can consider himself fortunate. Perhaps he has made his peace with the world in another day and is happy in his specialty, or in his cloistered home, or in his dream world. Yet, he can never be too sure, for in working in the editorial field—any and every phase of it—the writer comes up against new problems that constantly challenge him to exercise his higher social morality. And, of course, his tendency to act on his standards unless he withdraws entirely from society. A writer never wholly solves this special problem. He makes a series of compromises with life, realizing that if he is to retain his contact with reality and maintain himself in a complex world, he *must* adjust as much as possible to the *mores* of his society, whatever it is and wherever it is.

The problem of successful writers is that of measuring minutes. They want to get so much done, in a certain amount of time, and doing it all requires not only personal discipline but the maximum use of their time. Do you think that Erle Stanley Gardner can turn out four top-rate murder mysteries every year, and take part in all the other activities in which he does take part, by not measuring his minutes? Or how about Carter Brown, the Australian detective story writer who is under contract to the New American Library of World Literature to give them an acceptable manuscript *every month*? Can he do it and fritter away his time? I am told that when Georges Simenon is working on a novel, he gives himself 11 days— or some other breathtakingly short period—and during that time he will not let anyone get in contact with him for anything less than a major tragedy.

If a writer specializes in doing popular articles, he runs into a problem from the people whom he interviews. Some want him to send them a carbon—"so we can check it for accuracy." If he agrees to do this, he then finds that some press agent, public relations man, or someone else is going over the article with a blue pencil. He doesn't think it is "accurate" to refer to his man as "bulky," although the fellow may weigh 280 pounds.

I once did an article about a Senator who imagined that he was Presidential caliber. I had a tentative assignment from a magazine to carry a profile article on this solon. After I had finished the piece, as agreed, I sent a carbon to the Senator. He and his family and his press agent and public relations man all went over it, changing every reference that didn't make it seem that this was a man called by destiny to become our leader in a trying period. When I saw the mangled copy, I thanked them, and then voiced the opinion that when I sent it to the editor, that worthy would blow a gasket. This is exactly what happened. The editor sent me a check for the research, but he refused to carry any notice whatever about the Senator who had never made a mistake in his life. The Senator obviously did make one big mistake—he didn't get the publicity he wanted, and his "candidacy" amounted to nothing. His name was not even placed in nomination at the political convention.

Businessmen every day want to tell writers how to write, and so do many people who have never sold a line to any magazine. When the writer agrees to let the subject "see a carbon," he is letting himself in for a lot of headaches, sometimes. Yet, if he does not agree, he may not get the information that he must have to build the kind of an article that possibly will sell. The smartest thing to do is to send the piece to the editor first, then, when the subject has only a half an hour or so to make his corrections for "accuracy," let him see the piece, get it checked, and be on your way. If the subject keeps the piece for several days, he will suggest a new change every time he reads it. And so will everyone else who is "close" to him, either personally or professionally.

The successful writer has another special problem in that a lot of slow-minded people overemphasize his "wealth," and confuse his few thousands of earnings with the millions other men make in this society. Except for a bare handful of writers, even in this allegedly "affluent" society, about which John Galbraith waxes so eloquent, most successful writers are not wealthy. Yet, whenever they go to a dentist, or a physician, they are charged as much as the town banker, or someone else who may own a money tree. The disparity between what people *think* he should have—and what he actually has in life—sometimes can cause a writer a great deal of trouble. Not a few, but tens of thousands of physicians and dentists gross from $50,000 to $100,000 a year. A lot of service station owners who do not net $25,000 in a year think they are getting cheated. But if a writer sells one book, or a few articles to a major magazine, on which he may net a few thousands, the dimwits who are always jumping to conclusions wonder why he doesn't contribute $1,000 to the Community Fund, and a lot of ignorant real estate men will call him up, coyly telling him about the old Stone mansion which they can let him have cheap for $100,000. The writer's problem is to keep these people as informed as possible about his true situation, so as to keep such people from becoming nuisances.

Some people actually ask him personal questions about his income, his receipts from this or that book, play, or story. The average tradesman would never think of asking an insurance man, or a banker, how much either of them made the previous year. Yet, any writer will tell you that doctors, lawyers, dentists, waiters, shoe-shine boys, and numerous other people, knowing that the person is a writer, will ask him how much he made from a certain work.

A successful writer has problems with his editor, too. The biggest of the problems has to do with the *changes* that are taking place in the world, and in some fields with almost lightning-like rapidity. The fact that the subject of a profile dies, just as the writer has finished an article about him for a magazine that prints only stories about *living* people, is only one of a writer's special problems these days. The international situation changes every hour; new laws are passed, and some of them without publicity, making out of date (and even untrue) a random statement that a writer may have put down in good faith in an article. Individuals are changing their status all the time—some going up the ladder of success and some going down. Editors are changing all over the place. New magazines and publishing houses are being started, others are consolidating, and some are dying. Keeping up with these changes is as much a part of the successful writer's life as keeping up with the changes on the stock market are a part of a broker's life.

A writer has the problem of *competing with the past*. It is all very well for writers to talk about "appreciating" the great writers of yesteryear, and for them to recommend the masterpieces of the past. I do it, and so does every other writer. Yet, the fact is, we are competing with Rudyard Kipling, Zane Grey, Voltaire, Mark Twain, Booth Tarkington, and all the other poets, historians, scientific writers, playwrights, novelists, and essayists whose works are extant and may be published under various arrangements, or no arrangement at all (in case of no copyrights). There is no telling how many books of writers, long since deceased and a part of history, are published each year, in new editions, or how many anthologies are published, consisting mostly of writers who have fulfilled their life's purposes and have moved off the stage. But no one could deny that such printings are extensive, each year, and that every time one of these books is published, or articles and poems are re-published, it means that some living writer is being squeezed by the competition of men long gone.

A doctor does not compete with physicians of the past. The people who get sick today must be cured by today's methods. The doctor is paid at today's rates, and he can get rich fast, competing only with other doctors. Neither does a lawyer compete with lawyers of the past. Rather, he *uses* the knowledge of all lawyers of the past to build a new practice today. But he does not have to argue cases against dead lawyers.

In almost any other field, except that of writing, the tradesman competes not against dead masterpieces, but live-wires who must outdo *him*. But the writer competes against writers who are dead, and whose works are printed again and again.

Just consider the field of movies. A successful writer usually is thinking of selling his material to the movies. But here, as in the book field, he finds himself competing both against other living, producing writers, and writers who have produced and have quit writing. All of the works of the past are available for the movie makers. When they decide to make a movie of an H. G. Wells book, or of one of Jules Verne's books, it is a sale lost to some living writer.

Another problem of writers is that of finding out what environment he must have in which to do his best work. Writing is so energy-consuming, demanding a single-mindedness of purpose at the time the writer actually is composing, he simply must take into account every negative and positive factor in planning his working place and working time. If he, for example, lives in a downstairs apartment and is annoyed every time someone walks across the floor above him—the writer feels this annoyance in his work. He

he wants to have something to say. I think you are putting the cart before the horse when you worry about making more money by specializing than by not specializing. The first thing to do is to do the kind of magazine writing you want to do. If you want to do it badly enough, and have the talent, the money will take care of itself.

Frances and Richard Lockridge: This is a pretty vague question. We specialize in fiction. We have done non-fiction—about adopting children, cats, and, long ago, something about Edwin Booth. But most of this has been aimed, of course, at "popular general markets." Article writers need, of course, to specialize to a considerable extent.

Dora Albert: In most cases, I think a man will earn more if he sticks to one field of writing. However, I also believe that one should write about whatever one is most intensely interested in. If a man is writing about stocks and bonds and earning a good living at it, but suddenly becomes interested in gardening, metaphysics, medicine, or what have you, I think he should try to learn enough about his new interest so that he can attempt some articles in the new field, possibly by interviewing experts.

O. A. Battista: I specialize in two areas: science and self-help. My training and background permit me to be accepted by editors as a specialist in these areas. I don't have time to consider other areas, but must confess that I must discipline myself not to.

Fred Kerner: I have made a specialty of writing anything and everything. A newspaperman learns quickly to handle any kind of an assignment. In general, however, I think that the average writer might end up with better earnings if he sticks to one general field.

Pinky Herman: Writing a song is different from writing a story or novel, in that a songwriter often may write a song about a particular land or country or state which he may never have visited, yet he might come up with a hit song. "South of the Border" was written by two English songwriters who probably never visited

Mexico. Many writers of songs about Dixie never traveled as far South as South Newark, N. J. But their ideas of the subject matter, limited to 32 bars of music (sometimes only 16 bars) are brief, and thus the writers aren't apt to make errors.

Roger Burlingame: I am sure a writer makes more money when he sticks to one field.

Hugh Roy Williamson: Yes, I think that specialization is good if the writer wants to make money or if he has a fairly limited interest. As I have written plays, novels, theology, criticism and history in many forms and at several levels, I have been unable to specialize, except—which is most important—in an historical *period*.

A. C. Spectorsky: The danger of non-specialization is that one's efforts frequently are so diversified as to be spread pretty thin. To be known as a specialist has obvious values in terms of being deemed an authority and in terms of obtaining assignments. On the other hand, I have seen many writers become hopelessly typecast, so that when they try to diverge from their one most popular vein, they are hampered by seeming to editors to be out of character.

Erskine Caldwell: The writer does best if he sticks to what he knows best.

Senator Richard L. Neuberger: In my own writing, I participated in fields as diverse as children's books and articles on economics.

Emil Zubryn: I'm a Jack-of-all-trades in the writing field. . . . I suppose there's something to be said for both sides. You might say I'm a specialist on Mexican (and Latin American) affairs, but I've done humor, trade, medical, personality, general interest, exposé, movie, TV, and other stuff. I'd say it all depends on the individual writer.

Sloan Wilson: A real writer would never ask this. He writes what interests him—what he can write best—and lets the markets take care of themselves.

Evan Hunter: When I was struggling to earn a living as a writer, I wrote for any market that would take my stuff. I wrote Westerns, science-fiction, detective, light love, sports stories, and even occasional articles. I did not write confessions because I didn't think they would (a) advance my art, or (b) do anything toward establishing my name. But anything else I wrote was written sincerely (if commercially) with an eye toward learning something new about the craft in each story, and never, never selling a market short to make a fast buck. I think the beginning writer might do well to try *all* kinds of writing. If, for example, he's a Western specialist, he may wake up one bright morning to discover that all but two of the Western markets have collapsed. This is not sheer speculation. Magazines come and go, and pity the writer who rides a trend for a certain type of fiction and then discovers the trend has vanished.

Ben Smith: Anyone does a particular job better if he specializes. A man who is an airplane pilot and a plumber is never as good at one occupation as he is the other. It is even more true that no writer lives who can write everything equally well. He will have strong points and weak ones. However, specialization here refers to types rather than more minor components. Craig Rice specialized in mysteries, but she wrote short stories, novelettes and novels. She could do equally well with adventure or spy stories, since they are of a type. I write Westerns, but here again we have an adventure *type* and I have sold mystery, sci-fiction, straight adventure, off-trail, riverboat, gambling and airplane stories. Westerns, at this time, are the best avenue for steady income. Basically, though, a "tough" school writer should not write love stories nor a poet write treatises on the tax situation in the United States. Specialize by *types* of work.

Jesse Stuart: I do not specialize. I do not aim for markets. Never slant. I write what comes to me, what is in my mind and heart. I've written what I wanted to write, come hell or high waters. I've had ups and downs. Often, I've supplemented my earnings by public speaking and by teaching, or both. I've never worried a lot about it and have gotten along.

Thomas P. Kelley: I think a writer should play the field, but always have some knowledge of what he is writing about.

Scott Young: Some people specialize successfully. I prefer the broader fields, and keeping to one character or background would bore me stiff.

Deane and David Heller: On the contrary, we believe the more chances you can field without missing, the more you're going to sell. Our articles cover travel, history, current events, personalities, even sports. Many do marvelously well specializing, though. We find it more interesting to explore many fields.

John Gassner: It has been my experience that specializing helps a great deal. I don't believe the person who wishes to succeed as a writer must confine himself to one field, but he certainly must attain a reputation in *one* field. Thus, I have been published in the fields of theatre, motion pictures, and comparative literature, and I have also worked in radio and television. But I became known primarily through my work in the theatre and in the field of the drama. And one thing led to another.

Saul K. Padover: Nowadays, regardless of my personal experience, I should say that specializing would be more helpful to a beginner. There are numerous new fields opening up, offering good chances to young writers (scientific reporting, for example).

Kenneth S. Giniger: I think that, unquestionably, specialization offers greater opportunities for a writer than the buckshot approach. Once a writer has established a reputation in one field, the task of selling his product becomes very much simpler. However, it is important to note in this connection that various areas of specialization can diminish in importance fairly rapidly. For example, I know of one writer who did an excellent job of establishing himself as a specialized "anti-Communist" writer and found it a very profitable field; suddenly, the interest of his particular markets in this subject disappeared and he was left high and dry.

Georges Simenon: I never think about markets, earnings, or fields of writing. *I* don't manufacture sausages or pickles.

Joseph N. Bell: If a writer must specialize, he loses the fun in the work. In my view, writing is a wonderful field because the writer does not have to do anything he doesn't really want to do.

Frederic A. Birmingham: Specializing is a help, I believe, if your specialization is vertical enough to make you an authority and not merely a lay brother. A well known editor became an authority on automobiles—it has become a career for him, in part, as an author. The danger is, of course, that by remaining in one field you discover that you have barred yourself from the next, and the grass where you are is not thick enough to sustain your appetite. . . .

These are not all the special problems of successful writers, for each man in this field, of course, has his own special problems, and he feels them either slightly or poignantly, depending upon his mental and spiritual make-up. But they give you an indication of why I often have remarked, on the basis of the successful writers I have known personally, that many are more to be pitied than envied. And you also can better understand, I hope, why John Morley called literature "the most seductive, the most deceiving, the most dangerous of professions."

It is my hope that by the time you have finished this book, you will have a better idea of these problems than you had before you started it, and that, insofar as you can, you will not add to the woes of those few successful writers who are striving to make their maximum indentation before being felled by the cruel fate that awaits every man.

VI

The Advantages
of Being a Writer

*Life is surely given us for higher purposes
than to gather what our ancestors have
wisely thrown away.*

—BEN JONSON

THIS is one of my smaller chapters. Writers, if they stay in the
business long, try to persuade their sons to be dentists, doctors,
engineers, plumbers—or anything else to make big money and gain
community prestige without too much work. It seems natural that
a lot of the boys end up as psychiatrists, having had their curiosity
about *homo sapiens* aroused by watching the old man.

Considering what you've read so far about successful writers,
perhaps you are wondering why anyone in his right mind would
get into this activity. And when you consider all the people who
have gone mad, or died in mental hospitals, or ended up as paupers,
trying to make a living at it, no doubt a great big question mark
forms in your mind about the idea of making a living at the typewriter.

However, as it must be obvious to you, there are advantages to
being a successful writer. We can even say that there are advantages to being a *writer*, whether you are a success or not in this field.

For part-time writing serves as a release for many individuals who, if they could not write down their thoughts and feelings, undoubtedly would be bending the elbow or out creating trouble for themselves and others.

If you are a good writer, you will become far more famous than successful men in most other fields in life today. As an old obituary reporter, one way I use to keep up with the impact that men make on society is by watching to see how long a notice they get in the newspapers when they die.

Usually—not always, but *usually*—a successful lawyer, banker, doctor, dentist, or other professional man, gets very little space on his death, unless there is something unusual connected with it, such as the fact that he has taken poison, died in a gun battle, or otherwise has ended his life spectacularly.

But when a successful writer dies, the editor of the newspaper realizes that this writer may have an audience of tens of thousands, or even tens of millions, of people. Therefore, depending upon *how* successful the writer has been with his works, he is given an unusual death notice. The same is true of politicians, of course, for in a real sense, politicians and writers are kin to each other and are judged by the general public as being individuals of some importance, in both cases.

Let's not underrate the importance—in this society—of fame, or notoriety, or whatever you call the publicity that writers get. The desire for public recognition is one of the most basic drives in mankind. All of us possess this desire, with greater or lesser intensity, and most of us also have a desire to be *approved* by our fellowmen. So it is not a small thing—fame—that writers get in *lieu* of money.

I might emphasize that a writer *does* get fame in place of money, and that there is a kind of poetic justice in this. The writer who gets the most fame sometimes makes the least money, and the writer who frequently makes the most money gets the least fame. I know ghost-writers who would not think of working for less than $25,000 a year, and you very seldom see their by-lines. And I see lots of notices about this or that TV writer—who may write a play for one of the networks occasionally—who, in my opinion, do not average $10,000 a year. They *may* be lucky and make more, but on an average they would feel fortunate to be sure of $10,000 a year. Yet, they get plenty of fame.

One time, I gave a city editor two weeks' notice, saying I was leaving to go to another city. He pointed out that I was getting a byline every day and that I had the goodwill of every man on the staff.

"Bylines are wonderful things," I said, without trying to be snide. "But the truth is, I have to have more money. I went down to the restaurant the other morning and offered the Greek a byline in payment for my meal. He laughed at me."

Men who have become millionaires by making caskets, merging railroads, bribing Congress, or gambling in the stock market, look around them and say to themselves: "Now that I am rich, how can I get some favorable publicity so that I can be famous, too?" They go to all kinds of trouble to get their names and faces in the public eye. Some run for office. Others contribute heavily to a political party, hoping to be appointed Ambassador to Great Britain, or to get a Cabinet job, in case their man wins. In various ways, millionaires spend large sums every day trying to attain what a successful writer already has—fame.

Another advantage which a writer has over those in other occupations is that he gets to meet the leaders of his society—locally, on a state basis, and nationally. A writer who is working at his craft has to move about, interrogate people and interview participants in this or that episode he may be writing. I am thinking of a writer who likely is more successful than most, but not as internationally famous as, say, Ernest Hemingway. At lunch one day, he and I were talking about the various people around town we knew. He knew every member of the Cabinet. He had met the President on two separate occasions, before the President ran for office. He has known, on a personal basis, virtually every "important" man in the national political eye in the past ten years.

This, of course, doesn't make him "better" than anyone else, but it does help him to keep in focus the various subjects that arise in his life, and to assay more correctly the significance of this or that development in national life. Knowing the people involved—and, to some extent, their drives and their goals—he can judge their fitness better than the average.

To the average man, a visit with his Senator might be an occasion to comment on for years. To the average successful writer, it is an uneventful month when he does not encounter many people in the public eye. A writer who meets a large number of public notables is bound to run into some with whom he is on the same spiritual, mental, emotional, or moral plane. They "hit it off" together, and the writer has a new and powerful friend.

Another advantage to being a writer is that, little as you may have considered it, a writer has *power* in this society. Although millions of people, in their own ways, seek power, either the power to lord it over a small office, the power to direct the affairs of a specific club or civic group, the truth is that most of us live and die without actually tackling, and overcoming, any of the things that gripe us, or without helping to push forward the projects in which we are interested.

The writer *is* able to help whatever projects he wants to help, and to work against the men, forces, and projects that he thinks are bad. He has the chance to get into print ideas that may be influential.

Percy Bysshe Shelley, one of the greatest masters of the English language, said: "Poets are the unacknowledged legislators of the world." Shakespeare, in more than one way, indicated that he was aware that he was not only entertaining the people who would see his plays, but that he understood he was leading them to think and, in a fashion, to adopt his own philosophy of life, which was quite eclectic.

It is inherent in his work that a writer should be powerful. He can leave out important facets of a man's career, if he is writing about a particular individual, and hurt the individual more by what he leaves out than by what he puts in. A writer, every time he chooses a subject, is exercising his power. Working with a publisher, a writer can cause reforms to be undertaken by governments, can cause people now enjoying freedom to go to prison (if he exposes them), can give publicity to one group as opposed to another. One way to determine how powerful writers really are, or how powerful some selfish interests *think* they are, notice the publicity blurbs sent to writers. A typical successful writer finds himself on the mailing list of the representatives of the largest corporations, banks and most powerful Congressmen and government agencies. The men directing these enterprises know that the writer holds in his hands the power to help them or to hurt them.

The more a person finds out about a society, and the greater his economic stake in society, the more he wants to cultivate writers, if he is smart. The less a person knows, the less his stake, the less he thinks about writers, because this person really is not *living*, but merely existing in whatever society he finds himself.

The knowledge that he has this power—to help or hurt other men, movements, or causes—should serve to spur the writer to think carefully about the results of his actions. Most of the careless statements in print are written by individuals who are not aware of the great power of the printed or broadcast word. Sometimes, such acts are done by those who have obscure personal grudges, or reasons to be jealous or revengeful. But too many times, the injustice is caused by careless people who "know not what they do."

As a writer lives and works in his field, he *must* learn to think. If he thinks straight, he soon comes to realize just how much power he can wield when he sits down at the typewriter, whether he is writing an article for a local paper or for a magazine that is distributed to the farthest points of the earth.

Another advantage to being a successful writer is that it gives a person great opportunities to read, study, and become better informed about the fascinating world of which he is a part. Most people hold a job to which they must report day after day. Their regimen is the same year after year. They do not have time to read the books they want to read, to see the movies they want to see, or to get into all phases of the subjects in which they are interested. Not so with a successful writer. He has the advantage of being able to say: "I am interested in the Mexican War and I want to find out all about it." He can visit Mexican War specialists; interview the widows of Mexican War heroes; go to Mexico, if he can afford it, to get the views of the widows of the Mexican veterans who are living off Mexican pensions; spend hours, or days, in the public library, or at his home, reading about it.

Many society hostesses like to have an occasional writer in to their parties because this both adds color to the show and, sometimes, the writer is a brilliant conversationalist. He ought to be, considering the way he can pursue the subjects that interest him. The writer *is* better-informed, usually, than the men in other professions, or the vast masses who do not have time even carefully to read a newspaper. He is bound down only by the range of his own mind.

Yet, another advantage to being a successful writer is that he can travel more than other people, normally, and yet it need not be such an economic burden to him. If he can talk a magazine, newspaper, or book publisher into putting up sufficient money, the writer can fly to Hollywood, visit Canada, or go to any of the far-flung parts of the globe.

Another advantage in being a writer is that a writer has more-or-less complete control of his own time. This is no small advantage, when you consider what a wear and tear it entails on the body to rudely awaken it each morning, against its will, and push it, by sheer determination, off to meet the time-clock at 7:30 a.m., 8:30 a.m., or 9:30 a.m. Literally tens of millions of persons, I am told by physicians, go through life feeling tired and run-down. Most people, physicians say, feel tired and run-down because they *are* tired and run-down. They get old before they ought to, because they disrupt their sleep with alarm clocks, or other artificial devices that break into their natural rest. They then rush off to work in order to get to be first in line for the coffee break. They have to punch the time-clock. A writer, praise be, is spared this fate. He can sleep until he wakes up, which is *after* his body has obtained the rest it needs to rebuild itself.

Perhaps the biggest advantage a writer has is "freedom." He can come and go as he pleases; he can work when he pleases (if he works enough), or at least generally at his own convenience; he usually can choose *where* he wants to work, in his home, apartment, or wherever, less bound down by restrictions than others.

A writer, granted he is sure of his facts and is not libelous, can write *anything* he really wants to write. Somewhere, somehow, he can find a publisher, too. This is the greatest advantage, in one way of looking at it, for those who want to be writers, because they usually are the people who feel the restraints of subtle censorship which might be imposed by a boss, or "the company," or a particular neighborhood.

I know a clerk in a hardware store who is against segregation. He made one faint move toward expressing his antipathy for challenging the Supreme Court. It happens that he is in a border state, where the feelings on this issue run high. The man who owns the hardware store is a hidebound segregationist. He would do almost anything to keep from obeying the Supreme Court ukase. When his clerk had the audacity to speak up in favor of the Supreme

Court, the boss let it be known in no uncertain terms that he wouldn't have anyone in his employ who spoke out on this issue. The clerk, who has years of seniority and would find it very difficult to get a job elsewhere, naturally is caught in the switches. He wants to exercise his right to free speech, but he also knows that his employer has the right to do some firing, if the mood hits him. So the clerk cannot exercise his freedom. A writer who is earning his living by his pen is not bound by such restraints. True, he might lose a sale here or there, because some of the editors to whom he contributes his material do not like the idea of having him agitate in favor of constitutional Government, but most of the editors would respect the writer's right to believe as he wished, and to express himself as earnestly as he desired, on the issue, or any other public issue.

This freedom carries with it a responsibility, as the writers realize. The responsibility entails giving everyone else a right to his own views and not writing in a lop-sided fashion so as to make it seem that all who disagree with him are dunderheads, or nincompoops. It also entails sticking strictly to the facts, whether the writer is exposing a condition, a person, or an episode. It makes it necessary that the writer always be *honest* in his reactions and in his emotions and in his work, so that readers will get as true a picture as possible from him, no matter what he is writing about.

Because he is his own boss, a writer must be at times a cruel task-master for himself. When others are out dancing, or partying, *he* has a deadline to meet and he must stay home and work, much like a surgeon, who has to operate to save a life. I have known writers who might plan special week-ends, or vacations, who have been given assignments at unexpected times. They would forego their vacations and their other fun to do the work, realizing it was a part of their responsibility that goes with their freedom to be writers and generally to choose their own hours and work. So let's not get the false impression that merely because a successful writer usually is his own master, his life, *ipso facto*, always is a bed of roses. If he truly is successful, and intends to remain in the race, he must constantly be alert to opportunities for himself and to ways in which he can do more, in less time, in order to maintain his independence of thought and action generally.

VII

The Writer
and Society

*But words are things, and a small drop
of ink, falling like dew upon a thought,
produces that which makes thousands,
perhaps millions think.*

—LORD BYRON

*Since man learned print, no night is
wholly black.*

—CHRISTOPHER MORLEY

THE writer is in perpetual conflict with society, which, as J. B.
Priestley has said, sees the writer as an entertainer, while the writer
usually views himself as a dedicated person. Not *all* writers are in
conflict with society, I might add, for some of the best-paid ones
long since have lost any sense of mission, but when I say "writer,"
I refer to those who, in my judgment, deserve the term, both historically and in this modern era.

It is natural that the writer *should* be in eternal disagreement
with society, I believe. If a writer looks around him and sees a
perfect world, with everyone happy and achieving what he wants,
we can only say that the writer is blind, wearing blinkers, or living

in his own private dream world. This writer, seeing everyone acting safely, legally, logically and morally, isn't very likely to pay the price—in hard effort—to alert society to its needs. He will leave it to some committee to which he contributes several dollars a year to rectify the injustice. Besides, if the society is already perfect, as these few writers seem to believe, who in his right mind would want to write for it, since the only thing that could be said, in many different ways, would be that the society is perfect? Writing merely to please this perfect society, if a writer thinks it *is* perfect, will make a writer as inconspicuous as a quail in a haystack, and about as innocuous. The writer—like the quail—is fulfilling his destiny only when he is flushed out, takes off in flight, and begins to create some attention, even if it happens to be the potshots of a natural enemy.

The only writers worth their salt—the ones history remembers— are those who either personally or in their writings fight against segments, or all, of the society of their period. Shakespeare, like George Bernard Shaw, and other great playwrights of history and modern times, wrote always to expose men to themselves. In many ways Shakespeare revealed disdain for the foibles of society—and for "leaders" who did not lead.

From the standpoint of many successful writers, however, the principal characteristics of too many would-be writers, or beginning writers, or halfway successful writers, is that these fledglings these days seem to lack any real knowledge of society, and of the enormous problems facing our world. As a result, in spite of the tremendous number of publications, including newsletters, newspapers, magazines and books being printed and read in record volume, and a record-breaking number of people in schools (45,-000,000 in the 1959 school year), it still is demonstrable that millions of individuals are *not* learning what they must learn if this society is to work as it should.

How can this be stated so flatly and with such confidence? Because the official statistics—which measure the movements of our society much like a thermometer measures the fever of a patient—show clearly that this society, far from going onward and upward toward a better destiny, is deteriorating rapidly in many major areas.

For example, each six months, J. Edgar Hoover, director of the Federal Bureau of Investigation, makes his semi-annual crime report to the Department of Justice. As Mr. Hoover has stated more than once in recent years, his reports show that crime is increasing four times as fast as the population. This has been going on not merely for a year or two, but since 1950. In his year-end report for 1958, Mr. Hoover stated that major crimes increased eleven per cent in that year over 1957. Obviously, the increasing numbers of criminals are *not* learning from their reading and schooling how to adjust to this complex civilization.

But there are other authoritative statistics—released by many federal agencies—which show that millions, if not tens of millions, of persons are *not* receiving the valid information they must have to lead full lives, much less stay out of jail. As an instance, the Social Security Administration recently announced that more than 400,000 persons who are eligible for social security payments are not receiving the payments, apparently because they are not aware they are eligible. The National Safety Council has pointed out that the number of persons injured in automobile accidents doubled, on an annual basis, between 1946 and 1956—a 100 per cent increase in automobile accidents in a ten-year period. Obviously, these particular drivers (or *half* of them, anyway) in the collisions are *not* getting the information to help them drive safely on our public roads.

The truth is this particular society, in spite of its vaunted communications system and the great increase in publications, is not measuring up to its potentialities. Only one out of every ten persons who starts to high school finally finishes college. The number of college graduates this late in world history still is startlingly low, compared to the total population of this country (between four and five per cent). And while graduation from college does not necessarily make a person a genius, or even an ideal citizen, I still believe it is an important first step in building the kind of safe, sane, aware life that I believe all individuals deserve, and most of them want.

As J. B. Priestley has said, a writer probably views himself as a dedicated person. If he does, and he truly is educated and informed, the writer must see challenges wherever he happens to focus his gaze. He can see people living in hovels close to the mansions of millionaires. He can see those lined up in police court, convicted of drunkenness, disorderly conduct, or other charges, showing that they have not learned how to live in their civilization. Newspapers report policemen shooting their own loan sharks, and he realizes that millions of people are caught in the clutches of economic servitude.

Yet, even while he is in conflict with society, the writer feels a deep sense of charity toward most of the people in the society, because he knows that they have not become informed and aware, and are not likely to become informed and aware, of their rights, their privileges and most of all their opportunities in this best of all known civilizations. The informed writer realizes that millions are ignorant about the most elemental fundamentals of this enormous, changing, vibrating, challenging society. He wants to help these millions to find a better way, so that they can live in better homes, have fewer family problems, and enjoy the few years they have on earth in ways they have a right to enjoy them.

Heine said, "If one has no heart, one cannot write for the masses." Of all men, the modern successful writer must be a man with a heart. And the bigger his heart, the bigger his success. This is not to say that all of them are optimists, by any means. James

Branch Cabell said: "The optimist proclaims that we live in the best of all possible worlds; and the pessimist fears this is true." An optimist could not have written *The Old Man and the Sea,* the Nobel prize novel of Ernest Hemingway, nor *Dr. Zhivago,* which won the same prize for Boris Pasternak, revealing the weaknesses of Soviet society. Yet, in a real sense, neither man could be termed a true pessimist, for both reveal hope for the future.

Perhaps the decline of this culture, too, can be measured to some extent in the decline of really violent debates. People do not seem to be able to come to grips with events anymore, long enough intelligently to have a clash of wits. Everyone agrees that the national budget can't be balanced. Everyone agrees that all is being done that can be done in the foreign field. There is a committee for everything under the sun, with its own hired writers, so the writer frequently can feel, as many do, that there is no place left for him. Yet, history continues to show—as it has shown in the past—that there *is* a place for people who have something to say and will expend energy to distill the essence of their message on paper. There seems to be a uniformity of opinion building in this country that is frightening, when it is considered that all movement forward is created by friction and in turn creates friction. Milton said, "Where there is much desire to learn, there of necessity will be much arguing, much writing, many opinions; for opinion in good men is but knowledge in the making."

The fact that some writers, by writing innocuous pieces, do achieve a modicum of success, can be a reflection on the society and the type of people who buy books. Logan Pearsall Smith said: "A best-seller is the gilded tomb of a mediocre talent," and many a critic has echoed these penetrating words. André Gide declared: "A unanimous chorus of praise is not an assurance of survival; authors who please everyone at once are quickly exhausted." Perhaps some of these innocuous writers are succeeding—at least in making money—because, as Remy de Gourmont pointed out: ". . . We accustom ourselves like cowards to love only writing that is easy (on us) and that will soon be elementary."

The true writer, in my view, does not really break out until he has something to write that hasn't been written before, a message to carry, like Paul Revere, that has never been carried before. Oliver Wendell Holmes said: "Knowledge and timber shouldn't be much used till they are seasoned." Until a man has thought and felt deeply about what he is going to say, he should not inflict his utterance upon society.

The writer is one man who should do much thinking about society, for he is the only man who really works for every segment, never really knowing exactly for whom he is working, never knowing who may read his material and be helped or hurt by it, or influenced. This country does not have *one* society, but represents an amalgam of societies made up of almost 200,000,000 individuals, each of whom is experienced, educated and aware, at any one time, of only a limited number of facts about the whole society. Each of us knows himself, physically. Many of us do not know our own capabilities, or what we might do in times of strain, emergency, or under a new set of circumstances. Each of us is limited in his education, no matter how much he has studied, for there are still many books on many subjects that even the best-educated man may never have read. The writer cannot view problems as others view them, for if he did, he would be untrue to his innermost self. He can only strive to take into account the knowledge and feelings of the various audiences for which he may be writing and constantly bear in mind that each person who reads his material will do so through a different set of eyes. The writer *must* view his work as that of a teacher, remembering that he is reaching an incalculable number of persons instead of just a roomful of children in a certain grade.

The more the writer attains this feeling of responsibility, the greater will be his appeal and the greater his contribution to all elements in all the various societies which make up our country.

But there is a question in the minds of some writers as to what, if anything, they owe society.

"I don't feel that I owe this society anything," one writer told me. He has made a fair living in the editorial field for many years. "When I consider that the average disc jockey makes $18,000 or more a year, just talking a few hours a day, and how real estate men think nothing of making upwards of $100,000 a year, or more, and lots of administrative assistants to politicians get $15,000 a year for doing little or nothing, and considering all the other free-loaders in this society, then I don't feel that I owe any of them anything. I give the publisher what it takes to sell my books, or articles, and, as far as I am concerned, I am cheated every time I get paid. If they couldn't make a lot more out of the material than I do, they wouldn't use it anyway. Rather than *owing* society anything, I feel that society owes me a great deal for all the energy I have poured out, apparently in vain."

This is just one man's opinion, but you can't help wondering how widespread is this view among writers.

On the other hand, does society *owe* the writer anything, once it has read his books and articles and stories and cast them aside? I am sure that few, if any, feel they owe the writer anything. Because they have been propagandized, the members of the public feel that they owe the stockholders of this or that telephone company, or public utility, or bus company, at least six per cent on money invested in these enterprises. The public will agree that they owe at least a profit to most businessmen. Most tenants agree that they owe the landlord a fat return on his investment.

But owe writers anything? Not even editors agree that society owes anything to *them*! I once suggested to the editor of a popular magazine that he carry a "think piece" entitled, "What We Owe to Writers," in which I would bring out how much the world should be indebted to those who have created most of the amusing and interesting and thought-provoking stories, books, and articles which have helped our world progress.

He looked surprised.

"Ridiculous!" he exploded. "We don't owe writers a danged thing. They generally get paid more than they deserve."

The more I thought of how little he pays—considering even the poor material he carries—the more I could understand his feelings. However, if an *editor* can't understand about the debt society owes to writers, then I felt despair about ever getting any large number of plain people to understand.

How much any person in the society feels that he owes to writers, I think, depends in a great measure upon how aware he is about where he obtained his own knowledge and philosophy. Without writers—ancient and contemporary—we, as individuals, would be utterly confused in understanding what is going on around us, locally, nationally, or internationally. In a real sense, we *owe* the foundation of our education to writers, as well as to teachers, for without writers who had prepared the texts logically and interestingly, the teachers would have had a most difficult time pressing home the points that they drove into our minds. This civilization is falling down in many ways, and perhaps the way it is rewarding writers—very penuriously, as a general rule—may explain, as much as any other single point could explain, why it is failing so many in so many ways.

A society is stratified, at any specific period, just as there are lines of authority in any company, or any Government, except in times of chaos. The writer aims his material at one or various groups in this stratified society. Yet, there are very intelligent, reading people who are economically poor, and there are people who do not read who are among the richest. Whether the writer wishes to do so or not, everything he writes that is printed, that has any sense to it at all, changes something. If his goal is to lead his readers into this or that direction, or if his goal is to get them to love their present condition and be happy in it, or if his goal is to get them into the mood to work to go back to a certain condition they enjoyed in the past, it comes out in the writing. So no matter how much a writer balks at the word "reformer," he is one. If the writer's dedication to a certain ideas or ideals happens to be overwhelmingly strong, it will show up in his writing, and, if he has the ability, it will show up in *action* in the society, by this or that person who wants to help the writer to achieve the kind of society that the writer thinks ought to be. There really is no inconsequential happening in nature, as the scientists tell us, since there is a balance there, which, if upset, may have repercussions seemingly far divorced from the initially "inconsequential" happening. It is the same with writing. A man learns that he can't write anything that is without effect, if it has any reasoning power behind it and is motivated by feeling and determination. It may not sway millions, but it will sway one or two others, and those one or two in turn may influence ten, or twenty, or an incalculable number.

This is one of the wonderful things about being a writer. It also is one of the more dangerous aspects of the calling. Words are *powerful*, words are what move our society toward whatever direction it is moving.

Just how much a writer feels he owes to society depends upon the writer's own views about society, his role in society, and the motives he has had through his life. One writing only for money feels that he has only one responsibility—to turn out material that will bring him shekels. But a writer who feels—as does many a writer in the field of religion, for example—that he wants to please God as well as an editor, will realize that a writer, of all persons, must have a social consciousness. For a writer without a conscience is like a drunken sailor who is brandishing a powerful carbine in a crowd. A trenchant writer can cause great harm, not to just a few persons, but to many. He can wound society itself, although the

sailor might be able to kill or wound only a few persons before he
is arrested and imprisoned.

It is hackneyed to say the pen is mightier than the sword, but
many of us—including the editor mentioned earlier—frequently
forget this. We, as individuals in a society, owe a great debt to the
writers who feed us good information that helps us to stumble on,
and to see whatever light they can make available to us. We also
owe a great deal of scorn and contempt to those who, calling themselves writers and pretending to be learned, mislead us and either
through crookedness or purely for filthy lucre, will write every kind
of confusing half-truth possible to catalogue.

The writer is dependent on society, and the people in the society,
in many ways. He has to have food that others grow; he must have
his car fixed by men he may never have seen before. No man is an
island, and the writer, if he thinks at all, realizes this more poignantly than most others.

Yet, the writer must be independent of society, if he is to do his
best work. If he is writing about racketeers in the automobile business—mechanics who charge $100 to do $5 worth of work on cars—
or about bankers who not only abscond with millions, but, many
times, legitimately cheat their own customers out of millions, by
nicking each account some small service fee—the writer must not
let his friendship for one mechanic, or with one good banker, color
his views about these social menaces. A writer must strive to see
the picture clearly, regardless of pressures brought against him.
The public relations man once was hailed by many writers as being
the answer to their prayers. But in recent years, public relations
men for many industries and groups have become so clever at
hiding the evidences of corruption in their groups, or of diverting
the public attention from such corruption, many independent
writers have stopped using anything supplied to them by public
relations men representing special, vested interests.

The writer's goal must be not to injure society, or wound it, more than it has been wounded by the demagoguery of the politicians and the half-truths of the pressure groups. He must recognize his dependence on the society, and at the same time resolve, in his own work, to be as independent as possible. The writer might physically secede from the human race—and many do, by having minimal contacts with other human beings—but he can never run away from his responsibility to give society his best.

To sum up, in my view, the writer and his relation to society may be expressed as follows (with apologies to Benjamin Franklin):

> "For want of a word,
> The sentence was lost;
> For want of a sentence,
> The story was lost.
> For want of a story,
> The writer was lost,
> For want of a writer,
> The country was lost."

VIII

The Writer
and His Ideas

This itch for authorship is worse than the
devil and spoils a man for anything else.
—EDWIN ARLINGTON ROBINSON

WHERE does a successful writer get his ideas?

The variety of ideas that click, in the literary field, indicates clearly that writers get their ideas from *everywhere,* all the time.

One day a writer was chatting on the telephone with the editor of a popular magazine and he happened to mention a "gimmick" in the Social Security Act that would make it possible that year for a person who was turning 65 to work only three months, under Social Security, and be eligible for a pension that could bring him $25,000, if he lived long enough to collect it all. The editor said: "I don't believe it. But if it is true, I'd like to carry a story about that—and other gimmicks of other laws." Result: An article was born and sold for $500.

Another day, a writer walked past the Pan American Building in Washington. He stopped to admire some of the exotic, tropical plants growing in the patio. After a while, he asked an attendant if the Pan American Union really did any good. The attendant replied that the Pan American Union was like "a little United Nations." The writer did some investigation. Result: An article about the Pan American Union that brought him $1,000.

A man went walking in a country churchyard, thinking of a departed friend, whom he had admired greatly. The man went home and began a poem about the churchyard. Result: Thomas Gray wrote a poem that has been read for hundreds of years.

One day, Pinky Herman, a popular song writer, went to Toots Shor's place for lunch. He was pulling off his coat to give it to the hat-check girl when Johnny Andrews, the nationally-known singer and disc jockey came in. The two shook hands.

Johnny said: "You look happier than I've seen you in a long time, Pinky. Is it any of my business why you're beaming?"

"My first grandchild was born this morning," Pinky replied.

"How does it feel to be a grandfather?"

"Johnny, it's a wonderful, wonderful feeling!" Pinky replied.

Simultaneously, the two were serious.

"That's a darned good song title!" they exclaimed in unison. And, forgetting lunch, they went to a nearby piano and began to work on the song, "It's A Wonderful, Wonderful Feelin'." In less than an hour, both the words and music had been hammered out. When the song was published, it became an immediate success.

On Capitol Hill one day, a writer was chatting with a well-known labor reporter who had been covering the hearings at which Messrs. Dave Beck, Jimmy Hoffa, and many other labor leaders were being raked over the investigative coals.

"What's happening to the lords of labor today?" the writer asked.

"Nothing much," the reporter replied. "They have a minor official on now. He has stolen only $200,000 or so."

Later, the author's mind reverted to his expression—"The Lords of Labor." Suddenly, he thought: "What a book title that would make!" Within several weeks, he had signed a contract with a publisher to do a book called, *The Lords of Labor*.

A writer who is professional, i.e., one who earns his living as a writer, may *seem* to be just another fellow to you, if you see him walking along a street, sipping a drink at a bar, or chatting with friends. But there is one difference. The writer is getting ideas. He is *thinking* as a writer. This, I believe, is one of the biggest hurdles in becoming a successful writer. It is to discipline your mind to think always about ideas that are useful for one market, or a number of markets. A lot of would-be writers, you can tell from their stories, and their ideas, are thinking only of themselves. But the more successful writers are not thinking so much of themselves as they are thinking of specific editors, specific audiences in the society, and specific ideas that will fit these specific magazine and book audiences.

When I asked our panel of writers the specific question—"How do *you* get ideas?"—here is how they responded:

Alden Hatch: Since I am a popular biographer, I get ideas largely from the news; also from editors, businessmen, etc. I test these ideas by offering them for sale to the highest bidder among editors.

Harold Helfer: It is very hard, as a rule, to pin down just where an idea is born. Sometimes it seems to hit like a combustible explosion, an accumulation of myriad things suddenly clicking together, inexplicably. Or it could be something a little more explicit—a newspaper item, conversation overheard on a bus, something that happened to a neighbor. Often, one idea leads to another.

Will Oursler: Ideas come most fluently to me from following a specific course. I suggest:

(a) study the market for which you are seeking ideas;

(b) try to find out what is most wanted in the field or market you have been studying;

(c) creatively, rather than imitatively, let your mind seek to develop ideas to fit these needs.

Norman Vincent Peale: Ideas for writing come to me in all sorts of ways, but mainly from my personal contacts with other people. I believe there is a story of significance and general interest in the life experience of every human being. If you study people, love them and so get really close to them, exciting themes and ideas present themselves at every turn.

Richard Gehman: I get ideas in many different ways. Travel is an absolute necessity. I try to get to Hollywood three or four times a year and to Europe at least once, and the rest of the time I travel around the country as much as possible. I have also, believe it or not, dreamed ideas.

Harry Edward Neal: Where do I get ideas? From the same source as most other writers—everywhere! The idea for a short story in *Esquire*, called "The Last Match," was born when I tore the last match out of a paper matchbook. The germ of "The Lost Harpoon," which grew into a *Saturday Evening Post* yarn, came from a brief paragraph which I read in a Massachusetts guidebook. One of my favorite stories, "The Golden Goblet," which appeared in the *Family Circle*, was inspired by a sentence I had jotted down in a pocket notebook I usually carry. The sentence read: "Story about an old man who tells a boy a fairy tale and does something to make it come true." This was an idea that occurred to me "out of the blue," and which didn't take shape until several months after I had made the original notebook entry.

As for articles, they often grow from newspaper items or from conversations with friends and acquaintances. As you may know, I have six books in print, with more to come. One of these, *The Telescope*, published by Julian Messner, Inc., New York, in April, 1958, was developed as the result of a friendly chat with a buyer of books in a Washington bookstore. Knowing about my earlier books, this lady one day asked why I didn't write a book about the telescope. She received frequent inquiries from teenagers for such a book, she explained, but there was none available except highly technical works. I discussed the idea with the publishers, and presto—one book!

Frances and Richard Lockridge: We get ideas for stories by beating ourselves over the head—holding sessions, often long, of just trying to think up stories. We have got ideas for short articles by watching cats, and by hearing the pump of an artesian well start up. The only way we know to test an idea is to try it out on a typewriter.

Edison Marshall: I've traveled an enormous lot. I read everything but other people's novels, this prohibition being psychological. I search myself for ideas. If I were dissected and every layer of tissue put on a slide under a microscope, in every specimen would be found the writer. I live to write and writing is my right to live. This sounds pretty slick, but it is perfectly true. I don't test ideas. They test me. If I find they continue to haunt me, and I mull them over and over, in the end I write them.

Dora Albert: Ideas for articles may come from reflecting about one's personal experiences, and the experiences of others; from reading (especially newspapers), from conversations, from attending lectures. Sometimes a single exciting sentence in an article or lecture may inspire one with the wish to learn more about a subject or a personality. I try to write only about subjects that I am honestly interested in. Self-help articles usually are the result of coping with an individual problem—particularly when you find that others have had to cope with the same problem.

For instance, I sold an article to *Family Circle* on how to make decisions easily. Not only have I coped with the problem of making decisions—and gone through periods when I had difficulty in making them—but I found that many friends and acquaintances found this a problem that bothered them. In the same way, my book, *You're Better Than You Think* was the result of years of learning to compensate for a severe inferiority complex. In addition, I discovered that most of the people I met—some of them extremely successful businessmen and movie and TV stars—had to compensate for their own severe inferiority feelings. One good way of testing the value of an idea is to reflect on how many people over how wide an area would be interested. If the idea is of local interest, you may have an article for a newspaper in your own locality; if it is of national or international interest, you may be able to sell the resulting article to a national magazine, a book publisher, or a national syndicate.

O. A. Battista: Ideas? I read, read, read. In between reading, I think, think, think. Somehow ideas then click. I always now query editors on ideas—with major emphasis on picking a good title, followed by an outline of not more than one page.

Fred Kerner: Ideas come from everywhere and anywhere, ideas are sometimes tucked away in the smallest corners of the news columns. The test of an idea, as far as I am concerned, is three-fold: (1) Are people interested in it? (2) Is there a market for it? (3) Am I interested enough in it to do justice to it?

Pinky Herman: Ideas, especially for songs, often times come out of the blue. Unless one is faced with the problem of writing a specific song for a special situation, most of the popular songs are written "off-the-cuff." Seldom does a songwriter test a title or subject matter with a publisher beforehand. If an idea strikes him as a worthy subject for a song, he goes right ahead and writes it, because often a title may not be "great," but the song, once written, may be a "great song." So rather than have a publisher discourage him because of an ordinary title or probably simple idea, the songwriter simply goes ahead with his idea and takes the chance that the song might turn out better than the title might indicate.

Roger Burlingame: Unless a writer is bursting with ideas from the moment he is born, he had better choose some other profession.

Robert Payne: I don't think writers, or at any rate the writers I am interested in, *get* ideas. *The ideas get them.* It may be a mood or a melodic line, a girl's face seen in a crowd, a particular color on a wall under a street-lamp, and out of this there comes a whole complex of other related moods. Melodic lines, faces and colors take shape and absorb the writer, so that he must go on and

Basically, I begin with an interesting situation, implement it with likable characters, set it in an interesting background and go from there. I sometimes do my research before I develop the situation and find that a situation has developed automatically. Sometimes, I envisage a situation that, because of some peculiarity, demands a particular setting or background. Testing of an idea is simple. First, I visualize the situation as being enacted by live people. Does the piecemeal bit create drama? Does it demand an explanation of what went before and what is to follow? If so, it is a good situation. Mechanically it may appear at the beginning or the end of a book or story, but it is the situation from which the story grows. In skeleton form a situation might be built like this:

A MAN IS BEING HANGED

CRIME: HORSE THIEVERY   BUT HE IS INNOCENT

HE STOLE THE HORSE ON PURPOSE?

IN A WAY. HE HAD PAID FOR IT, OBTAINED A BILL OF SALE, THEN WENT BACK AND STOLE IT KNOWING THAT HE WOULD BE SEEN BY PEOPLE WHO DID NOT KNOW THE TRUE CIRCUMSTANCES

WHY?

DOES HE WANT TO COM-   DETAILS OF A HANGING
MIT SUICIDE?   Out of town. Judge is there. So
is everyone else.

DECISION

Horsethief wants everyone outside of town at a given time for a purpose of his own.

WHY AGAIN?

Most plausible is that he is a member of a gang who wishes to rob the unguarded bank.

PROBLEM:

How does he know he won't be hung immediately before bank can be robbed by his confederates?

SOLUTION

He pretends to be a Mexican and speaks broken English. He can, since he neither understands his questioners, nor is understood by them, draw out the impromptu trial longer than usual—or as long as he wishes.

QUESTION? .

How can he protect himself?

SOLUTION

By the above ruse. He simply pretends he does not understand what he is accused of doing wrong until he is ready. Then, suddenly, he does comprehend what is going on and produces the bill of sale for the horse.

DENOUEMENT

He is released. Rides away. But the robbery at the bank failed. Judge is also the banker and he carried all the cash with him in a sack under the seat of his buckboard. (He is suspicious, since the man who previously owned the horse had been in the bank for a loan and was turned down. Judge realizes that such a man might sell his horse to raise cash). Judge-banker, also smelling a rat, plays it safe by taking the money to the hanging.

SNAPPER

Pseudo horse thief rides to meet his companions but finds that they have fled from the meeting place. They are afraid that he will not believe that they failed to get any money at the bank. He thinks that they have run out on him, taking the loot with them. Holding his rifle at the ready, he rides after them.

That is, roughly, the way I would build up a short story, novelette, or a novel. Not on paper, but in my head as I go along. I never write but one draft—the first one—and sometimes (rarely) revise after a publisher has bought the thing and asks for minor changes.

Jesse Stuart: I never get ideas by reading, but by living, experiencing and hearing people talk.

Thomas P. Kelley: When I want an idea, I sit down and it usually comes to me.

Scott Young: My ideas come from everything I do. Can only

test them by trying to write them, or by seeing how long they last in my mind if not written.

Deane and David Heller: The newspapers are our most fruitful source of ideas. In every paper, every day, there are "leads" for at least a dozen salable articles. Travel is another good source. We seldom go anywhere without writing about it. Leads are no problem for any article writer worth his salt. Time and the opportunity to develop the leads represent the real problem. Unless we are really sold on a piece, or have some reason for wanting to do it at once, we immediately give it the acid test. We query the most likely editor or two we can think of. If we get the go-ahead, we do the article. Otherwise, we forget it. There are so many ideas kicking around that it's silly to work on any but the most promising.

John Gassner: I get ideas from traveling, reading, and human experience—as do all my students.

Saul K. Padover: My ideas come from a buried reservoir of (a) reading since childhood; (b) world travel; (c) government experience; (d) lecturing; (e) teaching; (f) listening to people—above all, listening.

Kenneth S. Giniger: I believe that I get my ideas (both for my own books and for the books I suggest to authors) from full and active participation in the life of our times. This means not only reading an enormous number of newspapers, magazines and books, but going to meetings, lectures, cocktail parties, the theatre, concerts and recitals, football games and what-have-you. The best way I know to test an idea is to talk it out in a discussion with someone who is knowledgeable on the particular subject.

Georges Simenon: Living.

Joseph N. Bell: I work in a specific area—the Chicago area—and I get ideas from all over the lot, by reading, observing, listening. The only way I "test" an idea is in answering the question: Am I interested in this idea? If so, I work on it; if not, I don't.

Frederic A. Birmingham: Since no idea is original, no doubt such stimulants as travel and reading may help, but not necessarily be relied upon in producing ideas. Good ideas are the accumulation of experience and sudden inspiration, plus a braking period for re-evaluation and then maturation. I do not think they can be pre-tested. . . . I believe the wisest thing possible is for you yourself to suspect in a thoroughly nasty way every idea you have. Did you plagiarize it subconsciously from another writer or a bright friend? Is it a distillation of common knowledge? Is anyone likely to be interested in it except your mother? Self-communion of this sort controls conception, and avoids abortion.

Lester David: One of the most fruitful sources of ideas, as far as I am concerned, is my own family. I have two children, I live in a small suburban community. I find a problem in my own home and then I ask myself: "Don't other people have this same problem? Isn't this a general worry?" I go out and do some digging. I learn that my hunch was right—other mothers and fathers are worried about the same thing. I dig some more, find a solution. I have a magazine article.

Let me cite a couple of examples: I discovered that our little girl, aged eight, was busy virtually every afternoon after school with Brownies, lessons of all sorts, school extra-curricular activi-ties. It sparked an idea for an article about parents who keep their children far too busy. Once my wife ruefully told me that I was going to find out how much she spent for my birthday present as soon as the bill came from the store. She said it was a shame she had to have me pay for my own present since she didn't have enough left over from her household money. The article idea: Wives Want Money Of Their Own. Another time, I was kidding my wife because she wasn't getting up to make breakfast for me. My wife retorted that few of her friends did this for their husbands. I dug around and learned that she was right. It made a fine article for *This Week* Magazine—"Should Wives Cook Breakfast?"

Robert Penn Warren says: "I always remember the date, the place, the room, the road, when I first was struck (with an idea). For instance, *World Enough and Time.* Katherine Anne Porter and I were both in the Library of Congress as fellows. We were in the same pew, had offices next to each other. She came in one day with an old pamphlet, the trial of Beauchamp for killing Colonel Sharp. She said, 'Well, Red, you better read this.' There it was. I read it in five minutes. But I was six years making the book. Any book I write starts with a flash, but takes a long time to shape up."

All of these answers make sense, at least to me, but I believe that Mr. Simenon made the most correct answer. Every successful writer gets ideas merely by living, and the more he lives—i. e., reads, thinks, moves about, mingles with people and looks at the endless pageantry of life, as well as meets its never-ending problems—the more ideas he will get. This, I believe, is why people who do get into the field, and stick to it long enough to become known as writers, are never at a loss for work. They become captives of the writing field, in a way, for their ideas about how to increase their usefulness to the world, and, of course, their earnings, become better and better year by year.

It may be, as Henrik Ibsen said in *An Enemy of the People* (Act II) that "the public doesn't require any new ideas. The public is best served by the good old-fashioned ideas it already has." This is the view of some politicians. However, writers are imbued with the belief that people *do* need new ideas, to meet new challenges. The writer is a man gripped with his ideas.

A lot of people retire, but writers seldom do. And other writers understand why. Their ideas just won't let them quit. Writers do not seize ideas. The ideas seize the writers, and sometimes the grip is incredibly strong.

IX

The Writer
and His Needs

*I want to walk a thousand miles and
write one thousand plays, and sing one
thousand poems, and drink one thousand
pots of beer, and kiss one thousand girls.*

—RUPERT BROOKE

*If one advances confidently in the direc-
tion of his dreams, and endeavors to live
the life which he has imagined, he will
meet with a success unexpected in common hours.*

—THOREAU

WE have seen, in an earlier chapter, that writers—in the judgment of many of those successful in this field—produce more copy
when they need money. I'd like to say that a writer has many other
needs, besides money. Many persons who are independently well
off still write feverishly, indicating that they have a drive to write
over and above their economic drive.

For instance, Emily Dickinson, a self-exile in her own home,
wrote thousands of poems, while literally shut off from the world,

voluntarily. For some decades, she was a wraith to her own people, in their own large home, and, except for meals, stayed strictly to herself. Yet, as we have noted, she apparently *had* to express herself in her poetry.

You get some idea of the needs—economic and otherwise—of writers in the case of Thomas Chatterton, born November 20, 1752, the posthumous son of a dissipated schoolmaster. As a schoolboy, he was considered dull. Actually, he began writing poetry in his tenth year in secret. He hid himself each day in the deed and record-room of the Church of St. Mary Redcliff, Bristol, and familiarized himself with the old handwriting and archaic spelling. When he was fourteen, he prepared a pedigree, based he said on the old documents, for a pewterer, tracing the tradesman's family back to the Norman Conquest. He sent the merchant a poem entitled, *The Romaunte of the Cyighte,* which he said was written by one of the pewterer's forebears. Actually, the pedigree and the poem were figments of Chatterton's vivid mind.

Intimate with many Bristol girls before he was fifteen, he fell in love with a Miss Rumsely. He wrote poems to other girls, but his mind was on the fifteenth century world he had learned to love in the record-room. He was apprentice to an attorney, but had no time for office work. Before he was seventeen, he went to London to earn his living by writing. He was overworked and undernourished, but wrote political letters, librettos for operas, lyrics, elegies and satires. He was often cold and always hungry, but never failed to send presents to his mother. He had wanted to be a singer but became a dressmaker. He wrote her cheerful letters, although he lived in a garret.

Once, his landlady offered to return part of his rent. Refusing it, he said proudly: "I have that here which will get me more."

However, he realized that he could not make a living as a writer, and he tried—without success—to get a post on a ship sailing to Africa.

His landlady, shocked on August 25, 1770, at his appearance, and knowing he had lived all week on a stale loaf of bread, invited him to eat with her. He refused. Instead, he went to the baker and asked for a fresh loaf on credit. Refused, he told a friendly apothecary that he wanted to rid his quarters of rats. Could he have some arsenic on credit? It was granted. Two days later, they found his body in his garret workshop, amid the litter of his manuscripts. He was three months less than eighteen when he was buried as a pauper in the burial ground of Shoe Lane Workhouse.

A person who wants to write *may* have a need for money, and frequently does. But in virtually every other instance, he (or she) has other needs that are quite important if he is to retain his sanity and exist in a crazy mixed-up world.

What are some of these other needs of those who want to write, or actually are writers?

Perhaps the need is for activity—mental activity—which the person cannot find in his regular, normal social contacts. It is difficult, as we all know, for men to "meet" each other in conversations, particularly if the two men happen to be of a different intellectual strata, or of different economic, or of different spiritual strata. Each occupation, in a way, has its own language. A carpenter uses one set of words. A dentist uses another. A physician uses still another.

In a certain sense, each of us is "boxed in" by his own profession. It is very difficult for a stock broker to enjoy chatting with, for example, a comptometer operator. There *are* areas of interest in the society that cut across financial, social and intellectual lines. A physicist and a railway clerk may sit together in the bleachers at a baseball game and both talk the same language—if they are rooting for the same team.

But there *are* many individuals—perhaps one or two per cent of the population—who simply cannot be interested in the things other people are interested in. These individuals have a need for mental activity, since their minds may have many facets and they are interested in many things that the average man finds dull. These individuals may find that through writing—which is an *intense* activity, when a person is interested in what he is doing—they get an emotional release and satisfaction they can get in no other way.

Perhaps the need for the intelligent person is to express himself. He is unable to do so because he can't get "close" to those on the job. I am thinking of a fellow who works for a large printing company as a linotype operator. He feels he has very little in common with the other men in the shop. He does not gather in the group at lunch to swap jokes, or pass the time of the day in aimless chatter. He is thinking about some problem. At night, he spends his time writing. Unable, in a sense, through his personality or for other reasons, to express himself in person to human beings, he nevertheless has a deep desire to communicate with others. Through his writing, in effect, he merges with the human race and makes its problems *his* problems, although he may seem, to the casual observer, to be aloof from his fellowmen.

Then there is the need for fulfillment. It is often said that there is a chance for everyone in this society, that everybody can become a millionaire, if he just wishes it hard enough. It isn't so.

This is one of the most stratified societies on earth. A few persons —and they are always well publicized—work out of debt and are able, by hook or crook, to become rich. But for the great masses of people who live and struggle and raise children and die, well, the economic fact is that they stay on a treadmill most of their lives. They seldom get a chance to be seen in the society columns of the daily newspapers; 174,000,000 out of 175,000,000 are never featured on "Strike It Rich," or other quiz shows, and don't even win a refrigerator. Anything they get, they have to work for, eight hours a day, and save, a nickel or so a week. Because they were poor, although intelligent, they may have missed college. Because of bad decisions earlier, they may not have entered politics. Not realizing they could become famous as singers, like Bing Crosby and Perry Como, they dropped singing. A lot of them didn't even jump into radio and become famous as disc jockeys. Some got into radio, but their teeth were bad and when they were photographed, they didn't look toothsome, like Art Linkletter, so they never became masters-of-ceremonies. In one way or another, all but a few thousand of the American people in the past fifty years *didn't* get rich or famous.

Yet, many of them still wanted to do more than live and die without making any mark. So a lot of them turned to writing. Writing, to these tens of thousands, represents the *only* method they can find of achieving fulfillment in life. They may feel that, through their children, they have fulfilled their destiny in some respects; they may think that in their church work, or lodge work, or civic activities, they have made a slight contribution; yet, many thousands of them feel that something more is needed, so they strive to become good writers. Writing offers them fulfillment.

Undoubtedly, some become writers because it satisfies their need for attention. In some respects, this need is pathetic, but that the need exists cannot be denied. So great is this need that men have been known to stand on top of tall buildings and threaten to commit suicide merely to get other people to *look* at them.

In this connection, I can never forget the time I went to address a writers' club, and took my seat in the audience while the "business" part of the meeting was going on. They were saving me until last.

At any rate, the President of the club asked those who had had material published since the most recent meeting to stand up and tell the others about it. A little old gray-haired lady—I later learned that she was a scrubwoman in a public building—stood up proudly.

"Since our last meeting, I have had a poem chosen to be published in an anthology by a New York publisher," she said proudly. There was a round of applause. Then, just as proudly, she added: "And, you know, they are going to charge me only six dollars!"

I didn't know whether to laugh or cry. Her need for attention was so great that she would do *anything* to get her name into print. Who am I, or you, or anyone else, to say that she did not get her money's worth—in case the "anthology" ever was printed?

These "needs," vaguely explain why some people write, and some do not. The people who experience these needs early in life develop a love for reading—which is communication with men and women (authors) who usually are far away in space or time. Because the child loves what he reads, he may fall in love with the *idea* of writing, or with the ideas he finds in books. Later, he realizes that he admires the best of the writers whose books, articles, or stories he has read. Sometimes, he is challenged, in what he reads, to do better. Thus, he becomes a writer, as well as a reader.

This discussion of the writer's needs goes back to the writer and his goals. Does a person write merely to get fame? Does he write only for money? Does he write to amuse himself? Does he write merely to be active, when he can no longer participate in sports?

Perhaps, if it were possible to find out *why* men (and women!) have chosen to become writers—rather than engage in some other occupation at which they could make money faster—it might be possible to determine whether or not it is wise for us to become writers.

I posed the question to many writers in this form: "What do you think impelled you to be a writer? Reform? Religion? Fame? Or other motivations?"

Here are the replies:

Alden Hatch: Force of circumstances. It was something I found I could do well.

Harold Helfer: Ever since I can remember, that's all I ever wanted to do. No one else in my family seems to have had that inclination. Just one of those things, I guess.

Will Oursler: I think I write because I had to write. I think I have something inside of me I want to say about the universe and I can say it best in words.

Norman Vincent Peale: I took to writing because I wanted to reach as many people as possible with truths which I had deeply experienced and in which I enthusiastically believe.

Richard Gehman: I think most writers start out with a desire to communicate something for various reasons. There is a certain amount of ego involved and desire to attract attention. I was never anything but. I started working on a newspaper when I was 14 and have been at writing ever since.

Harry Edward Neal: What impelled me to be a writer? Well, it all began in 1940 when, as a U. S. Secret Service Agent in New York City, I was transferred to Washington as a member of the Chief's staff. At that time Chief Frank J. Wilson began a "Know Your Money" campaign to teach laymen how to detect counterfeit money and how to outwit check forgers. The Secret Service had no professional writers, no public relations division, and I was assigned to write some magazine articles about counterfeiting and forgery, along with my regular work. The articles were published under Chief Wilson's name and he received editorial requests for more.

I decided I had better learn something about writing, so I enrolled in a fact-writing night course at the American University, given by William Dow Boutwell. The course folded after one semester and I enrolled in another course in Creative Writing, given by Professor Merritt C. Batchelder. This led me into fiction and the short story. In 1957, after nearly thirty-two years in the Secret Service, I retired as its Assistant Chief at the age of fifty, to devote all of my time to writing.

I liked and wanted to write, and I wanted to earn more money.

Frances and Richard Lockridge: Neither of us ever seriously considered any other way of living, or of making a living. But why this happened neither of us has any very clear idea. Certainly we never wanted to reform anything, nor did religion in any way enter into it. I suppose everybody is to some degree gratified by being known, but mystery writers don't, really, garner "fame." The advantages, for a free-lancer, of doing pretty much what you want to do pretty much when you want to do it are obvious. (So are the perils of free-lancing.) But I can't remember ever having anticipated those advantages. I started writing for *The New Yorker* while I was on a newspaper—where I did re-write—because we were spending more than we were making, and found this situation unsatisfactory.

Edison Marshall: I don't know why I am a writer. I just know that ever since I can remember I have been writing.

Dora Albert: I think the desire for self-expression, corny as that sounds, was probably the impelling cause in my case. When I attended college in the East, I was undecided as to whether I wanted to teach or to write, for a living. Actually, I preferred writing, but was afraid that it might be difficult for me to earn a satisfactory living. I did some substitute teaching, while I was working for a Brooklyn newspaper. That helped make up my mind. I found that I enjoyed writing more than teaching. Teaching paid better for me then—but I gave it up to devote all my time to writing.

Fred Kerner: I think it was sheer chance that I became a writer. While educational aptitude tests pointed the way toward my becoming an engineer—this in the late '30s before the race against Russia—there seemed to be a strong aptitude as well for the arts. I became bored with engineering in my first year at college and slipped quite easily into the field of general arts. My activities were equally divided between writing, acting, composing, playing music and directing in the theatre. As a free-lance in all these fields, while still a student, I think I made an equal amount of money in each. I sold to several magazines—including the late-lamented *American Magazine*—and was a high school and campus correspondent for several newspapers. I earned money as a radio and stage actor, earned money playing the piano and organ, was a professional director of little theatre groups. But finding myself in a strange town without a job led me to a newspaper office. I would say that was chance, or fate. Anyway, here I am still writing.

Pinky Herman: As a youngster, I personally liked to read poetry and when I was in fourth grade at grammar school, I wrote my first poem. As I grew older, I continued to write poetry for the high school paper and for the college daily. Naturally, I turned to songwriting right after leaving college and have been writing songs since 1929, when my first song was published.

Roger Burlingame: Because I was better at writing than at plumbing, banking or doctoring, all more lucrative occupations.

Abigail Van Buren: I write because I love to write . . . and that is the best motivation for doing a successful job at anything.

Robert Payne: I think I became a writer because of the sheer glorious fun of the thing. To watch an idea take shape, to follow its progress, to be in control of it, or at least to be in partial control. Writing is like chariot-racing, with a great team of horses roaring in front of you. But there is a sense, too, in which it is like the contemplations of a monk in his cell, with the sheet of white paper instead of a white wall. And these two concepts are not entirely contrary, for in both there is a pouring out of energy and the sense of some dedicated purpose.

Hugh Ross Williamson: I was asked by a publisher for a book while I was editing *The Bookman*, so I wrote it; and somehow it's gone on. I find writing very difficult—except plays, which are the only things I've ever really *wanted* to write. I have no urge whatever to spill myself in words, and I dislike intensely the *kind* of writing of, for example, Thomas Wolfe, although I liked him personally when I met him in the '20s.

A. C. Spectorsky: Writing for me is part of my profession as a communicator. Having worked in books, films, TV, radio, magazines and newspapers, I've always felt that writing was a tool— among others—rather than a profession.

Erskine Caldwell: Because I like to write.

Senator Richard L. Neuberger: I believe I was impelled upon a career as a writer because I always found it comparatively easy to express myself in prose.

Emil Zubryn: I knew I wanted to be a writer when I was nine years old. Don't ask why. It was not for reform, fame, religion. It just was a desire to put words down on paper, at which I was nominally proficient, without being a genius. And I've been able to make a living of sorts from this.

Sloan Wilson: The desire for money and fame impelled me to be a writer, but there were much deeper forces. I'm simply happiest when I'm writing.

Evan Hunter: I wanted to be a writer because it seemed to me I could best express my own creative urge in words. I had studied art, previously, with the idea of becoming a commercial artist. I discovered I wasn't expressing myself in what I considered terms of truth, and I began experimenting with writing. I now feel that writing is my medium, and I'm working toward the day when my expression will truly match what I feel inside.

Ben Smith: Money impelled me to be a writer. In 1933, I met Lee Bond, who at that time was writing for the pulps and making $400 a month and driving a new Dodge. My God! I thought. All he does is travel around the country, beat out a few thousand words on a typewriter, and he makes in a month what I make in a good year as a linotype operator for a weekly newspaper. That was, as I said, in 1933. I sold my first short story to *Blue Book* in 1944. So, after all, it wasn't altogether the money. It's a kind of loneliness that only those who have experienced it can appreciate. A desire to reach out and touch other people at a level beyond that of casual contact. To be able to make them laugh or cry or think so that they will forget that what they are reading had an author, and when they finish they'll say to their wife, "Goddam, that's a good story!"

Jesse Stuart: Reform, religion, or fame had nothing to do with my becoming a writer. I was born with the urge. I'd have to write even if never published.

Thomas P. Kelley: I was impelled to write to make money, which brings up the question: How stupid can a fellow be?

Scott Young: I wanted to do something in life that had the maximum amount of dependence on myself, rather than on an organization, economic situation, or whatever. I am impelled to try to explain why people do what they do.

Deane and David Heller: The utter need for a means of expressing ourselves led us to writing. We didn't want to be just ciphers in our community. We wanted what we think and felt about ideas and things to be important to others than just ourselves. Although money is important in the sense that we have no source of income other than our own efforts, we *have* to make enough from our time and efforts to make a living.

John Gassner: Everything "impelled" me to write. The need for self-expression, the desire for fame, and, above all, the sheer love of speech and literature—plus the conviction, formed early in youth, that the honest, independent writer is the conscience of the human race and the true proponent of both humanism and humanitarianism.

Saul K. Padover: I don't know. I've been a reader since childhood; always loved the printed word; always admired those who wrote and published; always wanted to do that, too. I don't care much about fame; I don't even understand it. I simply want to communicate, and teach.

Kenneth S. Giniger: I have been fascinated by books ever since I grew old enough to read, and, consequently, the making of books has seemed the noblest work of man. The opportunity to participate in this act of putting words on paper for eventual publication always has seemed to me to be an ideal occupation and I am very happy to be engaged in it.

George Simenon: Just a feeling. It's too easy, later, to invent motivation.

Lewis Broad: I wrote because writing was as natural for me as walking. No longer do I run the risks of the free-lance journalist. My books are commissioned in advance and I cannot find time and energy to attempt the uncommissioned.

Joseph N. Bell: I just wanted to be a writer.

Frederic A. Birmingham: I once laughed (mistakenly) at a man who said he thought he'd change his career (he was head buyer in a store) and go into railroading. I scoffed and described him chained to a desk in Philadelphia or New York City. But he just said: "I like to see the trains go by." And so they do, for every good railroader, wherever he may be, no matter how far from the tracks. So the writer must like words, must think of them in their double life as symbols for the spoken word, with a sound somewhere behind the page, and in their graphic form as symbols of a thought, an electronic impulse caught in type. There are other motivations, which you mention. But I would say they must be linked with this primary one. Otherwise, the pay can never be high enough.

Mark Twain, at a time when his grief over family tragedies was almost unbearable, and yet he was turning out some of his greatest works, write to a friend:

"It puzzles me to know what it is in me that writes & has comedy fancies & finds pleasure in phrasing them. It is the law of our nature, of course, or it wouldn't happen."

Perhaps, if we only *knew*, we would find that the needs of writers are what make it possible for them to write with feeling—either to make a reader laugh or make a reader cry. We do know that writing without feeling is as barren as earth without water.

It seems to me that Ken Giniger put his finger on it when he wrote: "I think that most writing is motivated by need—economic, social, moral, or psychological—and that the greater the need, the more intensive the work of the writer."

It always has been my belief that the people who want to be writers strongly enough to pay the price, are strongly impelled toward leadership in their society. Yet, for one reason or another, these people see the uselessness of expecting much in political action, since, as one of the characters in a fiction book I did one time expressed it, "government is the result of the combined *ignorance* of the people." If you have a roomful of idiots and one person with an intelligence quotient of 150 in a room, and there is to be voting, the idiots can out-vote the genius every time. If you have two geniuses in the room, they can agree to work together and keep the idiots in line. In such a case, you don't have democratic government, but a dictatorship of two. But if one of the two geniuses decides to throw his lot in with the idiots, for their votes, then you have government by the combined ignorance of the people. At any rate, writers recognize that true progress—if we ever make any—will come through the goodwill of the relatively few intelligent people helping the less intelligent to learn more, so as to make knowledge widespread. Therefore, writers eschew politics, on a formal basis, for the most part, and spend their time educating not only the people who now live, but, they hope, the people who will live. In this sense, the writer is seeking immortality.

People who are *not* writers should never feel envious of those who are writers and, as such, pay the price to do the writing that lives on and on. This is not a small price, for as Edison Marshall has pointed out, a writer can achieve greatly only by steeling himself to accept solitude—the insulation from his fellowmen that writing demands.

Most of all, then, it seems that the greatest need a writer may have is the sympathy of his fellowmen.

X

The Economics
of Being a Writer

For want of me the world's course will not fail;
When all its work is done, the lie shall rot.
The truth is great, and shall prevail,
When none cares whether it prevail or not.
—COVENTRY PATMORE

SUCCESSFUL writers are asked many questions, in the course of a year, about the economics of being a writer.

Seldom does a month pass, but someone asks me how much money he ought to have stashed away before he should try to be a full time free-lance writer. This is not a question that anyone can answer—truthfully—for all people. The person making the query might be an invalid, confined to bed. There would be nothing wrong with advising him, or her, to give full time to writing, as a pastime and stimulus for living.

To answer how much money to have in the bank before plunging into free-lance writing one also should know about other literary sales the person making the query has been able to achieve. A man who has had two books published—and still holds down a job paying him $9,000 a year—asked me if I thought he should devote *all* his time to writing. I told him that if he applied himself, he could make a good living at it. But he is a timid soul, and he still is a fulltime bureaucrat and a part-time author, which, of course, is *his* business.

Also, a lot depends on the person's own situation, family-wise. A young man who had been making $15,000 a year in public relations, and was unmarried, told me he was taking the plunge into free-lancing without any savings to mention—perhaps enough money to get him through three or four months. I said, "Okay, if you like to gamble."

I felt that, since no one else would suffer, except him, in case he failed, it wasn't up to me to discourage him. I think he is still going, although his earnings are nothing like they used to be, yet.

Another question frequently asked of writers, including me, is how long does it take to get established as a free-lance writer. Here, again, there is no pat answer, for it all depends on how much a person already has progressed in his ability to write copy that will sell and his knowledge of markets.

Generally speaking, my standard reply to both questions is that a person should have cash enough to maintain himself (and family, if he has family responsibilities) for one year. This might mean anywhere from $2,500 to $15,000, depending upon the person, his tastes and habits, and the number of persons dependent on him. Frankly, the older I get, the more I want to *increase* the amount of money a prospective full-time free lancer should have, and the amount of time I would estimate it might take for him to get established, granted he was not the luckiest person on earth. The editorial field seems to become more and more a "longtime" business, as the years pass. This is particularly true, I know, during a year of recession, such as was 1958. Why?

First, because the periods in which you receive reports from most magazines and publishers seems to become longer every year. This is particularly true when there is any hint of an economic downturn. During 1958, most of the publishers to whom I submitted book manuscripts holding them an average of *three months.* One publisher actually held a book manuscript nine months and seemed to resent it when I called him up long distance and told him either to buy it or send it back that day. Occasionally, I would get a report within a month, but this was definitely the exception. Many articles that I sent to legitimate publishers were held varying periods, ranging from two months to a year. The average time for a report on an article in 1946, based on my experience, was about three weeks. Today, it is closer to six weeks.

I can't go into all the factors that, in my judgment, have caused this long lead time on reports, but briefly, I believe, it is due to many factors, mostly beyond the control of any person involved. Magazines must stockpile material a longer time ahead now, in order to plan when to use it. The editor can save time by having on hand a number of articles from which to pick and choose. Also, he has to schedule his magazine farther in advance (to accommodate the printer), and this means, in the case of magazines paying on publication, a longer wait for the writer. Publishers now schedule books farther in advance (also due to the tightness in book production equipment) than they did ten years ago. The situation works a hardship on the writer who does not have funds to carry him along while his material is being considered.

Second, living costs have gone up tremendously in recent years, and give no signs of either stabilizing or tapering-off. Everyone with whom a writer deals—the plumber, the electrician, the delivery man, the mailman, the doctor, the dentist, the restaurateur, the grocer and the liquor store operator—wants more money each year.

After a person is established in the literary field and is earning, on an annual basis, from $5,000 to $10,000 or more, he still runs into "dry spells," in his intake. These are periods—generally about two months after he has taken a vacation—when, either because he does not have enough material of the right quality out, or because of specific situations in each of the magazines to which he, unfortunately, has submitted his material, he does not get in enough money to make even a down payment on his rent. In a "normal" year—writers usually are either way up or way down—the writer runs into difficulty collecting his money during the summer periods, when the bookkeepers are vacationing, or during the Thanksgiving-through New Year period, in which, it seems, everybody in the publishing office goes on one long round of cocktail parties, trips to Bermuda, Sun Valley, or somewhere outside the workaday world in which the writer lives.

To the average writer—if there is an "average"—who depends on the income he gets from writing, the field is hazardous even in years of high economic activity and magazines are bulging with advertisements. But in a year like 1958 when there was a noticeable economic downturn, things can really be rough, economically, even for a free-lance writer earning $15,000, $20,000 and upwards.

What happens when there is a downturn in advertising, as there *was* in early '58? Well, the publisher begins to cut the number of pages in his magazine. This obviously is to save printing and paper costs. But he cuts out relatively few pages, compared to the cuts he makes in the number of pages carrying purchased editorial material. He makes more use of his staff writers, who are close at home and who realize they may be fired if things get any worse. These staff writers begin to see more good article ideas, and short material, in the handouts sent to them by the carload.

Meantime, with millions of people out of work, more would-be writers become actual free lancers. They are drawing unemployment compensation, or severance pay, and while looking for other jobs, fill in the time sending in material to magazines. The existing free-lancers, noticing a downturn in their income, work harder. So the amount of material sent *to* editors goes up, at the very time his needs for such material are diminishing.

This may explain why, whenever free-lance writers got together in '58, they remarked wryly to one another about what a rat-race the editorial field was getting to be.

As you glance through magazines, or look through libraries, you will see that each year publishers reprint articles by writers who wrote their articles or stories years, decades, or even centuries ago. Not long ago, *Harper's Magazine* proudly featured four hitherto unpublished pieces by—of all people—Mark Twain, who has been dead more than half a century. Remember, whenever a book is printed that contains material already written last year, or last century, it is competing with books now being written by living, breathing writers. Besides, the "classic" is becoming better and better known, because, of course, the writer is dead and hasn't made any enemies among modern reviewers. Besides, the reviewers have been brainwashed. They grew up hearing that this writer —who is now dead—was a "genius," and his works were all brilliant, so no matter what is published by the long-gone author, it is real competition to anything published by living authors, who are having a hard time eating.

The same thing is true, of course, of new television and movie stars, who must compete with films made a decade and two decades ago. The competition these days between live actors and dead ones is intense.

I queried many writers about economic tips they might have for other writers not so fortunate as they in this field. I found that virtually every successful writer had solved these personal economic problems. None of them deprecated the importance of solving it, either, for more than one of them remarked that they really could not give full attention to their work or full play to their imagination, until they had made sure that the wolf at the door was firmly at bay.

Yet, I'll admit that the fact that these writers now are fat and happy—not literally, since many are lean and lithe specimens—may be one reason why writers from other countries, judging American literature today, say that the writing by the "best" writers is not showing any discontent, and that literary prophets crying in the wilderness are few and far between. Maybe it *is* difficult, in the context of today's society and the relative riches of those who buy and read magazines and books, for a writer who is hungry to sell to them, no matter how much his lines may burn with emotional fire. It is possible the *best* writing—and that which will live the longest —still is being written by men in the clutches of the loan sharks, or about to be evicted, with their families, from a new 20′ by 20′ rambler on which the writer could not meet the $92-a-month payment.

What are the ways by which the well-heeled writers *did* solve their economic problems? A lot of them became teachers, and on cloistered campuses, with a fair salary, began to write in extra hours until they had built up their name and a steady enough income to get out on their own. Still others held jobs until they had worked into the writing field, little by little.

A lot of them starting free-lancing early in college, and by the time they graduated, they had a good running start. Many held jobs in advertising agencies, on newspapers, or in related fields. Almost everyone of them worked in occupations that required them to handle words—or to be around those handling words. Since words are a writer's stock in trade it is natural that most successful free-lance writers come from occupations where they dealt in words.

"I've always found it doesn't pay for a writer to borrow money, since the interest charges represent a net loss to him," one writer told me. "The interest represents that many more words he has to write, and sell, to make the same amount of money, net, if he had waited and had bought whatever he did buy for cash."

This writer, like so many others whom I have encountered, early learned that bankers didn't consider him a good credit risk, even for small loans, and that if he borrowed, it would have to be from a friendly loan shark. He resolved—as has many another writer striving to get in the clear and stay in the clear, financially—to forego borrowing at all.

"A builder can afford to borrow money, since he can add the interest charges on the money he has borrowed into the cost of the houses he sells," this same writer pointed out. "So can a grocer borrow money to stock his shelves, for he can add the cost of the interest to his prices and get the interest from consumers. But the writer is only getting two cents, or five cents, or a certain number of cents per word, whether he owes anything or not. He is in no position to raise his price to get the cost of the interest back."

Another writer emphasized the necessity, from the writer's standpoint, of owning his home.

"The best thing for him to do—unless he is so successful money is no worry at all—is to buy a house, which he *must* pay for month by month, or in regular installments or three months, or six months. In this way, he makes himself save, and at the same time he hedges against the inflation. If a writer does not have a home of his own, it is wiser for him to get it first before investing his funds, if he has any, in stocks and bonds."

This makes sense, for unless a writer is affluent, he can't afford to keep an office. The rent is uneconomic. But the writer can use his home as a working place, and can deduct part of its maintenance and operation from his taxes (as we shall see in a later chapter), while saving the rental of other working space.

Naïve people—and who was it said that "naïve" is just another way to say "dumb?"—are always wanting to know what expenses a writer has? For them, let us point out that writing—and this goes for fiction as well as fact—entails research. Research may require letter-writing, travel, or going, at least, as far as downtown to the library. It also may require the writer to interview one, or ten, or 100 people. Some of these people will not loosen up and talk without a lunch, or sometimes, a few drinks. Gathering information—good, valid information—costs money. Telephone calls add up. So do taxi fares, and other fares for intercity or intra-city transportation.

Besides doing research on specific articles or stories he must write, a writer must be a researcher in a direction that never occurs to the average person. He constantly must be *looking for markets*, if he expects to make any really big money writing. Just getting the magazines that he ought to read for market information—such as *Author & Journalist, Editor & Publisher, Advertising Age*, and the like, the writer must read many daily newspapers and magazines merely to be sure he is keeping up with what is going on. These subscriptions cost money.

Even if a writer had no expenses except those involved in preparing his material for market, the cost could be substantial. I have been annoyed at editors who expected me—or any other writer— to work for the equivalent of $1 an hour, when the editors must know, if they would stop to think, that they could not even hire a public stenographer for less than $3 or $4 an hour. Preparing material on a minimum basis—in case the writer does it himself—requires paper, erasers, typewriters, typewriter ribbons (a typewriter cleaning twice a year at $25 a shot), envelopes, clips, staples, and postage. None of these is a small item anymore to anyone who uses them in quantity. If, of course, the writer is a sloppy final draftsman, he has to have someone copy his material before it is sent off— at about $3 an hour. If he hires a girl, then he is annoyed with becoming her tax collector and with filling out countless forms in the course of a year.

The actual costs of a prolific writer, who is striving to make at least $10,000 a year and up, easily can run into $5,000 and $6,000 a year these days. These are deductible business expenses, of course, for tax purposes, but this doesn't mean that the writer is "making" this sum without paying taxes on it, as many thoughtless people frequently imply. Money spent on business expenses is just as real a cost to a writer—and just as much of a cut out of his net income—

as money a businessman has to pay for the rent on his store. As noted, there is *one* big difference. The writer cannot add the cost of doing business to his price. He has to take what editors offer. The store owner can raise his prices to meet his costs.

If a businessman, worth a million dollars, wants to borrow up to $350,000 from the Small Business Administration, at a reasonable rate of interest, the way is clear for him to do it. But if a writer, who may need $1,000 to finish a book that might help millions, were to apply to the same agency for a loan at reasonable rates, he would be turned down. The agency has ruled that loans to writers might make them "venal." A writer has to wonder how many "venal" businessmen there are lolling on the sands at Miami Beach, while he labors away in a northern winter, and is lucky to be eating while he is waiting for his checks.

The economics of being a writer perhaps is the least-understood part of his whole life.

Bookkeepers of magazine and book publishers, I think, are the most important people, from the writer's standpoint. They all imagine him to be rolling in dough. A magazine bookkeeper will write out one check for $1,000 to a writer. The bookkeeper might know that this is the only $1,000 he has paid to this writer this year, but he reasons that if he has paid the writer $1,000, for one article, then the writer has sold perhaps 100 articles to other publications. Therefore, reasons the bookkeeper, whether or not the writer gets this $1,000 is a matter of great indifference to the writer. So the bookkeeper will sit on the check as long as he can. Bookkeepers, I am told, are very careful men in making entries and in notifying management about money due to the company. But writers can testify that when it comes to paying writers, bookkeepers are very careless and debonair.

How much money does a "successful" writer have to make to be in the "successful" class these days?

Everything considered, it is startlingly low, comparing "successful" writers with successful disc jockeys, successful news commentators, successful bank presidents and successful appliance salesmen or insurance and real estate men.

If you told the average real estate salesman that he would be considered "successful" if he made $10,000 a year, he would laugh at you. Even if you told the average meat salesman this, he would snicker. But virtually every writer I have interviewed has stated that if a writer is making $10,000 a year, he could be considered a success.

Referring only to *money*, I asked our panel of successful writers how much income they felt a writer should have annually to live comfortably in this society. The answers follows:

Alden Hatch: That depends on his tastes and background, but . . . no one can live *comfortably* on less than $10,000 a year.

Harold Helfer: This is a very personal thing. Some of us require less than others—our natures are that way. I don't think the fact that a man is a writer has anything to do with this problem.

Will Oursler: It is my opinion the writer should seek to run his work on a business-like basis, however high he may set his professional and creative standards. He should try to build his program so that he can earn enough to meet his specific needs. I do not think it practical to set a specific figure for *all* writers. It might vary from $2,500 a year to $25,000.

Norman Vincent Peale: A comfortable standard of living is no less important to the average writer—and no more important, either —than to people in other lines of creative work.

Richard Gehman: I don't know what the average income of the free-lancer is, but I think a poll taken about a year ago indicated that the range was between $10,000 and $20,000 a year.

Harry Edward Neal: A single man without dependents could probably live "comfortably" on $6,000 or $7,000 a year, whereas a married man with a couple of children and a mortgage might well have to earn $10,000 or $12,000.

Frances and Richard Lockridge: If I had to set a figure, minimum, I suppose it would be around $10,000 a year.

Dora Albert: Costs of living vary so much all over the United States, and individuals differ so much in their standards and requirements for comfort that I personally would not dream of naming a specific figure. I do recall, though, that one editor once told me that no one should continue writing who couldn't earn $10,000 a year through his work as a writer. I do *not* agree with this editor. I believe that anyone who has something to say that he feels might be helpful or interesting should try to find a market or markets for what he writes.

O. A. Battista: A steady-state average income of at least $10,000 a year is what I believe should be the minimum for a fulltime writer. If he really works hard at it, there is no reason why this could not be increased substantially.

Fred Kerner: I would think that in New York City a single man could live very well on $6,000 to $7,000 a year. A married man with no children would certainly require $7,500 to $9,000 to live comfortably. But, again, this is only judging on how I might want to live, and actually bears no reality as to how I have lived, and do live as a writer. I feel, from what I have seen among other writers I know, that in other parts of the country this minimum income could be scaled downward in some instances and would have to be scaled upwards in others. Perhaps, if a definite round-figure minimum were to be demanded of me, I would say that $10,000 a year would be the absolute minimum on which the average writer could live comfortably.

Roger Burlingame: The amount of money a writer needs depends on whether he is more interested in writing well or living well.

Robert Payne: Enough for Virginia Woolf's "room with a view," and that depends on where he is. It may be $3 a day in Spain or Greece, and, say, $15 a day in New York.

A. C. Spectorsky: I know writers who do very well on a few thousand a year. They have seceded from the rat race, have managed to find a life for themselves which does not require much in the way of material possessions or comforts, and have managed to keep themselves free of financial obligations. I know other writers who go along pretty hungrily on their $30,000 or $40,000 a year and try to find other ways in which to supplement their writing income.

Erskine Caldwell: As much as a bus driver or policeman or a fireman or bartender.

Senator Richard L. Neuberger: The amount of income necessary to a writer is totally contingent upon the size of his family, and their tastes and needs.

Emil Zubryn: You tell me you have a tough time at $18,000 a year—and I'm having a tough time down here just barely averaging around a third of this. I can't speak as to the States. But even in Mexico, if you want to live *comfortably*, you should really hit around $9,000 a year and not too many expenditures eating into this. My ideal—so far unachieved after ten years here—has been to *net* this amount. And I don't have to tell you that the first two or three years were rough.

Evan Hunter: I lived comfortably when I was earning $40 a week—and I live comfortably now.

Ben Smith: I would say that, in the United States, a writer with a family should have a minimum of $7,500 a year and more comfortably, $10,000 (that's with two children, for example). I suppose a single writer could live comfortably on $5,000 or perhaps a bit less. However, I am assuming one thing: that such a writer is established. A beginner should attempt to hold his income as high as possible until he can get a backlog to carry him through the dry times. And in no circumstances should he quit a paying job and attempt fulltime free-lance with less than a year's living expenses, *after all bills are paid.*

Jesse Stuart: Depends on where the man lives, and his family. I would have to make at least $10,000 a year.

Thomas P. Kelley: Today, at least $6,000 a year.

Scott Young: Depends on how large a family. I could live and be happy on $3,000 or $4,000 a year, if unmarried, or probably much less. But, married, $8,000 to $10,000 a year—to allow my family to keep up with the Joneses.

David and Deane Heller: $10,000 a year.

John Gassner: $10,000 a year net, after taxes.

Saul K. Padover: You can live on relatively little in Austria or Spain, but need a considerable income in New York City (at least $10,000 a year for a couple with one or two children, I should think).

Kenneth S. Giniger: I know writers who live comfortably on $5,000 a year and I know others who are up to their ears in debt on $50,000 a year. This is purely a matter of personality.

Georges Simenon: So-and-so needs a lot of money to write a Book-of-the-Month. Henry Miller, with very little money, is a happy man and an international figure in literature.

Joseph N. Bell: The idea is to do the work well and the income will measure up.

Frederic A. Birmingham: I would suggest a survey of the average incomes of writers' groups. Assuming that because they have the money for dues therefore they are consistent authors, I believe the average figure is still shockingly low. It is shockingly low for the national income figures on college men, too, but that includes a large group with bums, jailbirds, and the discouraged, which tends to pull the average down. In the writers' group, a small one, and seemingly made up of the leaders, the average is depressingly below $10,000 as I recall. But the big money writers who might pull the average up usually are lone wolves who do not need group protection and don't belong.

XI

The Writer
and His Health

The groundwork of all happiness is health.
—LEIGH HUNT

This is the great error of our day in the treatment of the human body—that physicians separate the soul from the body.
—PLATO

Every man is his own best friend, or worst enemy.
—ELBERT HUBBARD

THIS apparently-innocuous subject—health—is not one on which successful writers are in agreement. Perhaps some will say—as some have said—that a chapter on the subject of health has little or nothing to do with writing. On the other hand, I am deeply convinced that a writer's health has much to do not only with whether or not he can turn out really good material but, particularly, *how much* he can produce in a lifetime.

It seems to me that the writer is the one person in the society who is more dependent on good health—physical, mental and emotional—than people in any other profession, business, or trade. If a working writer loses time, due to poor health or bad work habits, he will lose income. Many writers can't afford to lose income, or they will be looking for work in other businesses.

A writer must keep himself in top form physically, mentally, and emotionally. All he really possesses is a machine—himself—to turn out the right words for the right audience. Any writer would admit that if his car needed new spark plugs, or had a flat tire, the machine would not perform as well as if it were in prime condition. *Everything* about an automobile has something to do with its performance. *Everything* about a body has something to do with its performance. It *is* possible to drive a car that is "missing" because a spark plug is out of whack. It also is possible to keep going personally, although "missing," because a part of your physical, mental, or emotional body is out of whack. But you can't perform your *best*, any more than your car can perform its best with parts worn out, damaged, or not properly oiled.

The writer should view his health as his most important asset. I have been sick only once in many years. But because of that one illness, my income dropped almost disastrously at a time when I had obligated myself to take on financial payments for certain properties. For two years, I looked back on that time of illness—about two months—and grimaced.

A bookkeeper on a salary can afford poor health much better than the average writer. The bookkeeper, if he feels bad, can take a day off without being nicked for it. But when a writer takes a day off, *he* feels it financially at a later date. This isn't true, of course, of writers who have books selling for them, or are on retainers to finish material by a certain far-off date. But these writers are relatively few. The great number of writers, I believe, are *dependent* on the material they produce each day, and each week.

Blake Clark, consistent high producer for *Reader's Digest* for many years, agrees with me. He has followed his diet carefully for many years, maintaining a regular weight. He also exercises regularly, swimming at the University Club or elsewhere. It is obvious to those who see him that he is in perfect physical condition. While I do not know his age, I am sure he looks ten or fifteen years younger than he is.

Although some successful writers, do not put much emphasis on health, scores of top-producing writers follow definite health rules. Not only do they think of their bodies, they think of their minds. They read regularly, and widely. They also think of themselves as social beings. They go to parties, go out to lunch with friends, and go to the races. Some of them are active in civic, church and community affairs. A lot of them take part in such sports as tennis, badminton, golf, horseshoes, and the like. They also think of their emotions. They strive to keep down the annoyances that can plague their minds and cut off the creative flow.

The typical successful writer, I judge from my various interviews, is a man who has learned *temperance,* in what I believe to be the true meaning of the word. He drinks in moderation. More important, he eats high-protein, vitamin foods and he *eats in moderation.* Of hundreds of writers, I do not know one who is overweight. This typical successful writer also does not overdo in any field. He goes out, but doesn't "live away from home," as so many society people do, because they have no inner resources and no happy family to keep them satisfied.

In this "happy medium" of eating, drinking, and partaking of social activities, the writer finds that he can get good or better ideas and produce most favorably. This undoubtedly is not true of *all* writers.

Questions asked of me by would-be writers indicate that they give some thought to health habits and also to working habits of successful writers. Something tells them that how a man *feels* has much to do with how good a job he does. Mary Roberts Rinehart, who wrote many best-sellers, was handicapped in later life by one ailment—writer's cramp. She always wrote with a fountain pen, and when she developed writer's cramp, she found that she could not dictate her material, or use a typewriter. Her production was cut immeasurably, but, fortunately for her, her fortune already was made. A simple ailment, a headache or a hangover sometimes can prevent a writer from fulfilling his destiny.

What is the best time for a writer to produce each day? A noted columnist, who began his professional career as a newspaperman, could never write unless he were in a crowded city room, with all its attendant noises. Another writer must have virtually absolute silence, except for the sounds of nature, such as the birds singing, the rain falling, or other natural sounds. Many people can write under tension, surrounded by noise; at other times, the same people find an early deadline or any noise distracting. Unless he *feels* like working, a writer can't do his best work. And his feelings, of course, are due to a large extent to what he has eaten, or failed to eat, how many heels he may have encountered in the course of his travels, and other factors, all having to do with his physical, mental and emotional health.

On this, let's hear from our panel of successful writers on "Do you have any special health tips for writers?"

Alden Hatch: Why should writers need health tips? I consider this a foolish question. I have regular working hours—four hours a day.

Harold Helfer: Never thought about this. A $1,000 check from a publisher probably will help to cure anything that ails you.

Norman Vincent Peale: I cannot very well urge the desirability of regular hours for a writer, as I myself often work late at night, until long past midnight—and at other times do my best writing in the early hours of the day. I feel a person has to write when he feels it in his blood and has the opportunity to do it. Working now early and now late will not tax a writer's health, if he thinks the right kinds of thoughts, eats correctly, and exercises ordinary prudence in conserving his physical strength.

Richard Gehman: My health tip to all writers is to refrain if possible from drinking more than one quart of whisky a day.

Harry Edward Neal: Each writer should gear his production and his working habits to his physical capabilities. The man who enjoys writing for four hours at a stretch might ruin his disposition, impair his health, and even lose some of his skill if he were to force himself into an eight- or ten-hour day. Conversely, the writer who has conditioned himself to write for eight hours or more daily might well build up to a nervous breakdown if he chopped this time in half. *Professional* writing is a business and should be treated as such. It is a business which requires hard and steady work, and in which inspiration plays an infinitesimal role. To my mind, the important goal for the established writer or the beginner is to set a definite working time to write each day, and to stick to his schedule, even though that time may be one-half, one, two, four, or ten hours a day. It is just as important for him to *write something* during his working time, even though whatever he writes may wind up in the wastebasket. Regular writing at a regular time establishes a desirable habit for the writer, and also improves his fluency.

Richard Lockridge: I write for not more than three or four hours a day, in the morning. I don't know that this is a "health tip."

Edison Marshall: I don't know any gimmicks. I glue my glutius maximus muscles to the chair. I work when I don't sleep and eat— a period of perhaps six months—five days a week. The other six months are divided between three months' research and three months' loafing, immediately following the writing, in which I can hardly bring myself to read a newspaper. I feel so "shotted," as my New England ancestors use to say of a herring that had spawned.

Dora Albert: About two years ago, the American Medical Association issued a report stating that it had found no reason for believing that some diseases are psychosomatic, and some are not. Apparently, however organic an illness may be, our emotional attitudes are among the causes of that illness. Therefore, as writers and as human beings, it is important for us to acquire the emotional attitudes that help lead to health. Of course, I believe in reasonably regular hours of sleep, sound nutrition, and the other elementary health principles. But over and above these elementary principles, we must look to and guard our emotional and mental health. We have to accept ourselves, with all our faults; learn to like ourselves; and learn to like others. Faith in a power higher than ourselves is a tremendous help, too. These emotional attitudes have more to do with out health than whether we work in the morning or at midnight. There are some people, as you must know, who are most creative in the early hours of the day—the so-called "morning people." I'm one of them. I prefer to do my writing in the morning, when possible. That doesn't mean that other writers, who do their clearest thinking at midnight, should follow my example. When you feel most energetic is the time to do your most difficult creative work, if possible.

I think writers who enjoy the particular type of writing they are doing are apt to enjoy good health than those who write without any particular sense of interest or achievement. If a writer had to choose between writing about subjects distasteful to him for large sums of money and writing about subjects he liked for smaller sums, it would be in the interest of his mental health to choose the subjects that fascinated him.

Fred Kerner: I think every writer will develop his own writing gimmicks. There are the night people—such as I—who find it much easier to write in the quiet early morning hours. There are those who find that they can get up at 6 a.m. and, after breakfast, write steadily until noon, and then take the remainder of the day off. Frankly, I think that the average writer would soon find when he does his best work and begin to schedule his day accordingly. As far as "health tips" go, I can only suggest that a writer keep as healthy as possible. Writing is downright hard work, and you have to be in top physical condition, as well as mental and emotional condition, to be successful.

Pinky Herman: Speaking only for myself, I often have awakened in the middle of the night to jot down a particular line or an idea for a song. Some writers prefer a special time to write, and I know many authors who go to the office and work from 9 to 5 p.m., just like millions of clerks. I wrote my lyrics and music whenever the ideas came to me.

Roger Burlingame: A disciplined writer should be able to write anywhere at any time. I have no "tips."

Abigail Van Buren: I don't drink, smoke or keep late hours. I work from 8 a.m. until 3:30 p.m., and that's enough for anybody.

Robert Payne: Writers write where and how they can; it is so personal a thing, depending on health, smoking habits, metabolism, where and when they sleep . . . I write mostly at night, because it is quieter and there are fewer interruptions.

Hugh Ross Williamson: My training as a journalist and my practice as a writer has made me distrust all "gimmicks" but two, which are—(1) write solidly in the morning from 8:30 to 12:30 p.m. and then forget about it, and (2) always prepare your first sentence for your paragraph for the next day, on the evening before, so that you don't waste the precious morning hours "trying to begin."

A. C. Spectorsky: This touches on an extremely important matter. Our society is such that a fairly rigid pattern of living is taught us from infancy. Yet, in my experience, all people and especially highly-creative people, have their own rhythms. They are very lucky if these happen to coincide with the 9 to 5 regimen and asleep-before-midnight national pattern. This is not often the case. One of the most successful writers I know does his best work from midnight to daylight.

Erskine Caldwell: Write whenever and wherever you can write.

Senator Richard L. Neuberger: Writers who do their best work in the early morning are what I describe as "larks," while those who succeed at night are what I call "owls." I, myself, am a "lark."

Emil Zubryn: I've been going for thirty years now. I've not followed any health rules. I've always slept fitfully, four or five hours a night (and now it gets down to three sometimes, and I feel it, but hate like hell to take sleeping pills, etc.). I get a checkup once in a while. *And* I don't *kill* myself with work. If it means my health suffers, or the word production per month suffers, it is the *word production* I give up. Generally speaking, these days, I sit down regularly at the machine from 9 to 1 (and this includes handling mail, rejects, etc.) and have the remainder of the time to myself. Now this schedule, of course, falls down when an important piece is in the works, or a special cable comes in for data, etc. But my goal is to stick to it—and cut it down to about three hours a day. . . . I find that what most writers lack is the self-discipline needed to sit down at regular hours. I can't write at midnight, but there are others who do. At midnight, I'm usually through poring over books or papers, magazines, etc., and settle down to relax with a science fiction story or book.

Sloan Wilson: Yes, I have some special tips. Stay off the liquor, and set a daily minimum of hours to be worked or pages to be written.

Evan Hunter: The only health tip I have is: keep writing. Whether you have an idea or not, whether you feel like writing or not, write. The only time a writer is unhealthy is when he's sitting around brooding and feeling worthless. I write every day. If the stuff turns out bad, I throw it away. But I've been working, and I learn even from the bad stuff I write. I have no superstitions about writing. It is not a profession wherein good stories or novels *happen* by luck. They are the result of hard work and the most rigid kind of discipline—which is self-imposed discipline.

Ben Smith: I have only one health tip for any aspiring writer.

Stay healthy. Writing is one of the most gruelling jobs in the world and it'll kill you if you don't play footsie with your doctor (yeah, I know, Somerset Maugham makes a liar out of me). I begin work when I sit down at the typewriter and stop when I get up. The hour doesn't seem to matter and I'm about as superstitious as a fence post.

Blake Clark: I get up fairly early and write, in longhand, perhaps 300 words, more or less. That is all I try to do in one day. I spend the afternoon in thinking and in research. I am a great believer in the proper diet. I have come to believe that a writer must get adequate proteins that he must have for the sustained drive which writing demands. Keeping your weight down, for example, is both good sense and good health.

Scott Young: I like working first thing in the morning, right after breakfast, and working right through without lunch break (maybe a sandwich at the desk) until I can work no more, and then quit entirely for the day. Usually five or six hours of work is plenty.

John Gassner: I have no health tips. Let the writer work whenever he feels like it and whenever he can.

Saul K. Padover: Some writers are helped by smoking; some by coffee; some by scotch or gin. I take only coffee. When I was young I did a lot of writing late at night; now I can't and don't. Now I prefer the mid-morning. Thomas Mann, I am told, used to write two pages every single morning, regardless of how he felt or what the subject was. He was guided by an inflexible routine—not a bad thing.

Georges Simenon: Some very good writers and some very bad work in the morning—the same goes for midnight.

Joseph N. Bell: Sometimes I work all night, sometimes in the morning, and at various times. A lot of writers are choleric about the work, how they hate to write, what a hard job it is, etc. My view is that if writing is so painful, you are in the wrong profession.

Frederic A. Birmingham: I personally prefer the very early morning, after a period of thought the night before over the content of my forthcoming work. The subconscious mind is a great arranger of scattered particles of thought, and a generous donor of thoughts seemingly lost forever in your gray matter. And in the morning, your body assists by being stronger and more alert and bringing more energy to your task.

XII

The Writer
and His Home

*The perfect place for a writer is in the
hideous roar of a city, with men making
a new road under his window in competition with a barrel organ, and on the mat
a man, waiting for the rent.*

—HENRY VOLLAM MORTON

WHERE is the best place for a writer to live and work? Is it in a
dingy hotel room, where, when the writer looks out, he sees poor
people shuffling along to their jobs, or engaged in their menial
work? Is it in a penthouse, looking out over skyscrapers that tower
far into the distance? Is it in a mansion on a knoll, where the writer
can open the venetian blinds and look out at rolling green hills in
the distance, and far away see a distant mountain top? Or is it in a
garret, where, working with little heat and less nourishment, the
writer fears to hear a knock because he knows it most likely will
be someone trying to collect an overdue bill?

A study of writers shows no hard and fast generalizations can be
made about *where*—and how!—a man must live to work. Writers
work in all kinds of circumstances, under all kinds of conditions,
and in all kinds of economic, marital, political and legal snarls. A

lot of them live and die without ever finding out whether or not
they could have produced brilliant material under ideal circumstances—in their own home, amid surroundings over which they
more or less have control, safe from the assaults of bill-collectors or
process-servers and behind a high board fence that keeps out the
noises of the city and the distractions of the populace.

Could Edgar Allen Poe, who gave the world *The Gold Bug, The
Raven,* and numerous other good and bad works, have written as
vividly and with such fire as he did if he had lived placidly in a
large home of his own? We'll never know the answer to that question, for the fact is, Mr. Poe never had what could be called a home
of his own, once he was dismissed from West Point in his twenty-
second year for disobeying orders (incidentally, the Poe Memorial
Gate at West Point features these words of Sir Francis Bacon:
"There is no exquisite beauty without some strangeness in the
proportion.").

Homeless and penniless, Poe went to New York, fighting a losing battle with illness, poverty and alcohol for the remainder of
his life. He wrote in every medium—essays, poems, short stories,
novels, analyses of handwriting, and even a plagiarized book on
conchology. Engaged as an editor intermittently, after winning a
$50 prize for *Ms. Found In A Bottle,* he regularly was taken home
drunk to his wife, Virginia, a cousin. When she died, Poe wooed
many women, in more or less platonic fashion. He tried to commit
suicide when he was thirty-nine, but his stomach could not toler-
ate the poison and he vomited it up. He died in a Baltimore hospital October 7, 1849, having been found in a tavern four days before
with "his face haggard and unwashed, his hair unkempt, and his
whole physique repulsive."

Would Poe have even been a writer if he had lived a sedate life,
making friends and holding menial jobs faithfully? Could his genius have worked just as well in the pleasant surroundings of a well-

kept home as it did in the back-alley kind of rooms he occupied most of his life?

Richard Lovelace, the English poet of the seventeenth century, was heir to four estates in Kent, but he went with the wrong political faction. When he was twenty-four, he was committed to the Gatehouse Jail, where he wrote his most famous work. Out on bail —estimated at from 4,000 to 40,000 pounds—he raised troops for the Royalists, even as a prisoner on parole. He followed Charles I to France, was wounded at Dunkirk, and when he was thirty, went back to England. Again imprisoned, he started writing. When he was released from prison, he spent the last ten years of his life in abject poverty. The youth who had started out dressed in silver, befitting a king's courtier, haunted alleys for scraps of food in his last days. He lived near Shoe Lane, in Gunpowder Alley. When he was forty, he was consumptive. One cold morning they found his body in a cellar.

Would Lovelace have given the world the poetry in *Lucasta*, if he had lived an idyllic life in one of the great estate houses he inherited? We cannot say. But, had he lived calmly and sedately, still would have had the same *capacity*—in his brilliant mind—to turn out whatever he would have wanted to turn out. But would he have *wanted* to produce literary material if he had not been imbued with a cause for which, in effect, he gave the last full measure of devotion?

Sir Walter Scott, who was a lawyer—clerk of session for twenty-five years—before he determined to make a reputation in literature, *was* financially successful as a writer. So successful in fact that he went into partnership with his publisher, John Ballantyne, and built the magnificent estate of Abbotsford. Although the company failed, Scott refused to take advantage of bankruptcy. Ill, and fifty-six years old, he worked feverishly and strove to pay off his creditors. But the work hastened the end of his life. His doctors

prescribed a sea voyage. When he knew he was dying, Scott in-
sisted that he be taken to Abbotsford to meet death. He was carried
across Europe and died in his home September 21, 1832.

Robert Louis Stevenson's *Requiem* indicated his love for a home-
site, but it also revealed that he realized he could never have one.
These are the lines on his epitaph in Samoa, where he was buried
December 3, 1894:

> *Under the wide and starry sky,*
> *Dig the grave and let me lie.*
> *Glad did I live and gladly die,*
> *And I laid me down with a will.*
>
> *This be the verse you grave for me:*
> *Here he lies where he longed to be;*
> *Home is the sailor, home from the sea,*
> *And the hunter home from the hill.*

Stevenson, born in Edinburgh, planned to be a lighthouse engineer, as was his father before him, but he was a consumptive. He
studied for the law, but never practiced, and began to travel to
find a place to prolong his life.

He went to France, met Mrs. Fannie Osbourne, and followed
her to California, almost dying during the rigorous journey. They
were married in his thirtieth year. He wrote *Treasure Island* and
The Strange Case of Dr. Jekyll and Mr. Hyde, and other works
which have become classics.

Fighting against his disease, he went to Saranac Lake, N. Y. A
winter there gave him some respite from his illness. He sailed from
San Francisco on an excursion among the South Sea islands. But
what began as a lark became an exile. Sixty natives carried him to
a peak on Samoa, facing the broad Pacific, upon his death.

Alexander Pope expressed the hopes of a home better than many
writers who came after him could. In *Solitude* he wrote:

Happy the man, whose wish and care
A few paternal acres bound,
Content to breathe his native air
In his own ground . . .

Blest, who can unconcernedly find,
Hours, days, and years slide soft away
In health of body, peace of mind;
Quiet by day.

Sound sleep by night; study and ease
Together mixed, sweet recreation.
And innocence, which most does please,
With meditation.

Thus let me live, unseen, unknown;
Thus unlamented let me die,
Steal from the world, and not a stone
Tell where I lie.

Ralph Waldo Emerson's home burned down in his seventieth year, when he was the most famous living American writer. He was weakened both by exposure and the loss of his precious books and furniture. But kind friends sent him to Europe. When he returned, he was gratified to learn that admirers had rebuilt his home and furnished it to the last detail.

Consider Wilfried Scawen Blunt, a famous English poet who married Lord Byron's granddaughter. He entered the diplomatic service at eighteen and served in various European and Latin American countries before retiring at thirty to settle down at Crabbet Park, an estate in Sussex, where he bred Arab horses.

This interest caused him to go to Arabia. He became a passionate Mohammedan sympathizer, at a time when this was definitely against British policy. He defended the Egyptians—almost a hundred years before the short-lived Suez War of 1956—and when he was forty-seven, he was arrested for helping the Irish. He served two months in prison for that.

He lived most of his life at Crabbet Park, in between his various jaunts to other lands to take the side of minorities. When he was eighty, he published *My Diaries*. But it blistered British diplomacy with such withering scorn the faint-hearted publisher withdrew it from distribution.

Blunt once wrote in one of his poetry books as follows:

"No life is perfect that has not been lived—youth in feeling—manhood in battle—old age in meditation."

He had experienced it all when he died in 1922, a contented man, at eighty-three.

Oliver Goldsmith was a man without a home. Considered the village blockhead—and he looked the part because his features were harsh and his face was pitted by smallpox—he acted like a clown in school. When he was persuaded to go to college, he got his degree at twenty-one, the lowest on the list.

He squandered a small inheritance left to him by his father. He became a tutor, but lost the job in an angry dispute with the head of the household. When his uncle gave him fifty pounds to study for the law, Goldsmith gambled it away.

He once started for America, but changed his mind and went to France determined to be a physician. It appears that he spent his time playing music for country dances. He earned his board and lodging by playing a flute in the streets and taverns.

Before he was thirty, he returned to England and lived among the beggars. He was, successively, an usher, a bookseller's hack, a reviewer, and, in time, a professional writer. But he looked upon writing as drudgery.

He was forever in debt and being pursued by the sheriff. Sometimes between his thirtieth and fortieth birthday, he met Samuel Johnson. Johnson learned that Goldsmith was about to be dispossessed from his room for not paying the rent. Johnson sent the writer a guinea. Goldsmith bought wine with it. A little later, Johnson stumbled on *The Vicar of Wakefield* in Goldsmith's room, and sold it for sixty pounds. Then *he* paid Goldsmith's rent.

When he was forty, Goldsmith turned to writing plays. He got 500 pounds for *The Good-Natured Man*. And *She Stoops to Conquer* became enormously popular. By the time he was forty-five, he was prosperous, but his dissipation—continual drinking and gambling, at which he lost—ruined him.

He fancied himself a physician. Because he could not get patients, he would say: "I prescribe only for my friends." But jokesters said that if he were wise he would prescribe only for his enemies. When, finally, a physician went to Goldsmith, the physician asked: "Is your mind at ease?"

"No, it is not," Goldsmith said. And then he died. His home had been a room since the death of his father decades before. And yet he gave the world some of its greatest poetry and at least one of the greatest plays.

Consider David Herbert Lawrence, who published thirty-seven books in his lifetime and ten more have been published since 1930 when he died at forty-five on the French Riviera.

Lawrence was the son of a miner in Nottinghamshire, England, who drank and beat his wife. D. H. had an attachment to his mother, and shortly after her death, he fell in love with Frieda von Richtofen (sister of the famous World War I flying ace). She was seven years his senior and mother of three children. They eloped, lived abroad, and were married some years later, much like Ingrid Bergman and her Rossellini. Because she was German, they became the victims of spy-hunting fever in England and Lawrence left, denouncing, as Byron had done "the artificial complexities of civilization." He lived in Italy, France, Ceylon, Australia, Tahiti, Mexico, and the U. S. Lawrence pretended to hate colonies, but he was always trying vainly to start one of his own.

Carl Sandburg, who is living in his own cottage in retirement

near Asheville, North Carolina, did most of his best writing while
following his wanderlust. He started work delivering milk when he
was thirteen in Galesburg, Ill., where he was born Charles August
Sandburg in 1878. He earned his living as a barbershop porter,
truck handler, dishwasher, turner's apprentice, and harvest hand.
He enlisted in the Sixth Illinois Volunteers and served in Puerto
Rico in the Spanish-American War.

Back at Lombard College, in his home town, after the war, he
worked as editor of the college paper, captain of the basketball
team and gymnasium janitor. When he graduated, he became a
salesman, advertising manager and journalist. At forty, he began
to roam, during which period he wrote his monumental five-volume
work, *The Life of Lincoln.*

Whether or not it pays for a writer to have a solid home base,
Sandburg has never said.

However, many modern successful writers seem to feel that, with
a family, and their responsibilities, they *must* have a home, preferably one that is capacious and paid for. Edison Marshall lives
at Breetholm, a beautiful home near Augusta, Ga.; W. Somerset
Maugham lives in a mansion on the French Riviera; it is said that
in Hollywood, a writer is not considered one of the top men unless
he has a mansion, a swimming pool, a dog, an extra sweetheart,
and a psychiatrist, not necessarily in that order.

On the basis of my visits in the homes of successful writers, and
my interviews with others whose homes I have not seen, I would
say that *thousands* of writers in the United States live in bigger
and better homes than the one hundred *top* writers of any other
country. This undoubtedly is due to the fact that in America, the
writer has reached closer to economic freedom—as represented by
dollars in the bank or in stocks and bonds—than the writers of
other countries. And this, in turn, is due, of course, to the great
publishing industry of this country, which has the greatest array
of successful periodicals of any country on earth.

Yet, the question legitimately can be raised—as it *has* been raised

by more than one visitor from abroad—whether or not the affluence
of all these talented writers actually helps them to look clearly at
the society for which they are writing? It is difficult for a man with
a big bank account, a home without a mortgage, and a big new
car (plus a small, more costly European car) to believe that there
can be much wrong with a civilization that has produced these
things for *him.*

Perhaps a hundred years from now, or a thousand years from
now, the writers who mistook their mission in life will be forgot-
ten, while some youngster writing in a share-cropper's home (and
there still are plenty of them) on an L. C. Smith, 1927 vintage, he
picked up in a second-hand shop, is turning out material that will
be considered lively and valid in that far-off day. This is such a
whacky business, and history has such a way of confounding the
most self-assured prophets, it isn't likely that we can determine
whether or not this is happening, or will happen.

Those who believe that writing is more a task of the spirit than
the result merely of a desire for lucre always will believe that men
will produce good literature as long as they need anything, no
matter how wealthy they may become. And those who write purely
for beautiful homes and all the accouterments will continue to do
so and will not worry too much, since this is their temperament,
about whether or not they ever will be remembered.

Besides, the most sophisticated among these will say, who gives
a damn about 100 years from now? Isn't one life at a time enough
to keep us busy and active?

Their philosophy may well have been summed up by Edward
Robert Lytton, Earl of Lytton, who wrote:

> *We may live without poetry, music and art;*
> *We may live without conscience and live without heart;*
> *We may live without friends; we may live without books;*
> *But civilized man cannot live without cooks.*

XIII

The Writer
as a Diplomat

Diplomacy is to do and say
The nastiest thing in the nicest way . . .
—ISAAC GOLDBERG in *The Reflex*

JOHN HAY said that "there are three species of creatures who when they seem coming are going, when they seem going they come: Diplomats, women and crabs." I'd like to add a new species to that list—writers. For it is my belief that successful writers—if they become successful and remain successful—must be diplomats *par excellence.*

But why do I devote a chapter to the writer as a diplomat? What has writing—and selling that writing—have to do with diplomacy? Let me answer these questions with a couple of true examples.

Not long ago, I read in a syndicated New York gossip column about a youthful writer who, according to the critics, was a man of great talent. A major publisher had published his first novel and was on the verge of giving him the publicity treatment—lots of promotion, autograph parties at Macy's and Gimbel's, heavy exploitation through advertising, *the works.* Then, unexpectedly, the publisher let it be known that it was dropping the author from its lists. Instead of pushing him upwards, the publisher was pushing

him out. Why? Was it halitosis or body odor that ruined a budding
career for our hero? Could it be that he had antagonized Steve
Allen, Dave Garroway, or even Elvis Presley? Not at all. The gossip columnist gave the reason in one phrase: "Too boorish."

This phrase told much to those who understand the publishing
field. No matter how much talent a man may have, he must learn
to adjust to the rhythm of those with whom he works, in whatever
phase of publishing he intends to work.

The publishers have learned what Pope knew some centuries ago
when he wrote: "Some judge of authors' names, not works, and
then nor praise nor blame the writings, but the man." Publishers,
at least these days, are in the business of selling both a book (the
author's product) and its creator (the writer himself).

The mere fact that this young man had his wings clipped, just
as he was learning to fly, so to speak, doesn't mean that he is any
less talented than he was before. It may not mean that he is "dead,"
from a literary standpoint, as some would predict. But it does mean
that he is going to have to learn what he can do, and what he can't
do, in relation to those with whom he works in the literary field.

A year or so ago, I was acquainted with a writer who was "on
call" for a major magazine. The magazine, while not keeping him
under contract, nevertheless gave this fellow enough assignments
—at $1,000 or more a throw—to keep him well fed and well clothed.
For some reason—lack of comprehension of his role in the scheme
of things, a psychological quirk, or something, this writer began to
antagonize virtually everyone he contacted. Perhaps he had read
somewhere that Edgar Allan Poe had no friends and became a great
writer. Or perhaps he just figured that word of his stupidities never
would filter out of town into the offices of the magazine which was
paying him so handsomely.

Whatever the reason, or reasons, he failed to realize that his job
was as much that of a diplomat—for himself and for the magazine
he represented—as it was to write clever, forceful material. And,

in time, he was given to understand that he had received his last assignment from that particular magazine.

The successful writer—until he has made such a pile that he can afford to tell everyone to go jump in the lake—realizes that he is as much of a diplomat as he is a writer. He must find outlets for his material. He must maintain contact with people—those whom he interviews, librarians who can help him or hinder him, and editors and their associates and assistants. He has to cultivate public relations men, and sometimes men with private relations. He finds that he can learn—and benefit—from disc jockeys, press agents, press relations men for private and public agencies, and all their assistants and associates. If they really go out of their way to help him, depending upon his treatment of them in his personal contacts, they can make him into a "comer." If he treats them like dirt, as the saying goes, they can figuratively push him down, stab him in the back, and make life pretty difficult. In the case of publishers, they can cut him off and let him drift to other, less lucrative fields, if he doesn't learn what he *can* do and what he *can't* do, in relation to them and their organizations.

Sir Arthur Wing Pinero once remarked: "How many 'coming men' has one known! Where on earth do they all go to?" If there was one quality these "comers-who-never-arrived" seem to have in common it is their failure to learn how to be diplomatic.

Francis Hackett, in a book review, once stated: "In a diplomat's soul you may find iron ore, but it is usually oil—and in a whale of a diplomat you'll find the whole equipment—the blubber of charity, the whalebone of flexibility, the oil of commodity. A great diplomat is a regular Moby Dick."

In *L'Aiglon*, Act IV, by Edmond Rostand, a bear asked a Chinese woman: "How do you know I am a diplomat?"

"Why, by the skillful way you hide your claws," she replied.

Ely Culbertson said that "power politics is the diplomatic name for the law of the jungle."

And Leon Samson chimes in: "The diplomat sits in silence, *watching* the world with his ears."

Walter Hines Page, in his book, *A Publisher's Confession*, made a statement with which every writer—although not every editor— may agree: "Every letter of declination ought to be written by a skillful man—a diplomatist who can write an unpleasant truth without offence."

In a very real sense, this ability to "write an unpleasant truth without offence" is the challenge the writer faces in this modern era, when there are so many different individuals at varying stages of their intellectual development.

The writer, after he has a story, or while he is working on one to sell, is his own envoy to various "foreign countries." The people whom he studies are "strangers," to him, and they become less strange only as he learns more about them. To learn more about them, he must exercise all his skills to pull information out of them —information about themselves. Sometimes, this writer—or envoy —is thwarted in getting the information he wants from a specific individual. He must go to others to learn from them. After he has the article, story, book, or whatever, in hand, the writer must be salesman enough to sell it.

If he has written a book, the writer must be a diplomat in other ways. He is called upon to lecture, or to appear at public gatherings, in connection with his work. He learns that the sales job of the publisher is not an easy, automatic process. The publisher sends out salesmen, who in turn must talk booksellers into ordering our hero's tome. If the bookstores do not stock the book, our hero is prevented from becoming a millionaire because no book can become a best-seller resting in the publisher's warehouse. To sell, a book must be seen, and read, and reviewed, and talked about. The writer learns that he must develop a diplomatic technique in realing with book reviewers, some of whom are most powerful and can help to make the writer, or, by ignoring him, can help to destroy him. The writer learns that book reviewers are a motley crew, and that lots of them don't even read books, preferring, when they review a book, to reprint the material the publisher has sent them concerning it.

A writer, like a diplomat, *must* watch his words. In the *War-Song*, John Davidson wrote:

> *"Some diplomat no doubt*
> *Will launch a heedless word,*
> *And lurking war leap out."*

The writer, in his use of words, can either inflame the people into hatred—for him, if he is not careful—or lull them to sleep among social evils of vast magnitude. It is the writer's role to get action, but not to incite the people to riot, which is the difference between demanding a jury trial for a suspected murderer and haranguing a crowd to lynch him.

Laurence Sterne said that "writing, when properly managed, is but a different name for conversation." Most of us—writers or not— learn how to hold our tongues early in life, disciplined by parents, teachers and the world at large. Writers must learn how to guard their words so as not to "cross over the line," and undiplomatically kill the article, story, or book they want to see in print.

The writer comes to agree with Henry Brooks Adams, who said: "No one means all he says, and yet very few say all they mean, for words are slippery and thought is viscous."

It is surprising how many actual diplomats can be found who were writers, or, perhaps more accurately, how many writers actually were in the diplomatic service of this or that nation.

Edmund Spenser who wrote *The Faerie Queene*, dedicated to "the most Mightie and Magnificent Empresse Elizabeth," in 1580 became secretary to the Lord Deputy of Ireland. He believed so much in the cruel theories of his chief, in fact, that he defended the tyrannical Lord Deputy in a long piece of prose and made him an

idol as the Knight-Errant of Justice in *The Faerie Queene.* Spenser
became famous, and was given a pension by the Queen. Profiting
by the same methods used by his mentor, he acquired an Irish
estate, Kilcolman Castle. It was burned during the Irish Rebellion
of 1598 and Spenser, his wife and four children fled to Cork. When
he returned to London, he was destitute and actually died in a
cheap lodging house, after having lived the life of an aristocrat, despite the fact that his father was a clothmaker. Spenser was buried
in Westminster Abbey, his funeral expenses paid by the Earl of
Essex.

Aphra Behn was in the diplomatic service of Great Britain, too,
before she turned to writing and won her fame in English literature. The daughter of a barber, (her mother was a domestic serv-
ant), Aphra Behn was reared in Surinam, then British, and married
a Dutch merchant. She went to London when she was nineteen and
became the toast of the town. They called her "the Incomparable"
and she was known at court for her wit, light humor and startling
coarseness. When her husband died, she was twenty-six. Charles II
sent her as a spy to the Netherlands during the Dutch war and she
sent back plans of great import.

Because of enemies at the court, she fell into disfavor and poverty. In this period, she determined to be a writer. She established
herself in two years as the first Englishwoman to earn her living as
an author. In the ensuing fifteen years, she wrote and produced
fifteen plays, and, in between them, she wrote novels and poetry.
She became more and more popular—both as a playwright and
socially—as she matured. She was the center of scandal at the time
of her death, but nevertheless was buried in Westminster Abbey.

Matthew Prior, who became known as one of the most skillful
writers of the early eighteenth century, was appointed secretary to
the British Ambassador in Holland after graduation from St. John's
College, Cambridge. He was a secret agent in Paris during important negotiations and the Treaty of Utrecht, signed in 1713, was
known as "Matt's Peace."

Being both partially deaf and extremely dour in appearance, he nevertheless won friends in every circle by his good nature. It is said that even as a diplomat, his easy humor could turn to sour wit. He would not hold back the quick thrust.

Like so many others, he went from affluence to poverty with startling suddenness. Admirers subscribed four thousand pounds for an edition of his poems, and a British nobleman gave him the money for an estate in Essex. Although he moved in the circles of the nobility, he consorted mostly with women of the lowest class. One time, a wench whom he kept in his house stole his silverware. He was on the point of marrying a woman who kept an alehouse when he died. He left her most of his estate.

Sir Thomas Wyatt, whose poetry and essays became famous by the time he had received his M.A. (at seventeen) from St. John's College, Cambridge, served as Ambassador to Italy from Great Britain when he was only twenty-five. He translated Petrarch while there.

Wilfred Scawen Hunt served in the diplomatic corps of Great Britain from the time he was eighteen until he was thirty, being stationed from Athens to Madrid and from Lisbon to South America. Then, he married and inherited an estate and became one of the most undiplomatic writers in the British Empire, tweaking the British Government until his death.

Some of the ways in which the writer must be diplomatic are as follows:

Getting interviews from difficult people or those who are not particularly interested in publicity, or say they are not.

Obtaining free pictures from these people from their family albums, or enlisting their aid in having pictures made, or agreeing to pose for pictures for the publication that is interested in the artcle.

Cultivating and cooperating with book reviewers, reporters, and others who can help to publicize (and popularize) the writer's work.

Working on the same wave-length as the editor himself wants to work, so that the contact between the writer and editor will be pleasant, or at least tolerable, on both sides.

Researching and planning the material sent to editors so that they will not be embarrassed by having carried false statements, libelous matter, or material that will lay the editor open to charges of plagiarizing the works of others.

Finding a way to get along with his family and acquaintances so as to minimize misunderstandings, mix-ups and heartaches.

The writer doesn't have to look at the world through rose-colored glasses. Writers are necessary to help society progress, rather than retrogress. Whether we like it or not, it *is* necessary for a writer to work with other people at almost every step of the way in both preparing his material and in getting it published. He *must* learn to be diplomatic to do his best.

XIV

The Writer
and the Editor

A good many young writers make the mistake of enclosing a stamped, self-addressed envelope, big enough for the manuscript to come back in. This is too much of a temptation to the editor.

RING LARDNER

IT IS appropriate that a discussion of the writer and the editor should follow a chapter on the writer as a diplomat. For the writer must learn to get along with editors if he is to subsist. The more successful the writer—financially—the more likely he is to have found a way of working closely with an editor, and the editor's representatives.

If the writer is successful enough, as was for instance Mary Roberts Rinehart, he can start his own publishing company and see that the editor for whom he writes is someone pleasing to him. (Sir Walter Scott, as we have seen, tried this and went broke!) But many writers do not have the means to cause heads to topple, in case they are displeased.

A writer early learns that there is no generality applying to all editors. All editors are different. Each has his own distinctive tastes, ideas, likes, dislikes, ideals, and hopes and fears.

Successful writers have not standardized their practices in their contacts with editors, and their efforts to sell their material. Some professionals never write more than a one-page résumé, even of a book, before "making a deal" with an editor or publisher. Others actually finish a manuscript before putting it out for judgment.

Here is what our panel members answered when we asked the question: "Do you submit outlines to editors, or do you, when you get an idea, work on it and finish it before you try it out on editors?"

Alden Hatch: I seldom write a word until I have a contract.

Harold Helfer: No. I prefer to take my chances on the finished product.

Will Oursler: On articles particularly I always submit outlines—preferably a letter outline of no more than a few paragraphs.

Norman Vincent Peale: Before actually starting work on a projected piece, I sometimes discuss the idea with an editor, but I submit no manuscript until the piece is complete in its entirety.

Richard Gehman: Yes, I submit outlines to editors. As one gets more experienced, these outlines need not be very long. But most magazines operate on the committee system these days and an outline is required in most of the markets I work for.

Harry Edward Neal: In writing short stories—fiction—I never submit an outline to editors; only the completed story. Often, however, I do write the yarn from a working outline prepared for my own use. In writing articles I customarily send the editor (through my literary agent) an outline which includes the full lead as I propose to write it, and a conclusion. As for books, I prepare a chapter outline and one or two sample chapters.

Lester Velie: No magazine writer should invest time and energy to do a piece unless he has an assignment from a magazine. He may find, if he does research and writing and turns it in, that the magazine has a piece like it in the works or doesn't like the idea. I would say that even a beginning writer should check with the magazine before going ahead.

Frances and Richard Lockridge: We don't submit outlines.

Edison Marshall: I tell my agent an idea, as far as I have developed it, before I start writing. He reads about half of it when I get that far. Once or twice he has shown me I have attempted an impossible project and I abandoned it. Often my relations are close enough to an editor that I can tell him, also. Usually I am committed to a novel by the close of the second or third chapter. I won't accept money from an editor, or any kind of advance, until the novel is completed. Then, if he contracts for it, he is supposed to know what he is doing. My outlines are in my head, rarely put down on paper. Mainly, what is in my head is the concluding, climactic scene. To get there in an exciting way is my *job*.

Dora Albert: If I personally believe an idea is of national or universal interest, I prefer, as a rule, to submit a letter briefly outlining the idea. If an editor shows interest, I am willing to work out a much more detailed outline. Most times, I may prefer to query. However, when the article is to be very brief, I'll sometimes take a chance and write the article without any previous query. It is possible to sell an occasional editorial to the *Saturday Evening Post*, but normally it would take about as long to explain what the plan for the editorial was as it would to write it.

Sometimes, if a writer has a number of ideas for brief articles, it might be possible to outline each briefly. I used to do this with *The New Yorker*, many years ago, when I lived in New York and contributed brief items to their "Talk of the Town" series.

I think it usually is desirable for the non-fiction writer to outline his ideas to some extent; otherwise, the magazine he considers his prime target may already have assigned that very idea.

O. A. Battista: I always now query editors on ideas—with major emphasis on picking a good title, followed by an outline of not more than one page.

Fred Kerner: Inasmuch as the majority of my free-lance writing these days is ghost work, I am usually commissioned to do what

some editor wants. Ideas of my own I will submit in the briefest
outlines, because I feel that every editor with whom I deal knows
my abilities and there is no need for me to work out an idea before
submitting it. I feel, however, the beginner should work out every
idea and submit all but book-length manuscripts in full. The beginning writer has nothing to lose by writing articles and submitting
them. In fact, he has a great deal to gain.

Roger Burlingame: Editors demand outlines before they will
sign an agreement. I therefore submit brief ones which I do not
necessarily follow in detail.

Hugh Ross Williamson: The publishers have always been kind
enough to commission books after, usually, a talk over luncheon.

A. C. Spectorsky: I'm happy to say that it is many years since I
have completed a project before submitting part of it written, but
the bulk of it in outline, to the market I deem suitable. This works
for non-fiction but can hardly work for less-than-book-length fiction.

Emil Zubryn: I always work on an outline basis.

Sloan Wilson: Sometimes I submit outlines, but sometimes I finish it first. In general, beginning writers usually work more closely
with editors than do mature writers. The mature writer knows his
work will be published; the beginner needs reassurance.

Erskine Caldwell: No outlines. Short stories and novels need to
be written first of all.

Evan Hunter: I very rarely submit outlines to editors. I find that
many excellent editors are too quick to judge the skeleton of the
story as bad when it does not contain the essential fire of creation—
the emotion an author brings to the actual writing. Some of the
greatest scenes in *Hamlet* would have sounded like the corniest
sort of melodrama in outline. Too, I don't like to *discuss* ideas, I
would rather *write* them. I find that whenever I talk something out,
I am giving half of the act of creation to talking, so that the writing
is cheated later on.

Ben Smith: I rarely submit outlines. Once or twice, as I remember, I have sold novels with a sample first chapter and synopsis treatment, but never do any more. . . . Ninety per cent of my nonfiction work is done on order from someone who knows me.

Blake Clark: The best way I've found to sell an idea to the *Reader's Digest* is to send in a rather complete, 600-word outline, giving the: (1) Title; (2) Theme, expressed in a single sentence with a verb; (3) The subject, which may not be shown in the title; (4) The treatment. I put down, "I would begin this article in this way" —and actually write the lead, or a tentative lead. I then add: "Among others, I would make the following points, naming the various points."

Jesse Stuart: I have never submitted an outline.

Scott Young: On books and articles I always use outlines. Short stories I wrote and sold in full.

Deane and David Heller: We usually query, by an informal letter.

John Gassner: Publishers have come to me with ideas for books since 1934; I have never waited for completion of any manuscript, but have sold it in advance, sometimes with and sometimes without an outline—usually a very scanty one. But my experience is, I believe, unusual.

Saul K. Padover: Editors usually ask for outlines. I don't like outlines. I prefer to write out the whole thing.

Kenneth S. Giniger: For my own books, which are anthologies, I have always worked on the basis of submitting an outline.

Georges Simenon: Outline? Gosh, never!

Joseph N. Bell: I submit outlines on article ideas, but not on humor or fiction.

Frederic A. Birmingham: The technique on outlines should vary, I believe. A fact piece, by a competent writer whose qualifications are known to the editor, should be based on a detailed outline. The editor then may steer the writer into what may be desired channels, and save them both a lot of time and grief. However, in specialized

subjects, in humor, or personal experiences, etc., the writer may as
well do the whole piece to create his effect, and gamble on the
result....

I have been amazed, in my study of successful writers, at the
percentage who actually have worked on publications, either under
the eye of an editor, or as an editor themselves. Probably 95 per
cent of the most successful writers of this period either have worked
on the staff of some newspaper, magazine, book publisher, or literary agent. In such jobs, the prospective writer—who expects to be
"on his own" some day—learns all phases of the editorial process,
from the actual gathering of facts, to the copy-reading, the editing,
the proofreading, and, finally, the actual designing of it for publication.

Sometimes, it seems to me, the people who want to be writers
would make better editors and associates than the ones who actually *are* employed on publications. The people who work in publishing tend to get into a groove—from the standpoint of the outside
writer—and to·rebel against anything outside that groove.

Henry Brooks Adams said that "chaos often breeds life, when
order breeds habit." The writer's mind sometimes is chaotic but
from it comes life that makes for good reading—literature. But the
editor wants order. He is thinking of printing schedules, sales and
distribution problems, promotional ideas, as well as getting sharper
and better articles and stories. In trying to achieve this order, he
sometimes breeds only habit among his subordinates.

Professor Floyd G. Arpan, chief of the magazine department,
Medill School of Journalism, Northwestern University, challenged
a forum sponsored by the National Business Publications with these
words:

"What is editorial quality? Can you educate a staff to it? I think
you can and the staff which has adaptability, which has its main
purpose of communication, which is non-rigid in its approach to
its editorial problems and sees the romance of the business as a

stimulating, driving force, almost invariably achieves editorial quality. . . .

"Whenever a publication starts losing money or circulation, the efficiency experts or magazine 'doctors' invariably gather round to diagnose the difficulty. Invariably, too, they come face to face with that intangible and oftentimes undefinable 'something' known as editorial quality. A magazine which has editorial quality almost never has trouble securing subscribers or selling at the newsstands. Those magazines which do not have editorial quality soon disappear from the market under the stress of severe competition.

"Whenever a magazine is unusually successful, or if it dies, I usually call the attention of my graduate students to the special characteristics of the publication and what makes it a success or a failure. And, whenever I am called into a magazine office as an editorial consultant, I usually sit down with staff members, much in the way that I do with my graduate students, in an effort to analyze the particular positive and negative aspects of the editorial production, in an effort to diagnose the exact reasons for a magazine's success or failure. . . .

"What works on one magazine will not necessarily work on another. However, I do want to call your attention to four areas of thinking on this problem of editorial quality. For, I have usually found that these four principles apply in almost every instance, where a magazine is experiencing difficulty with its editorial output.

"1. *Adaptability*—There seems to be a popular concept that, if you write for an engineering publication, you must sound like an engineer. Likewise, if you are writing for a medical publication, you must talk in the doctor's terms, use his language, use his bedside approach. Perhaps it is not immediately evident, on reading one or two issues of magazines written in this manner, but sit down some time with a whole year's issues or perhaps five years' issues and read through these publications. You will notice a thoroughly deadening and uninteresting effect. The monotony becomes almost unbearable. I always tell my students in writing classes that 'there are no uninteresting subjects in the world. There are only uninteresting writers about those subjects.' This statement is particularly applicable to many of the writers for the Business Press.

"What is needed, primarily, is more interest-development—making the writing suit the particular problem—and getting away from the assumption that, because the magazine is presented to a doctor and the doctor has an interest in medicine, he will read anything, no matter how poorly written it is. Many of the writers for the Business Press need to adopt the standard rules for interest-development which the consumer magazine has used to its advantage. Each article and subject should be approached as a challenge to the writer to make it interesting, to find some new way of presenting it, even though it has been done a dozen times; to establish some new spark of interest on the part of a reader who may already know considerably more about the subject than the article contains.

"Can this be done? I assure you that it can. . . . There is more than one way of saying things; more than one way of approaching things; more than one way of getting an idea across. Adapt-ability, to my mind, is one of the main stumbling blocks on the part of writers who are attempting to gain editorial quality.

"2. *Communication*—In the Business Press, about the only reason for writing is to be understood. A good rule-of-thumb on writing is to ask yourself the following questions. (a) What am I trying to get across? (b) What is the best way to get it across? (c) Did I get it across so that the reader understands it?

"There are in the world today many people whom I classify as 'intellectual illiterates.' They are very well-trained people. Many of them are top experts in their fields. They make an incalculable contribution to the welfare of mankind. Yet, when it comes to explaining to someone else what they are trying to do, they stand nearly mute. In recent years, we have broken the sound barrier, the heat barrier, but there are thousands of these great intellects who are writing for the Business and Scientific Press who can't get through the 'word barrier.'

"Many of these writers feel that placement of a phrase or word is not important. They write in the way that they can understand and leave it to the reader to make out as best he can. I would like to emphasize that every word that is written is important in communication. A misplaced word can befuddle a reader, becloud the issue or explode with all the violence of a time-bomb, with all of its destructive force, if it is misinterpreted at a crucial point.

"As an example of what you can do with a single word, let me suggest to you the following sentence. 'She told me that she loved me.' Now, use the word *only* at the beginning of that sentence. Each time you use the sentence, move the word *only* one word forward. You will find that you will come up with eight shades of meaning. This illustrates the reason it is so important to think carefully about what you are trying to say and to make sure that the word gets in the right place.

"3. *Non-rigidity*—Many magazines suffer from rigor mortis. By tradition, some editorial staffs have gotten into the habit of doing things in a certain way. The net result is that such staffs have placed a strait-jacket on thinking. New covers, new layouts, new typography, new editorial approaches are all part of the changing magazine theme. There is little excuse for continuing to do something the same old way simply because you have been doing it that way for thirty years.

"The world does not stand still around you. If you insist on standing still on your magazine, you will find that you are soon left behind. This does not mean, of course, that you should be completely experimental, changing with every whim. It does mean, however, that you should keep your staff alive to the possibilities of change, when a reason can be found for logically making the change.

"4. *Romance*—Perhaps this element of editorial quality will startle you somewhat, but I insist that there is a lot of romance to be found in the Business Press. Even if you have been writing forty years in the same field, don't allow yourself to get into a routine rut. Many magazines die not because of the idea being unsound but because editorial writers allow their interest to lag and the readers quickly spot it.

"There is just as much romance in writing for the Business Press as there is in being a foreign war correspondent. There are just as many problems, just as many challenges. . . . If your writers have gotten into a rut of routineness, I would suggest that you get them out of their ivory tower. . . ."

If the writer's idea is just to do a passable job, it is possible that he will make sales. Enough magazines do carry enough mediocre material to justify the time and effort of writers who are satisfied merely to "fill a need." But I think that very few writers who become known as successful writers are motivated merely by a desire to "get by." They actually want to help the editor to do his job better by striving to prepare material for him that is better than any he has printed heretofore. When such a writer comes along there are editors who recognize him. Then it is only a matter of time until the writer is famous and the editor rich for having recognized the writer's true worth.

Yet, it is strange that the same editor cannot recognize all the brightest authors, or budding authors, in the world. If it were so, then one publishing house would print all the best-sellers and the others would go out of business. Trying to figure out why certain writers get along with certain editors (and can't get along with others at all) is as useless as trying to determine why two teen-agers get a crush on each other that may or may not turn from infatuation into love and marriage. At one stage of every editor's life, he *can* perhaps see with a clearer vision that he could earlier or he might be able to see later. Every piece of material he chooses is "on the beam," and his magazine soars in popularity. At another stage of this same editor's life, his decisions are repetitive failures. He has stood still, while the world has moved on.

Each generation has its needs for its own kind of writers, who fit into the texture and fabric of that particular generation. It is doubtful if Elbert Hubbard, for example, would have achieved the success during the post-World War II world of today that he achieved in an earlier, more rural America, when aphorisms and brief sayings were the vogue. Will Rogers was a phenomenon of his time and period, as was Gertrude Stein and Mark Twain. It is doubtful that if they had lived earlier, or later, they would have made the same impress on the world. But who will ever know?

Just so, each generation has its needs for the services of its own kind of editors. Charles Dana, Bernarr MacFadden, William Randolph Hearst, and Horace Greeley, for examples, each seem to have "fit" his own times. Each was instrumental, in various ways, in helping to push great writers into the limelight. Yet, if they were active today in the editorial field, the odds are that they would have to act in vastly different ways to become "successful," in the context of today's "committee" meetings on magazines and in book publishing shops.

There are two schools of thought—among successful writers—as to whether or not they should try to become friends with the editors for whom they write. One school believes that it is profitable for them to get out and mingle with editors on every possible occasion. The other school feels just the opposite. They shun all contacts with editors and publishers, except those which are demanded by a standard of minimum courtesy. To these writers, editors are never friends, but usually if not always, actual enemies who are striving to bring the writer's ideas and ideals into conformity with their own.

The writers in the first school usually are the more extrovert among our modern band of scribes. They love to go to cocktail parties, they revel in being at publishers' banquets, and nothing seems to make them happier than to be the center of attention at an autographing party.

Those in the second school are more introvert in their psychological make-up. They are not the "pushers," and they are not "sensation-a-day" men or women. They are writing more for the next generation (or "the ages"), than for the dimwits who are inhabiting this rather uneducated world of today.

There are many writers, of course, who do not fit either groove. They strive to meet editors whenever this is convenient and logical, without being "eager beavers," or becoming social lions. They realize that the average successful editor already has a wide acquaintance and that it isn't likely he will have much time to spend with a writer who contributes only one article every once in a while to them, or one book every several years.

It might be well for *all* writers to bear in mind that, as William Ralph Inge said, "Literature flourishes best when it is half a trade and half an art."

A writer has to be a persuader with an editor, in a sense, but the editor ought to be a "hidden persuader," in the sense that he tries to bring out the best in the writer through the proper encouragement. A writer has to be a politician, too, to some extent, in selling articles with viewpoints that may not be in sympathy with the strongly held views of some editors. A writer also has to have a sense of direction in seeking out the sources of power on a publication for which he may write. He may find that he is trying to appeal to an editor who has been relegated to innocuous tasks, while the man who makes the decisions is in another office entirely. The writer's desire to find out who is important must extend all the way from the people whom he chooses to interview to those to whom he sends his material in hopes he can sell it. Persuading the editor, sometimes, of the importance of a biographical subject, for example, may be conceivably difficult if the editor himself is not aware of who is coming down and who is going up in the society. The object in doing such biographies is to find the people who are "will-bes," and not to be confused by the noted "has-beens" who dot the political, economic, literary and cultural landscape.

Successful writers keep in mind what Henrik Ibsen wrote in Act II of *An Enemy of the People*: "An editor cannot always act as he would prefer. He is often obliged to bow to the wishes of the public in unimportant matters . . ."

One of the most crucial "peril points" in a writer's dealings with an editor may come over editorial changes that the editor wants to make, or wants the writer to make, in the contributed material. The more successful the writer, the more apt he is to see the point of the changes suggested by the editor. Beginning writers are apt to feel keenly that everything they write should be carved in stone, and resent changes made in their copy. As time passes, if they continue to write regularly, their attitude will change to one of gratefulness to the editor for helping them to express better what they want to get across to the magazine's public.

As one who has attended many editorial conferences in magazine and book-publishing offices, I may say that the successful writer usually is not too perturbed when editors suggest they are going to delete this or that chapter, or this or that paragraph. The writer may defend the material, but in my experience, the more successful writers do this openly and straightforwardly and without rancor. They give the reasons why, in their judgment, the affected material is vital and how its inclusion may well increase the sales value of the magazine or book. The editor, if he is worth his salt, will hear out a writer who makes sensible points, even if the writer is talking about his own brain-child.

Writers should remember that editors have lots of problems and keep to a minimum the number of times the editor is annoyed, disturbed, or contacted. Unless the writer and the editor are close friends, the writer does well to think before sending the editor a memo. When he does, the memo should be as concise as possible, so as to require a minimum of time lost by the editor in reading it, since, it must be kept in mind, there are scores of other writers also sending memos. Projects that seem very important to a writer—since they are *all* he is thinking about—may appear to be very trivial to an editor, who is hard-pressed on a hundred different activity fronts.

The important point is that the successful writer usually thinks of the editor—as well as of himself—and by so doing he builds and maintains friendly relations with many different editors. These friendly relations do not make a man a writer. But they help him to market his ideas and to learn more about the wants of various editors. Having friends who are editors won't make you a writer, but unless you drink with them too often, knowing editors will not prevent you from learning how to write, or writing.

XV

The Writer
as a Ghost

Every man's work, whether it be litera-
ture or music or pictures or architecture
or anything else, is always a portrait of
himself, and the more he tries to conceal
himself the more clearly will his character
appear in spite of him.

—SAMUEL BUTLER

A GHOST writer, according to *The American College Diction-ary*, is "one who does literary work for someone else who takes the credit."

But it is well to bear in mind, if you plan to do any ghost writing, that while the other person will get the credit, you likely can collect the cash. This is why a large number of successful writers become ghost writers. They find that ghosting material, for other individuals who have made their money in the oil busniess, as bankers, or in insurance, can be very lucrative—sometimes far more rewarding than sales even to some of the very largest magazines.

When a writer goes into ghost writing, his problems are compounded. And people who make use of ghost writers should be forewarned of the truth of what Samuel Butler pointed out above

when he said that "every man's work . . . is always a portrait of
himself. . . ." In other words, if *you* hire a ghost writer to write something for you, always remember that whatever he writes for you
will be more a reflection of his views on that particular subject than
your own. Since many persons—even those who dabble in politics—
are philosophically immature and do not really know *what* they
believe, it poses no great problem to them to have someone ghost
write their material. As long as it sounds literate, they are satisfied.
Such people may be extremely wealthy, very famous, and even
aware in their own specialized field, but they have given so little
thought to other subjects that they really have no convictions. They
make ideal "clients" for ghost writers.

If you will forgive a bit of personal history, I'd like to relate some
ghost writing experiences I've had, ranging from college football
players to candidates for President of the United States. One of
the early ghost writing jobs I took on—in order to get through college—was that of writing the English themes for a certain college
football star, who was having trouble passing his courses. The football player was on a "scholarship," and drew a regular monthly
stipend from the college for "work," such as raking leaves. Actually,
the only "work" he ever did was to play football, which he enjoyed
immensely.

One day a group of faculty members visited the football field
where our team was working out. This particular player came over
to speak with one or two members of the faculty. I happened to be
standing nearby. When the player ran back into the scrimmage, I
heard his English teacher remark:

"That fellow is brilliant. He doesn't know much about the history of literature, but he writes some of the most beautiful themes
I have ever read. I am sure he is one member of our football team
who will become a writer!"

I had to restrain myself from laughing. If she only knew the
truth!

Alas, our football hero never did become a writer. In fact he flunked out of other courses—in spite of all the professors could do for him—and before the year was over, he was kicked unceremoniously out of school. The last I heard of him, he was assistant manager of a service station, in charge of the pumps.

In this same period, although I was just a college boy, I was ghost writing for the Governor of the state in which I lived. The day I drove into that strange state, to attend college in the most economical way possible, the thought occurred to me to pay my respects to my new Governor. Forthwith, I went to the Governor's office and—my lucky piece was working that day!—I actually was ushered into the presence of His Excellency. During our brief conversation, I told him I was there to write my way through college, if possible, and before the conversation ended, I had my first client! Stranger things may have happened in the world, but I declare I can't remember them.

When I received my sheepskin and left town to take a job elsewhere, I felt keenly that ghost writing couldn't be such a bad way of making a living if dealing with others were as pleasant as dealing with this Governor. Three or four years later, I was in Washington, in the vortex of Government and ghost writing. Although still hardly dry behind the ears, I was enlisted to become a ghost writer on the team of a Presidential candidate. This proved to be quite rewarding, from the standpoint of experience and financial remuneration. I never realized, until that experience, just how much money certain businessmen will put up to assure themselves a few years in the limelight as Ambassador to Guana, or minister-without-portfolio to the Hottentots.

It was then that I came to the Great Realization regarding ghost writing. It is, that by the time a person has become anxious enough to get into the limelight—particularly politically—he usually has become wealthy enough to pay any price demanded by the ghost writer. This is one of the most important lessons, I think, that successful ghost writers learn—i. e., they can demand, and get, much higher prices for their ghostly work than they can for material they might write and sell to a magazine under their own names.

Some time ago, a rather well-known ghost writer in Washington, whose name has never been in the newspapers (the more anonymously a ghost writer operates, the better known he becomes), told me about when *he* came to this Great Realization.

"I was determined to be my own boss and resigned my job with a magazine," he related. "The first assignment that came my way was to ghost write a speech for a trade association executive. I did the speech with ease and the executive liked it very much. He told me to send him a bill for the job. That is when I really ran into a problem. I worried over that task for several days before I finally made up a bill. I realized that I couldn't charge him a word-rate, for it was just a brief speech and even at the rates of the best magazines, this would not pay me for the time I had invested in the preparation—including the various calls I had made on the client. Finally, I arrived at a figure which I thought was fair. I took it to the client. He looked at it and laughed. Then he said: 'I know you are new in this field, for you have told me so. I am going to give you a tip about pricing. You are not used to making your own professional fees. From now on, when you arrive at what you consider to be a fair fee, then just *double* it and bill the client for the top amount. You'll never get any complaints, in my opinion, and all your clients will feel prouder to have employed such a top-price man. They'll even boast about using your services among themselves!'

"Forthwith, he handed the bill back to me and told me to revise it in line with his advice. When I found out that his trade association had a million dollars in the bank, I didn't feel too bad about it. Most people who employ ghost writers expect top service—and they are able to pay top prices."

The amount of money a successful writer can make from ghost

writing will vary widely even among individuals in one city. It may depend sometimes on the writer's reputation, his luck, his ability to make "contacts," and, of course, on his own imagination and the time he wants to devote to ghost writing. Many successful writers do ghost writing as "a breather" from their regular type of writing.

Ghost writing is at least as old as George Washington's Farewell Address and as new as the latest magazine on your favorite cigar counter. President Washington, never very proficient at expressing himself in writing, enlisted the aid of Alexander Hamilton and perhaps even Thomas Jefferson to polish off his Farewell Address, which still is read every February 22 in both the Senate and the House of Representatives.

Just how much Hamilton and Jefferson got is hard to say. But the ghost writers who work these days can draw down sizable sums. Bob Considine, who makes $100,000 a year as a reporter, also ghosts books for others. It is fair to guess that he demands upward of $25,000 for a book project. Some ghost writers would settle for $2,000, depending partly on their ability to bargain.

There is nothing unethical about ghost writing, although some purists hint it isn't quite fair to people who listen to comedians, politicians, radio and television commentators, and entertainers. If the people had to listen to these entertainers very long—with the entertainers using only their own words—there would probably be a hue and cry for a return to the old system of ghost writing. Ghost writers know the words to make a speaker's words sprightly, for sense, or nonsense. The ability to *deliver* a speech is a talent in itself; but the ability to create a good speech, or words of comedy, tragedy, or pathos, may not be possessed by the same man who has a wonderful platform manner. That is why ghost writing has become so popular.

While ghost writing is honorable work, it pays more in money than in fame. Whoever pays you off can forthwith claim full credit.

Under the rules of the game, you can't do anything except enjoy spending the money. If you ever claim to have authored the material, you will have violated a confidence. You also will find it more difficult to get future ghost writing jobs, if the word gets around you are a fellow who will "kiss and tell."

Occasionally a writer will ghost-write an article and his name will be carried at the top of the piece, with the name of the person furnishing the information. If a submarine captain drives under the North Pole, the experience is one the world may be waiting to hear. But the experience itself does not imbue the captain with the ability to plan and write a best-seller. The captain knows engineering, while writing a fascinating yarn might best be left to a man who is accustomed to working with words.

The ghostly arrangement—carefully outlined in legal documents —*can* prove profitable to each. The captain can dictate his experiences to a tape recording machine, and answer the questions the writer may ask him. The writer can give his time to a book that may bring him royalties for years. The publisher will profit if the book sells well. If all three do their job, they *can* benefit handsomely. The book may be serialized. Later, it may be syndicated. Then it may be sold to the movies.

At least 500 ghost written books are published every year. More, probably, if we consider the books subsidized by various businesses and industries to celebrate their anniversaries, or their coming of age in various ways. The number would include many "autobiographies," as well as fact books. I doubt that many fiction books are ghosted, although lots of writers of fiction in one field will use pseudonyms on their own work in another field.

A writer gets assignments in many ways to ghost books. I once agreed to ghost a book for a physician in exchange for an operation on my wife. I'm happy to report that the operation was a success, and so was the book. I sold it to the first publisher to whom we submitted it.

What is the best way to get the leads on material which you may ghost and sell under the name of someone else? The successful writers whom I interviewed tell me that the best way they have found is by reading omniverously—newspapers, federal reports, and by keeping their ears open all the time for news about individuals and their activities.

Many years ago, I happened to see a news release about a social study group. It told of how the director of the project ran into difficulty in making the study being released. I got in touch with the woman director, who proved to be a dynamic, public-spirited citizen. I got permission to write a story by her, as told to me, for a national magazine. She was most pleased to get the public recognition (which she deserved!), while I was pleased to work with her and to get the money for the article.

I know a writer who was reading a Lions Club bulletin in his home town one day and learned about a unique project being sponsored by the club. He investigated and found that the man behind the project, to help youngsters, himself had a son who had died tragically. The writer asked the man to let him tell the story of the club's project in the first person, i.e., in the name of the man who conceived the idea. Permission was granted. The article sold to a national magazine and won wide notice.

Many magazines besides *True Story* and *True Confessions* like to feature first person material. The general magazines, of course, use only an occasional story in the first person—i.e., among the articles—but experience has taught the editors that, when the story is gripping, it creates more reader interest if it is told in the first person.

Writing teachers constantly are often asked what is the most lucrative field for ghost writing. Political ghost writing can be very lucrative, for the men at the top, but there are as many writers who are poorly paid in this field as in any other. Some writers wouldn't think of taking less than $1,000 a speech, but others will write a speech for $25. The men who write speeches for Presidential candidates get $18,000 a year and up.

But *location* has a lot to do with earnings. A talented writer in Big Springs, Texas, who wants to ghost for the local or state politicians would have difficulty getting more than $100 a speech. A knowledgeable writer at the state capital might get $250 to $500.

The political ghost writer soon learns, if he observes the ways of politicians very carefully, that it is not what *is* that is important in politics, *but what it's called.* If a politician, in his personal life, is a rough-talking, picayunish person the ghost writer, is supposed to think of expressions the speaker can use to prevent the public from forming a true impression. Politicians rise or fall on the use of words, and writers are more responsible for this rise or fall than almost anyone else to whom he may call for assistance.

Timing can be an important factor in many kinds of ghost-writing. If there is a big catastrophe in which someone suffered greatly or performed heroically, the time to get this person and find an editor who wants a first-person yarn, is *immediately*.

Another question that constantly arises is arrangements for payment on ghost written material. Get these arrangements straight before you invest much time.

In ghosting, the writer must keep in mind the amount of *time* he expends on the idea, plus adding a professional (or knowledge) fee. A physician gets paid for what he *knows,* as well as for what he *does,* and so should a lawyer or a writer.

In articles which a writer might volunteer to ghost in hopes of selling the first-person article to a magazine, the writer gambles that he can make the sale. He usually agrees to do the article, under the other person's name, if the other person will accept the fame and let the writer get the financial rewards. On book projects, the writer might have to share 50-50 with the celebrity whose "autobiography" he is writing.

Successful writers make sure of certain points before they enter into any ghost arrangements. They do not pledge to put up any of their own money unless they have an iron-clad agreement from a publisher who wants the particular story or book.

If people are hesitant about giving the story free, the writer must decide just what kind of a deal he can make. He might offer 10 per cent, 20 per cent, or even up to 50 per cent, of the income, to get the story and full rights to it. In one such 50-50 arrangement, in ten years, one writer made $250,000 from the arrangements and a well-known hero made the same amount.

The smart writer will get the agreement down in writing, setting forth exactly what both parties will be expected to do, who is going to handle the money, etc.

Writers usually take their "final" draft of their writing to the principal, if there is the slightest doubt in the writer's mind about some phase of the subject, so that the subject can go see if it accurately reflects his views, emotions and experiences. This is not only good manners, it is good sense, for the best-trained reporter sometimes can make mistakes in taking notes. Many times, the writer will want to use a tape recorder, to guard against misquotation of the principal.

Even the best-laid plans of the most skillful writers can go awry, however. Quentin Reynolds once interviewed a fantastic "Canadian war hero," whose exploits published in *Reader's Digest* were the talk of Europe and the United States. Alas the story was too fantastic to be true. When the "hero" was at the height of his popularity, and the money was rolling in, he was revealed to be a fake.

This is not the only pitfall that lies in the path of the ghost writer. The ghost writer must not only understand the man for whom he is doing the job, he must please this fellow, for this man holds the purse-strings. The writer also has to keep in mind the wants and needs of the editor. No ghost job is as simple as it sounds, for it introduces new phases into the creative job. Sometimes, these phases are new stumbling blocks and the writer fails because of psychological factors, although he may be a competent writer on his own working for himself. In such cases a writer might well be warned to leave ghost writing to the fellows who seem to have the flair for it.

Whatever the campaign, and whoever sponsors it, if you value your good name and a clear conscience above riches, it will pay you many times to investigate carefully any group whose sponsors, aims and goals are not known to you.

A man came to me one time and asked me if I would ghost some speeches for him. He offered good pay. The name of the organization he represented sounded legitimate to me. It was in a big building and was well-furnished. The speeches he wanted seemed innocuous enough. But the second time I went to see him, in his office, I became quite suspicious. The neighboring office was the headquarters for the Ku Klux Klan. I excused myself and did not take the job.

As a ghost writer, you want to be sure you see through the groups for which you may work, so that you will not be defending the indefensible, no matter what the financial stake. You also want to be able to see clearly the real aims of the politicians, and others in the society who may enlist your aid, for part of your role as a writer is to help society, not wound it more.

XVI

The Writer
and His Goals

*We know what we are, but know not what
we may be.*

—SHAKESPEARE: *Hamlet*

THE trickiest thing about writing is that many of us, at different
times in our lives, take a good look at ourselves, re-examine our goals
and decide that what we are doing is not what we want to do at all
and that we would be happier if we were doing something else.
Some people arrived at this conclusion after trying for two weeks to
become a writer; some people don't arrive at it until they are already successful.

John Clare, in a letter to a friend many decades ago, wrote: "If
life had a second edition, how I would correct the proofs!" Apparently, many modern writers—who fall into the "successful" classification—feel the same way he felt. They not only would correct the
proofs, they would see to it that there would be an entirely different
set.

We all have personal goals—for ourselves and members of our
family. For the long future, our goal may remain the same as it was
when we were young and idealistic—to become so well-known that
wherever we go, men with microphones will ask our opinion and

listen respectfully as we give it in Shavian humor and with Jovian authority, mixed with Socratic depth and Shakespearian cleverness. It is the ultimate goal of every writer, I think, not to be as big as the President, but to be far better known, and more in demand at social and public functions.

The truth seems to be that these are not only the goals of the writer, but of virtually everyone in the society, whether he admits it or not. The writer merely makes some feeble steps in that direction, while the average man gives up and reconciles himself to being a small fish in a small pond.

By the time a writer has become what we would call "successful" he has become a very knowledgeable person as to what kind of a society he finds himself living in; what he can do best in this society, and what he *really* wants to do with the short years remaining to him. At this point, many a writer decides that what he wants is money, rather than spending his life entertaining or informing or teaching the people. Many get out of the writing field, and become public relations consultants to big corporations, or publishers, or take well-paying information posts in the Government.

Others go into teaching. Colleges and universities have many fine writers on their faculties. Occasionally, one will write a best-seller and make a pile, and yet he continues to teach, for teaching is his primary goal.

Each writer is many men. He is pulled in this or that direction by his interests, his family, his friends, and forces that he, himself, cannot quite isolate.

The person who stays in writing against all discouragements and disappointments usually is the one who becomes the most successful. Writing is an all-encompassing task. The more this society becomes specialized, the less possible it becomes for a writer to practice other professions part of the day and to be a writer the other part. He finds that taking the pains he must take, doing his research, and thinking the thoughts he must think, takes *all* of his time. If a writer cannot satisfy his goals by writing alone for his living, then he lives with a sense of futility and a feeling of failure. He either must change his goals—the short-range ones at least—or lose his touch with reality.

In questioning our successful writers, it seemed to me they had no particular goals, beyond making money, taking care of the family, enjoying life and entertaining the public. Yet, I discount this, in many cases, because many individuals have goals that they keep locked inside their minds. They have found that making these goals known to others can cause misunderstanding and, sometimes, leave the person who expresses his goals publicly open to ridicule.

But whether or not a writer ever expresses his goals—to anyone but himself—the fact that he formalizes these goals, in his mind, helps him to develop ideas, attributes and characteristics that make it possible for him to reach his goals.

Even if the goal is merely a short-range goal—say, writing a book —the mere formalizing of the goal helps the writer to focus his thinking, his activities, his research, and his writing. Thoreau said: "If one advances confidently in the direction of his dreams, and endeavors to live the life which he has imagined, he will meet with a success unexpected in common hours."

Charles Darwin formalized his goals, early in life, for virtually everything he did. The son of a country physician, Charles Darwin was sent to Cambridge to become a minister. But he was more interested in science than in theology, and he went on a Government-sponsored scientific exploring cruise—as the naturalist member—to South America. The cruise, on the now-famous *H.M.S. Beagle,* lasted from 1831 to 1836, and while he was on it he made the observations that he later embodied in his famous *Origin of Species,* and his later book, *The Descent of Man.* Twenty years elapsed between his famous voyage on the *Beagle,* and in that time he married his first cousin, Emma Wedgwood, by whom he had five sons and two daughters, and in which he studied patiently in spite of his astigmatism, nausea and long periods of illness. *Origin of Species* was not published until he was fifty years old, but it created such a furore, even before publication, that it sold out the first edition in one day. Preachers denounced the book throughout the world. When *The Descent of Man* was published twelve years later, in which he contended that man is descended from apes, his books were not only condemned, they were banned in many areas. Tennessee had a statute which made it unlawful even to teach about the theory of evolution in any public school. Eventually, this resulted in the trial of John Thomas Scopes, a teacher, who was defended by the noted attorney and free thinker, Clarence Darrow. William Jennings Byran, known as the boy orator of the Platte (River) and secretary of State under Woodrow Wilson, served as special prosecutor and won the conviction against Scopes. Incidentally, the county attorney who drew the indictment against Scopes was a young man named Tom Stewart, who lived to become a United States Senator.

Because he knew where he was going, and headed toward it all his life, in spite of infirmities and other difficulties, Darwin met with "a success unexpected in common hours."

What are some of the goals of successful writers?

The principal aim—i.e., the principal goal he will *make known*—of one noted writer is that of making his thoughts simple and clear. This is a worthy goal, but not as easy to attain as many novices in the writing field think. Henry Brooks Adams once said: "Simplicity is the most deceitful mistress that ever betrayed man." W. Somerset Maugham told a reporter that one of the letters he treasured the most came from an American serviceman during World War II. The soldier wrote the author that he liked to read Maugham's books because it was not necessary for him to look up the meanings of any of the words.

One of the great pitfalls for many would-be writers is that of trying to appear pedantic, learned, or erudite by the use of "scholarly" words. Many of these would-be writers persist in thinking that those who advise them to write simply are urging them to "write down" to the masses. They could not be more wrong. The greatest writers of the centuries have been those who learned how to express themselves in the language of the people of their day, so that millions could understand them. It has been pointed out more than once that Jesus of Nazareth, whose words are captured in the four Gospels, used simple illustrations whenever he talked to the people and spoke in terms to which they were accustomed, and about things familiar to them. He told his hearers to "consider the lilies of the field," and He mentioned sparrows, and prodigal sons, and men set upon by criminals, and other human experiences and natural phenomena with which his hearers were familiar.

Abraham Lincoln is another who mastered the art of simplicity in composition—in speaking and writing. Laurence Sterne says, "Writing, when properly managed, is but a different name for conversation." Lincoln once said "No man ever got lost on a straight road." This is a simple statement, but it means many things, to many men, and it rings true to all of them.

The goals of simplicity—of staying on a straight road—of developing a feeling for the people—all are worthy goals. Every successful writer has them, in one degree or another, otherwise he could not have achieved even a modicum of success. But the greater the writer, the more he has these goals and the more he must develop and accentuate them in himself, if he is to grow continuously.

To say that the writer's goals change constantly is to state a truism, at least to those who know philosophy and life. Life itself is changing constantly and the way we live today is not the same as the way we lived yesterday and it will not be the way we will live tomorrow. The changes go on constantly and regularly, like deterioration, and expansion and contraction. It often is said that the only time a man is static is when he is dead, but this is not true, for even then chemical changes take place each hour in the corpse.

Merely because the writer's goals change does not mean that

he cannot keep them higher and nobler. And merely because he literally never achieves the ultimate goal—i.e., to be as perfect in expression as the greatest men who have lived—does not mean that he must wreck his career on the shoals of impatience, or self-abnegation. He must realize that few ever have achieved, in this world, all that they wanted to achieve and felt they could achieve. He comes to know that, if he does his best, he achieves more as a writer than he would if he tried to become a banker, a real estate man, or a mortician. The true writer's central goal is, as it has been, to remain a writer—free, unyoked, unafraid—all the days of his life. If he achieves that goal, who is there to say that he has failed in any way?

William Faulkner, in *Writers At Work*, said: "All of us failed to match our dream of perfection. . . . That's why he (the writer) keeps on working, trying again; he believes each time that he will do it, bring it off. Of course he won't, which is why this condition is healthy. Once he did it, once he matched the work to the image, the dream, nothing would remain but to cut his throat, jump off the other side of that pinnacle of perfection into suicide. . . ." "An artist is a creature driven by demons. . . ."

XVII

The Writer
and His Pleasures

One hates an author that's all author.
—LORD BYRON

WRITERS are human and most of them—away from a micro-phone or a TV camera—act about as normally as other human beings who are bookkeepers, lawyers, physicians, teachers, and even editors.

You can learn of the pleasures of some rich writers by reading the newspapers. Ernest Hemingway likes to go deep sea fishing. (Some say the biggest fish he ever caught were the critics who laud him.) Robert Ruark likes to go big game hunting in Africa, although sometimes he prefers Manhattan. Ben Hogan (who wrote a book, remember!) likes to play golf. I mention these he-man activities—in which he-men play a role—because the impression has gotten around that male writers generally are rather effeminate people, who prefer pink teas to the more robust games in which wholesale grocers and financiers take part. This impression is akin to the one that all female writers are deep-voiced creatures with their hair cut in a boyish bob and that you usually find them in jodhpurs, or some other type of male attire. I can say truthfully that I never saw a successful woman writer who wasn't completely feminine in every way. Most of them (there are a few exceptions) are downright beautiful.

What a successful writer does for pleasure and recreation, of course, depends upon his economic situation, his family status and his location. If he lives in a little town, he doesn't spend much time touring night clubs. If he lives in Washington, D.C., he either joins an after-hours club, or goes home to bed when the midnight curfew sounds and the city workers begin to roll up the streets. Washington is an early-to-bed, early-to-rise city, which may explain why all the people are healthy, wealthy and wise. If he lives in Paris, or Hollywood, or New York, the writer may have more trouble getting to bed early.

Writers have all the usual hobbies, and others, too. Some writers are do-it-yourself fiends, and many, like Artie Shaw (who writes books, too!), seem to have marriage as their hobby. The same goes for the female writers. Kathleen Winsor (who was Mrs. Artie Shaw one time) has been married many times.

The successful writers I interviewed agree on one thing: a really successful writer *must* enjoy himself away from the typewriter, otherwise his work will suffer and his income will drop.

"Personally, I make a hobby of staying in good physical trim," Blake Clark told me. "I have worked out for years at the University Club, or at the YMCA, and feel that it is necessary for my well-being to get in some form of physical exercise almost every day. I like to swim. I also work out with bar bells, and do gymnastics."

Many writers are walkers, or hikers. Some writers get their greatest pleasures in the roar of a downtown street in a big city, watching *people*. Others, disgusted with people, are bird-watchers. But a lot of bird-watchers confess that they are people-watchers, too. They find that there are just as many species of odd people going around, as there are unusual birds flying around.

A writer is a brain-worker, and the brain needs rest just as any other part of the body needs it. The trick in getting pleasure is *diversion*. If a writer has specific editorial tasks to do, and learns when his "exhaustion point" is reached, he should make it a point to divert his interest at that time, and go outside for a brief walk, or stop for a cup of coffee and read the comic page, or otherwise relax his mind. Most writers find that this slight relaxation is invigorating and actually helps their minds to work better when they do get back to the typing grind, or to writing with a pen. These "breaks" should not be artificial interruptions (i.e., by someone else, who breaks into a writer's chain of thoughts), but should be natural and taken by the writer himself, when he feels like making the pause that refreshes.

Most successful writers feel that to produce well they must see life in all its facets. So writers go on motor trips, they play golf, they go to bridge parties, they like to go to stage plays and motion pictures, and a lot of them like to go to night clubs and cut the rug occasionally.

One of the most unusual writer-companion teams in history was that of John Fletcher and Francis Beaumont, who bemused early seventeenth century London by working together on plays. They lived together for years and were said to have shared the same clothes and the same mistresses. The pair was called "a perfect union of genius and friendship."

In order to be near the theater, Beaumont and Fletcher lived not far from the Globe. Beaumont died when he was thirty-one, while Fletcher succumbed to the plague when he was forty-six. It can be said that their only true hobby was women during the years of their greatest productivity as playwrights.

Being unlucky at love—in the sense of being married to a shrewish woman—seems not to have disturbed some geniuses of literature. John Dryden married Lady Elizabeth Howard, who was several years his senior, and the marriage went sour, although they never separated. Dryden became so cynical on the subject of mar-

riage, however, that he scarcely even mentioned it without making
his feelings evident. Long before his wife died, he wrote his famous
Epitaph to His Wife:

> *Here lies my wife; here let her lie!*
> *Now she's at rest. And so am I.*

At different ages, a writer—like any other person—will enjoy
doing different things. Sooner or later, it seems, travel is the one
goal of virtually all writers.

The desire to travel for pleasure is natural for a writer. He learns
about the people of other nations and reads about castles in Spain
and the sunrise o'er Galway Bay, and he yearns to see these places.
The great writers who have been wanderers are many—including
Robert Louis Stevenson, Sir Walter Scott, Lord Byron, Percy
Bysshe Shelley, Rudyard Kipling, Edgar Allan Poe, Rupert Brooke,
Ezra Pound, Sir Walter Raleigh, Walter Savage Landor, Stephen
Foster, Robert Browning, Herman Melville, and W. Somerset
Maugham.

Successful writers have learned that finding some pleasures in
each day helps them to live a happier and fuller life. Most writers
avoid the organized pleasurable activities of the world, although
occasionally they do belong to organizations. Since a writer essentially is an *individualist*, he finds that the kind of life that pleases
him apparently is not the kind that pleases so many others. To many
writers, society always has been slightly off kilter. The writer is
too analytical, and some would say, too self-centered, to enjoy the
antics of others for long at formal parties and the like. That is why,
when writers have parties, they usually are for small, intimate
groups.

Many individuals who are interested in writers ask whether or
not it is true that writers drink more—for pleasure—than other
people. The publicized lives of Edgar Allan Poe, F. Scott Fitz-
gerald, and some others among the *literati* no doubt stimulate

such questions. I would say that there are no more topers among the writing fraternity than other professional groups. There is not nearly as much drinking among writers, I think, as there is among people in "show business," or in politics.

"What's drinking? A mere pause from thinking!" Lord Byron once wrote. It cannot be denied that most writers do imbibe, to some extent, in order to get their minds off problems—either those involved in their work, those involved with editors and those involved with the general state of the world.

Determining how much of a social life a writer may have, or can have, is not an easy chore. At some periods of his life—for example, while engrossed in writing a book on a deadline, or completing a long article or fiction story—the writer may be a recluse. Later, the same writer, because he has completed his task, may become a social lion, of sorts, in that he will be on the lecture platform at times, at cocktail parties at other times, or entertaining friends in his home.

Here are some responses from specific writers as to whether they considered themselves to be recluses, or social lions:

Alden Hatch: In non-fiction, it helps enormously to have wide contacts. Besides, I like roaring.

Harold Helfer: Certainly I am not a social lion, but I am not quite a recluse. It depends on the mood I am in, I suppose. But there's this for sure: When I'm actually at work, writing, which is bound to be a great deal of the time, I have to be a recluse, all by myself and on my own.

Norman Vincent Peale: I am neither. The life of a Christian minister is incompatible with being a recluse, and it seldom affords much leisure for social lionizing.

Richard Gehman: I am a little of both. I enjoy being with people, but I think I like to be alone and working more than that. It becomes more and more difficult for a magazine writer, especially if he is fairly prolific, to get as much solitude as he needs—because he feeds on his friends and acquaintances for ideas, material, and even inspiration. I have now worked out my life so that I have about four days a week in town and three pretty much alone in the country. I have been trying to get four days alone and three in town, but it just hasn't worked out that way.

Harry Edward Neal: I'm neither. I go to very few parties, mostly because I'm not invited to many! I like people and I enjoy interviewing those who furnish information necessary for my books and articles. I'm curious, as all writers ought to be, and my curiosity often brings me into contact with new acquaintances and new fields to write about. I do have a sort of hideaway, a study, at home, and I reckon that when I'm hard at work on a book, an article, or a story, I'm in the recluse class. I'm confident that a lot of other writers are also "typewriter hermits" when they're in the throes of actual production.

Frances and Richard Lockridge: We live quite normal social lives. Certainly, we seldom roar.

Edison Marshall: A real writer has no real companions. He likes people and occasionally is liked by people, but friendships are too expensive, in time and energy, for a dedicated writer to maintain. Oddly enough, I thought I had to be a social lion from 21-41; now, I am a recluse. I go to no parties, but we do have formal dinners at our home, Breetholm, when editors, publishers, etc., come through, and they are pleasant diversions.

Dora Albert: I'm sure there is a golden mean here. Frederick Collins once told me that a writer could spend so much time at social affairs he would have no time left to write. On the other hand, I'd hate to live in an ivory tower, surrounded only by books and newspapers and magazines and not know the stimulation of meeting other people. I don't know of anything more interesting than people. Although some hermits write very well, no doubt, I wouldn't like to be one of them.

O. A. Battista: My successful self-help books prove, I think, that

I like people. Much of my free time is spent with my family, how-ever, doing things with my wife and children exclusively. If I did not do this deliberately, I would be letting them down. My type-writer and tape recorder get much of the time that my friends fritter away at bridge or cocktails.

Fred Kerner: I can hardly call myself a recluse or a social lion. But if I have to point the indicator at one direction, I would say I am probably closer to the recluse side. While I find people in-teresting, I don't like them in large crowds and I tire of people rather quickly. I guess I pump them for all they have and then look to fresh fields. I enjoy reading and enjoy classical music, so that I am quite often content to be alone. However, I sometimes find myself lonely. This will probably be rectified if and when I marry—but this is not an ad for a wife.

Robert Payne: The recluse prays; the social lion presumably is the man standing in the chariot. I do not see why one should not lead a full social life and still, during the act of writing, be a recluse. The recluse has however one advantage: in his cell, he can do what he pleases. And without the enjoyment of freedom, I do not see how one can write at all.

Hugh Ross Williamson: I'm said to be a recluse. Desmond Mac-Carthy once told me I was the most inaccessible man in London! Personally, I don't think I am. But I've no time for literary parties and all that sort of thing, which bore me to distraction; though I like to be with *people*.

A. C. Spectorsky: I am neither a recluse nor a social lion—except at home. At home, I am definitely not a recluse. Unlike many writers, I find that having a room set aside where I can have peace and quiet and a closed door and be all by myself makes me feel lonely and left out of things. I am selfish enough to want my writ-ing desk in my living room. My family knows when I'm working, manages to be quiet and unobtrusive during these periods—and I get a sense of importance and moral support from their behavior which helps my morale immeasurably. This is a hardship on them, but they are most gracious about it. Frequently, of course, they go out and leave me all to myself. In such cases, although the house is empty, I am still working in the largest, pleasantest room in the house and this fills me with a sense of well-being which I could never have sequestered away in some den or study, where, in any case, I might be interrupted.

Emil Zubryn: I'm a recluse—definitely! (Mr. Zubryn moved to Mexico many years ago to get away from so many people).

Sloan Wilson: I'm a recluse, with occasionally regrettable exceptions.

Erskine Caldwell: I stay to myself.

Evan Hunter: When I'm working—which is between ten in the morning and four in the afternoon—I am neither a recluse nor a social lion. Writing is essentially a lonely profession. I work at home on the second floor of our home in a rather small office. I look out at the woods behind the house. I rarely see anyone during the day except my own family. Therefore, I welcome their intrusions (except when I'm red hot on something I've been trying to express all week and one of the children pops in to ask if I will tie his shoelace!). I welcome the ring of the telephone which connects me with New York and the outside world. My concentration, except on those intensely red hot occasions, is not a thing which—once shattered—cannot be reconstructed. When I end a phone conversation, I reread the last paragraph I've written and am immediately back in that other world of fiction. But without the interruptions, without the voices from the *real* world, I imagine writing would become a terrible ordeal. Writing, despite the hard work involved, is still fun for me. The day it stops being fun is the day I'll quit. I don't think that day will ever come.

Ben Smith: I never knew a writer of any consequence who was a social lion. In the first place, writing is the occupation of loneliness—you have to be alone to work. That necessitates long hours away from other people. You get out of the habit of being with people and soon you forget how to make yourself interesting to them. A writer must straddle the fence. Contact with people is part of the grist for his mill. But after the contact has set his literary wellspring bubbling, then he is a recluse.

Jesse Stuart: I am neither a recluse nor a social lion. I am, perhaps, in all appearances a regular person, but can be explosive.

Thomas P. Kelley: Friends call me "The Hermit."

Scott Young: I am a normal member of the community, neither recluse nor social lion.

Deane and David Heller: Neither, although we're engaged in politics and several other things which take up time. Ever so often, we just "slow up" on our outside activities and cut 'em back to a desirable point. We find, however, that they are often a fruitful source of articles. Often people will come to us with ideas which are useable.

John Gassner: I am not a social lion, nor a recluse either; my activities keep me continually involved with people, but I always long for a retirement from the heat and chatter of the world.

Saul K. Padover: I lead a normal life; go out socially whenever time permits.

Kenneth S. Giniger: I am not a recluse.

Georges Simenon: Not a recluse, nor a social what-you-say. A very ordinary kind of man.

Joseph N. Bell: I am known in our block of a suburb as the neighborhood handyman, since I'm likely to be the only man at home on most days. Writing to me is fun and the life of a writer can be fun.

Frederic A. Birmingham: I am neither a recluse nor a social lion. I enjoy being with people and I like them, but not under social conditions. I shrink from cocktail parties but not from crowds. I enjoy being alone but what I gain from solitariness I believe is best used in relation to other human beings rather than in further singu-

larity. I enjoy any group animated by a combination of personalities, rather than a uniformity of idea or background. I am actually a reclusive lion.

Lewis Broad: For the last ten years I have been applying my
skill gained as a journalist to the art and craft of biography. Your
questionnaire has brought me to realize the extent to which I have
come to devote myself to writing. I feel myself now to be almost
dedicated to authorship. I lead a solitary life, living much of the
year on my own, with dog and cat, in a Tudor farmhouse in the
heart of the country. I do not entertain. I have few social contacts.
I frequent neither pubs nor clubs, my friends are few. I am ready
to abandon all distractions that interfere with my writing, prepared
even to sacrifice the playing of bridge.

As a journalist I should not have thought it necessary or proper
to cut myself off from the world in this seclusion. Is an author so
compelled? Not, perhaps, inevitably, but authorship is an unsoci-
able occupation. It is a job that has to be done in the solitary
silence of the study, cut off from human contacts while the labour
of composition proceeds. The solitary hours of concentration do
not end when the pen is put down, or the typewriter is closed, for
when he is not engaged on composition the author must be brooding, and even biographers, relying on facts rather than imagination, have need to brood to produce their conceptions of character
and to evolve the stages of their narratives.

These solitary habits do not conform with the needs of matri-
mony and domesticity. Authors, I suspect, do not make good husbands. Women for the most part do not admit rival interests and
hours devoted to any subject but themselves.

Not long ago I induced one of my friends to turn author. He
produced a good novel but declined to undertake a second—it
would wreck his marriage.

XVIII

The Writer
and His Agent

Let every eye negotiate for itself,
And trust no agent.
—WILLIAM SHAKESPEARE,
Much Ado About Nothing, Act II

IF YOU want a heated discussion, start talking about whether or not literary agents are necessary.

A writer like John O'Hara, author of *Ten North Frederick* and other best-sellers that have become big movies, for instance, feels deeply that agents are not needed. He recently told a reporter for *Publisher's Weekly*: "Why should I give 'em (agents) ten per cent of my earnings? I don't need an agent and I get along very well without them."

And when you read about some of the deals he has made with movie producers, you realize that Mr. O'Hara is no slouch at the bargaining table. But the question arises as to whether other writers would be able to negotiate competent contracts for themselves as well as Mr. O'Hara.

Evan Hunter, who is just as successful as a novelist although somewhat younger than Mr. O'Hara, once worked for a literary agent and he has a firm tie-up with that agent today, one of the best-known in the country. Apparently, *he* has found that it is helpful to have the guidance on the "big" deals, where an agent might get a writer an additional amount extra far greater than the total fee of the agent. In other words, some writers believe that the agents might *earn* money for writers, instead of actually *costing* the writers money, if the agents fulfill their roles well.

About half the writers I interviewed have agents, and defend the idea vehemently. But the other half do not use literary agents. These writers say that they don't want agents, use them only as a last resort, and can't see any basic reason why anyone should use an agent and lose ten per cent of his earnings thereby.

There are so many kinds of "literary agents" nowadays it may be well for us to define our terms. When a successful writer talks about his "literary agent," he is generally referring to a man from whom he gets money, not one to whom he sends money. When the average *beginning*, or would-be, writer talks about a "literary agent," or asks questions about one, however, *he* usually is referring to an agent whose advertisement he has seen in a magazine for writers, or on the Sunday page of his local newspaper.

The two kinds of agents are not synonymous. Most "literary agents" who represent successful writers do *not* advertise that if writers will send in material, with a "reading fee" attached, the agents will send the writers a report on whether or not the sender has capabilities as a writer.

Usually the kind of literary agent who represents successful writers does not advertise. The only kinds of advertising he does is an occasional letter to some writer who, he feels, is becoming a big timer and may be helped by having an agent attend to his marketing problems. This kind of agent usually does not want to handle anyone who is selling less than $10,000 worth of material a year.

The second—or advertising kind of "literary agent"—obviously is looking for lots of amateur writers, would-be writers, or individuals who are hopelesly without talent, but not without literary hopes, to send him reading fees, so that he can play on their vanity and get other fees from time to time in the future. These "literary agents" of the latter type undoubtedly *do* sell an occasional article, story, or book, out of the thousands of manuscripts sent to them. Yet, it is a matter of record that they handle very few of the really "big" writers, i.e., writers who are writing and selling best-sellers that make big money. The successful writers—if they have literary agents—usually have agents who are relatively unknown to the general public and whose advertisements seldom, if ever, are featured in writers' magazines.

As a prolific writer, if not always a "successful" one, I have blown hot and cold on the subject of literary agents.

It is my belief at this time—and it is no more than a belief—that literary agents are becoming fewer, although the publishing industry is getting bigger. *If* this development *is* taking place, it is due, I believe, to the increased economic pressures on writers, who find that they can't afford ten per cent for an agent, particularly on work sold in the United States. If a writer lives here and is selling to English, French, or foreign markets, an agent would appear economical for international sales. Likewise, if a writer lives outside the United States, it might pay him to send his material to an agent in this country for transmittal to likely publishers.

One of the first questions that arise in classes for writers, usually has to do with literary agents. A large part of those who want to become writers think in terms of spending their money—on agents —before they are even earning any on their writing.

Potential writers ask: "What about literary agents? Should I try to get an agent before or after I am selling my literary output?"

Usually, these would-be writers are thinking of the "literary agents" who advertise, the only ones known to the public.

First, a writer should be told not to worry about getting a literary agent until he has earned at least $10,000 in a year by writing.

The *bona fide* agent's job is *selling*, and getting the writer the top dollar for the material he sells. It stands to reason that a reputable agent couldn't make any money of an individual writer unless the writer were producing enough material to bring the agent at least $1,000 a year.

"No reputable literary agent has ever been known to advertise in writers' magazines," one nationally-known author told me. "The reason is clear. If he is a top marketer, word of his ability will spread without his advertising himself. The best-known writer *about* salesmen in the U. S. is Elmer Wheeler, but he isn't the most successful salesman, by any means. Some salesmen for big companies make hundreds of thousands of dollars a year, and they deserve it, but only occasionally does the general public ever see their names. However, *everybody* who is anybody in that salesman's specific field knows he is good and gets results. That salesman doesn't have to put display ads in the newspapers. Neither does a good literary agent have to advertise."

Second, successful writers almost uniformly agree that it is silly to send money off to a "literary agent" for reading fees.

"Whatever advice such a 'literary agent' gives you *may* help a beginning writer, and it may not," one successful writer commented. "However, the writer could get just as much help—for no fee at all—from discussing it with friends in a writing group, or by studying the story or article closely, in case it is sent back by a magazine editor, and then rereading the magazine to which he had sent it.

"The way to crack any particular market—or sell to any specific magazine—is to study the magazine, and try to learn what the editor is striving to give to his readers. Even if a 'literary agent' says that a specific piece is 'good,' it doesn't mean anything to the writer, unless the agent actually *sells* it to a specific editor. Many would-be writers go through life nourishing their starved egos by repeating what some 'literary agent' to whom they have sent money and stories said about their material. These people are more to be pitied than censured, but they most certainly should be warned. However, I don't think the warnings do much good, for the same people, year after year (and new ones come up all the time), send their manuscripts, accompanied by a 'reading fee' to these 'literary agents.' And the agents seem to have plenty of money for full-page advertisements."

Successful writers warn beginning writers to discount the idea that an agent, or anyone, can sell material to an editor by "pull," "contact," or by any device except furnishing him material that properly fits into his editorial plans.

"Numerous people have some idea that there is some kind of 'club' to which selling writers belong that other people can't join, unless they are born to the writing purple, or happened to have come into the world under the proper sign of the zodiac," a noted novelist told me. "They want to be known as 'literary,' but they will not pay the price of foregoing teas, receptions and cocktail parties long enough to get down to the hard job of writing.

"Until they realize that the only way to become a good writer is by hard, dedicated, regular work, they never will become successful, selling writers. Most of these people never become writers. But they always are up there in front *talking* about writing."

Perhaps it would be well for such people to consider these points about the writing profession, and the people in it.

First, editors are *not* ghoulish, spiteful, frustrated men who are determined to put you in your place by returning your material, with snide comments, as fast as you can prepare it and mail it off. They are usually looking for material to buy and they will buy it from anyone *if* the stuff is written as they want it and is on a subject that fits into their program.

Instead of considering the editor an enemy the best way to think about any editor is that he is a friend to the beginning writer. The editor *wants* the neophytes to write and he hopes that, if there are new names in the slushpile, some of them will turn out to have the kind of background and energy and ability to write which the editor needs. Material almost always is purchased on its own merits, without regard to whether the author is young or old, experienced or inexperienced (as long as he has been competent enough to prepare the specific property under discussion), or other extraneous factors. Naturally, if a contributor is discovered to be a crank, crackpot, or a propagandist, his material might be turned down, no matter how cleverly or competently prepared. By and large, *influence* does not sell literary material. Merit counts most vitally.

Writers who *talk* about agents before they have produced and sold articles, stories or books, are often striving to make an impression on their friends, or whoever is listening to them talk about "literary agents." Such writers really have the hope that there are *easy* ways to succeed as writers. They apparently think that a literary agent can smooth the rough spots, can correct their material, and help them to receive a bonanza without earning it the hard way, like most other writers have had to do.

"Writing material to sell to specific editors does not lend itself to any basic shortcuts," a noted writer told me. "True, as each of us writes, day by day, he learns how to express himself better. He learns personal management shortcuts. But the advantage the successful writer has over the unsuccessful writer is in the knowledge he has gained by hard study, hard writing, hard thinking. The writing field is *not* an easy field. The newcomers who want to take shortcuts secretly think that they are 'smarter' than the older heads in the field, and they believe that it is possible to get something for nothing. But all of us must pay a price for whatever success we have. The greater the success the greater the price. The writing field usually is too hard for people looking for an easy life and they end up working for the government, or administering a pension fund, or as a disc jockey, or something on par with that."

There is so much hocus pocus connected with the subject of

agents. I visited several, in making preparations for this book, and was able to get the lowdown on agents right from the horse's mouth, so to speak, although from what some writers say about agents, I may have used the wrong approach.

These agents were mature people—and some of them evidently have passed the age of maturity—who have been in the literary field for a long, long time. They do their work in comfortable offices, often located in big apartments, with one of the rooms set aside for the agent's office. The agent has a secretary and perhaps one or two other employees. I understand that they usually have an arrangement with a lawyer who reads contracts for them, or pay lawyers for specific legal advice at various times, usually relating to copyrights, specific provisions of contracts, or for other legal niceties.

Most of them are on friendly terms with publishers. They cultivate the staff among these publishers, not so much in favor of their writer-clients as to get these people to refer prospective writers (who have submitted material to publishers) to the agents. The publishers generally prefer that a writer have an agent, for it is easier for them to deal with one agent, who may have a stable full of writers, than for them to keep up with a great many writers. Publishers also have found that agents are much more professional, as a general rule, in their behaviour toward publishers, than a lot of individual, more-or-less Bohemian authors, particularly when the writers are young and full of individuality and will power.

All of the agents whom I contacted either had purchased the agency which they operate from someone who had operated it for years before them, or they had inherited it. Literary agencies apparently go on for century after century, like famous restaurants, or like the Taft family, the Lodges, the Wanamakers, and various mercantile families in America.

The agent, I learned, is a fiduciary, in that he handles, at times, large sums of money for his client, and clients. He is both a literary and financial adviser, too. The latter is true when he has sold a book that becomes a best-seller and then earns a great deal of movie money for the client who may not have the first idea about how to handle it.

The agent must be a good business manager, for he handles money both for himself and for others, and, as everyone knows who handles any money, this is a touchy subject. He is obligated—morally, if not legally—to get the very top dollar for the various legal rights the author can sell, both in this country and in others. It is the agent's job not only to wait for orders for a writer who is successfully writing a lot of salable material, but to get suggestions from editors about specific articles they are seeking and to pass these along to his client.

When the agent has sold a book in this country, let us say, he is interested in exploiting the writer's work in every legitimate way. He will, if he can, get an item about the sale into magazines designed to catch the eye of the book sellers throughout the country. He also will try to get notices about the book in various gossip columns. He realizes that the more publicity the book gets—if it is a novel, in particular—the greater the chance that it will become a best-seller. He also is interested in exploiting other rights. He might approach a syndicate with the idea of trying to sell someone on the idea of getting the writer of the newest best-seller to do a special series of articles on some subject of which the writer is an expert. He may approach various motion picture producers, about the idea of buying the literary property on which to base a movie. He may offer the book to a paperback publisher. He may approach publishers in London about bringing out a British edition, or a publisher in Paris about a French edition, an Italian publisher about an Italian edition, etc.

The agent, as it can be seen, actually can handle, and do justice, to the work of only a limited number of top-flight writers. There are just so many hours in a day, whether you are a literary agent, a President, or a popcorn vendor. If an agent is handling, let us say,

William Faulkner, John Steinbeck, Ernest Hemingway and Erich M. Remarque, and a few other internationally-known, prolific writers, he isn't going to have time to welcome just any would-be writer who sticks his head in the agent's door. This agent can afford to pick and choose among the budding literary lights who are always pushing upwards. That is why it is sometimes not easy to get the agent you want to handle you. They are busy—competent and hard-working men who have gained their reputation by actual performance for writers through the years.

There are so many individual factors involved in the question whether you should have an agent that it is one each writer, or would-be writer, must answer for himself. I know people who represent themselves as lawyers—and do a good job of it. I know others who "freeze" when they approach a courtroom and couldn't defend themselves against overtime parking charges even if they had never driven a car in their lives and don't own one. It all depends on the person's temperament, experience, knowledge, poise and a number of other factors—whether he can be his own agent, or his own lawyer, successfully.

XIX

The Writer
and His Taxes

*The optimist proclaims that we live in the
best of all possible worlds; and the pessimist fears this is true.*

—JAMES BRANCH CABELL

IT MAY not seem so to you, as you look at the placid-faced successful novelist or writer on the lecture platform waiting to be introduced (and wondering if the master of ceremonies will mention
that his latest book is now on sale at all bookstores!), but this successful writer is seething inwardly. He is not only a mass of talents,
he is a mass of resentments; and most of his resentments are directed against one agency of the Federal government—the Internal
Revenue Service.

Why should this successful writer be so bitter toward the income
tax man? The biggest reason is that the writer, usually interested in
words instead of figures, doesn't catch on, until he has become
successful, just how many loopholes there seem to be in the tax laws
for everybody else but him.

The writer knows, for instance, that a businessman who owns
machinery can take fast depreciation on the machinery, deduct this
(for tax purposes) from his gross income, and that, in effect, Uncle

Sam helps the businessman through this fast depreciation to get rich. Yet, the writer, whose principal "machinery" (besides his typewriter and a few scattered pieces of furniture) is his mind and body, realizes that he is wearing himself out every day that he sits down to work. The writer, however, can take no depreciation, from a tax standpoint, on the wear and tear his body suffers, although it is self-evident that he has only so many years use of it and then he is gone for good. The writer wonders why it can't be made plain to people that *his* machinery—his mind and body—deserves a tax-break just as much as the machinery-using businessman.

The writer, of all people, is a well-read person. The more he reads, the more successful he becomes, and the more successful he becomes, the more he reads. As a result, a successful writer usually is quite a curbstone expert on taxes and the inequities inherent in our present tax methods and procedures. He learns—to his chagrin —that some of the wealthiest people pay the fewest taxes, legally, and that many struggling people—notably writers—pay at much higher rates, proportionate to their true earnings, than many others.

It is possible that some selfishness enters into this feeling of writers. On the other hand, it is apparent that selfishness entered into all the other deals, agreements, and shenanigans that were pulled to give certain groups favored tax treatment, so the writer might well be excused if he now reacts selfishly—even though too late.

Although some are fortunate enough to be born rich, and others are talented and/or lucky enough to make money while they are still single and able to save some capital on whose unearned increments they can amble through life, the vast majority of successful writers did not attain a modicum of success until they had reached what is euphemistically called "middle age." At that point, with family responsibilities and all the other expenses that are a part and parcel of this civilization, these writers have found that a man must be superhuman to live on any income, however large, *and* to retain enough to assure them of staying off public welfare in case of illness. At the same time, these writers are old enough to realize that in a relatively few years, they will be older, their walk will have lost its spring, and perhaps their writing will have lost a lot of zip. They *know*, anyway, that by the time they reach this period, their literary production will diminish. In short, the writer at middle-age is worrying more about his own future than he is worrying about the future of the world. Virtually everyone else, he observes, has made plans for retirement. The writer decides it is time for him to plan.

Looking around, he sees that minor executives of big companies contribute tax-exempt payments into a retirement fund that will pay them handsomely, besides their small social security checks, when they get too old to cut the mustard anymore. He reads and understands that there are not just a few of these pension funds, but thousands of them. When he investigates, however, the writer finds that they are, in effect, closed corporations to the people who work for this or that company which has set up a plan of its own. The writer, if he is a superhuman, *can* set up his own retirement system, out of income. But he still has to pay the taxes on the income, even if it is set aside for his specific retirement, just as the income of corporation bigwigs is set aside for this purpose.

For some years, the Authors League of America has sponsored legislation in Congress which would make it possible for writers (and other professional and self-employed persons) to set aside a certain sum of money each year, for retirement purposes, and to deduct this as a business expense, on the same order that corporations and their executives may deduct retirement payments from their income each year before computing what they owe Uncle Sam. Congressional leaders, however, have found it very difficult to get into their heads that writers, and kindred self-employed persons, deserve any official attention.

Legislation was advanced to the point at which it was reported out of committee, but it never yet has been acted upon by the Senate and the House of Representatives. Among others who spoke against it, when it came up in the Senate, was Senator W. A. Purtell (R.-Conn.), a very wealthy man who never delivered a single speech against pensions for Congressmen but found against the idea of having writers, and kindred people, actually set aside their own money for retirement purposes, without having to pay taxes on the money set aside for such purposes. The Senator, we might add, didn't last long after the votes were counted in November, 1958, only a few months after he delivered his diatribe against self-employed persons.

There also have been bills introduced in Congress to make it possible for writers to depreciate their bodies, as manufacturers depreciate machinery. Successful writers almost all approve of such legislative measures. But it is a sad fact that writers, even if every one in the country were to be in a parade, would hardly make up as inspiring a group as the members of a couple of big American Legion posts in one of our big cities. There are fewer than 20,000 writers who earn their full incomes from free-lance writing in the United States, so for writers to get through legislation which will benefit them, they must band together with doctors, lawyers, house-to-house salesmen and similar self-employed professionals or tradesmen.

Several years ago, a noted book writer took his family on a long cruise in a boat he had bought for the purpose of taking the sea voyage to gather material for a book. He was gone for many months, with his wife and two small children. Upon his return, he entered the total cost of the trip—less the amount of food his wife and children actually had consumed—as a deductible business expense.

This deduction—which ran into some $8,000—was challenged by the Internal Revenue Service. He appealed to the U. S. Tax Court, which every taxpayer has the privilege of doing through payment of a $10 fee, and, through his attorney, argued in favor of his deduction. He won, too. It was firmly established, by the U. S. Tax Court, that if a writer goes anywhere to collect information for a story, article, book, movie, or whatever, that he can deduct the total cost of the trip. It also was established that merely because he takes his wife and children along is no sign that the trip is not a business trip (if it had been classified as a vacation, he would not have been able to deduct his own expenses, of course), although the writer is not able to deduct the actual cost incurred by his wife and children during the trip.

Successful writers become more tax-conscious the more money they "handle," for they become aware of the difference between gross income and net income. They realize that merely because they are taking in $18,000 or $25,000 or $50,000 a year, they do not necessarily "make" that much money, any more than a groceryman who takes in $100,000 "makes" the full amount. The groceryman realizes that, to compute his true net profit, he must deduct, among other things, the rental of his building, the cost of the utilities, the cost of the clerical helpers, the payments he makes to wholesalers, the license fees he must pay, the money he must spend in going to market and return, and so on *ad infinitum*.

The successful writer realizes that he has expenses which do not hit the average man. The writer must deduct from his gross income, among other things, the cost of travel to get information, the cost of intracity travel, when he goes to interview people or to get facts that he must have in his work, the cost of entertaining either interviewees or editors, the cost of maintaining a working place, the cost of paper, typewriter ribbons, depreciation on his equipment and machinery, and a number of other items, not the least of which is his telephone bill, for he must keep in mind that it costs even to call the typewriter repair company.

The successful writer keeps strict account of his income and outgo. If he has a secretary, he keeps a day-book of income and expenditures, in cooperation with her. If he does not have a secretary, he keeps a day-book himself, or enlists the aid of his wife, or sweetheart, as the case may be. Sometimes, he may enlist the aid of both his wife and his sweetheart. There are some cases in which a successful writer has been found to have several wives and several sweethearts, and here, no doubt, special problems arise.

At any rate, the keeping of a day-book, whether by wife, sweetheart, or secretary, is about the best way most writers have found to keep their expenditures, with a minimum of fuss and bother. The writer lists, each evening, the source of the income he receives and the amount, in the "income" book. Then, he puts down the exact expenses he incurred during the day.

If the writer goes away on a trip, to visit editors, to gather material, or for other valid business purposes, he is particularly careful to jot down his expenses.

"I never realized just how important my day-book could be to me until I was checked by Internal Revenue agents a few times," one nationally-known writer told me. "If someone had told me, years ago, that I would incur as many expenses these days as I actually do incur in my work, I would have thought he was exaggerating. But the sad truth is that it costs a great deal of money for a writer merely to move around and to contact the people he must contact. A trip to New York, which once cost me $50 for a few days, now runs into hundreds of dollars."

Here are some stratagems that writers have used to assure themselves of income for a good while to come, and at the same time not have to pay taxes at the prohibitively high rates after a man passes the $25,000 net income mark in any one year:

In selling the rights of a best-selling book to a motion picture producer, a writer was offered $200,000. Instead of taking it in one lump-sum payment (which would have made him liable for taxes of upwards of $140,000), the writer specified that, instead, he would rather have the money paid to him $25,000 a year for eight years. His total taxes on it (depending, of course, on what other income he may earn in each of the eight years), most likely will be only $50,000 or so, altogether. It is important—according to tax court rulings—that the agreement specify flatly and irrevocably that the writer cannot demand payment of the residue owing to him whenever he wants it. In other words, if he has the privilege, in the agreement, of asking for the remainder due to him and getting it any time, then the Tax Court has held that, in fact, the whole amount of the agreement *is* taxable income in the year in which the agreement is made. In short, the agreement must be irrevocable that he be paid only $25,000 a year and that he has no rights to the other due to him until it actually is due to be paid to him, at which time, of course, it immediately becomes subject to the income tax.

A writer might swap his services, as a writer, to someone who needs the services of a writer, in exchange for some service which the other person may render to him. Since no money passes hands, in either case, there is not a tax situation in either case. For example, a writer had to have an operation. He sought out a noted specialist, whom he knew was interested in writing a book. The specialist normally would have charged several thousand dollars for the operation. The writer normally would have charged to help a noted physician write a book. In this case, neither man charged the other for his services. The writer got the operation and the physician got the book finished on which he had been working for years.

Similarly, a writer of my acquaintance was approached by a woman who wanted some expert editorial assistance on a book. The writer said that he couldn't help her, since he was very busy on his own work. She mentioned that her husband was a painting contractor and the writer perked up. He knew two things (1) that his house needed painting, and (2) that the cost to him to have it painted would run close to $1,000.

"I'll tell you what I'll do," he said. "If your husband will paint my house, to my specifications, at no charge, I'll help you write your book at no charge."

And so the swap was made.

Successful writers have found that they can swap their services for a number of other useful services in this society, besides simply a paint job on the house, or an expensive surgical job. Writers have swapped their editorial know-how for an all-expense trip around the world (one went by air, another by boat); for a vacation trip in the Adirondacks (where a certain hostelry wanted publicity); for trips to Alaska, Honolulu, and many other points on the globe; for dental services; for public relations assistance; for legal assistance and for a wide variety of other services. The beauty of "swapping," from the standpoint of taxes, is that no money changes hands, and both parties are exempt from having to report the transaction, since no "income" was represented. A dentist can charge what he pleases for an expensive bridge job, and a writer can charge what he pleases for editorial work on a book, but when the two men swap, they have a right to exchange their services.

Successful writers, on major economic transactions, have learned enough either to consult with tax lawyers and/or certified public accountants, or to study the ins and outs of tax rulings so that they can proceed with sureness both in claiming the deductions they do take, in making special income "deals," or in claiming losses that other people might overlook. Many Americans have heard so much about how rich men use loopholes in the tax laws that many of them come to think that these regulations apply only to rich men, who can afford to take the time to find the loopholes, or to pay to have it done.

Writers should remember that they are just as eligible to use these provisions of the tax law, to their own advantage, as are very rich people, or those in the business of studying taxes for their profession. I know a writer who took back a first trust note when he sold a piece of property. The trust note was for $20,000, payable in small monthly installments. But the time came when the writer wanted cash for his other activities. He sold the note, which had a face value of close to $20,000, for $15,000. This gave him a carry-forward tax loss of $1,000 a year for five years. This carry-forward (of losses) was one of the vital points he kept in mind in making his decision to sell the note, rather than to borrow money against it and hold it until the entire $20,000 had been paid to him over a period of years. He figured that he could use the $15,000 to finance undertakings that would make him far more than $20,000, and at the same time he would have a $1,000 automatic deduction each year for five years. Also, when he sold the property, he had received in cash (over and above the $20,000 note) approximately what he had paid for the property originally. So, all in all, he came out of the transaction happy.

It is estimated that tens of thousands of persons, who have the right to claim carry-forward tax losses do *not* do so, because they are not aware of their rights.

"I've already urged my son to take courses in economics and taxation in college and after he finishes college, even though he plans to be a physician," one successful writer commented. "It is my theory that, as the years go by and as local, state and federal taxes become more onerous, and the tax laws more complex, a man in any field of endeavor who strives to understand taxes, in every phase, is the man who will be able to retain what little it is possible for any person to retain of his income any more."

A successful writer these days must—and does—give a great deal of time, thought and effort to his tax records, and to the tax rules and regulations in effect in his community, his state, and his country. If you look at the furrows in the average writer's brow, you can assume that not all of them were caused by pondering on his writing—many were caused by the problem of his taxes.

XX

The Writer
and His Reading

*Knowledge and timber shouldn't be much
used till they are seasoned.*

—HOLMES

*A man will turn over half a library to
make one book.*

—BEN JONSON

IF YOU have read this book, or *any* book, this year, you may feel
sure that you are a bit better informed than the average American,
for Joe Doaks—or Tom Jones—or Henry Smith—is no longer a book-
reader.

Although around 14,000 books are published each year, and
there are tens of millions of volumes in the Library of Congress,
perhaps 100,000,000 (or more) Americans never crack open a single book during a typical year. Some individuals read a book a
week, some read one or two a month, and some read only one or two
a year. But most Americans do not read even one. This may be
considered a reflection either upon authors, because of the dullness
of their writing, or upon readers, for their lack of respect for "book
larnin' " upon which our forefathers set such store.

Still, if you have read thus far into this book or have read *any* book lately, you have taken a step to becoming a better communicator—a writer. For every successful writer I have ever known started out as a *reader*.

The more successful the writer, by and large, the more he reads. However, many writers, like persons in other professions, sometimes think they have learned everything and stop reading. Those who quit reading are those whose names become known less and less as time passes.

Millions of Americans have quit reading, for all practical purposes. They depend on the quick newscasts on the radio or TV to give them a fill-in on a world teeming with problems. Even if the announcers were supermen they could not pack into five minutes even a smattering of the important happenings going on in the world. And merely to transmit adequate news about any *one* significant happening, so that a hearer could understand it halfway intelligently, an announcer would have to speak for thirty minutes or more on just one subject.

Men can learn about the world and its problems only by reading. Writers, if they are to keep up, *must* be omnivorous readers. And the earlier they start reading the sooner they are likely to become successful. It is understandable, of course, that a brilliant concert pianist at eleven or twelve must have started playing the piano at five or six years of age. It is just as understandable that good writers are those who started reading early in life.

Most successful writers confess that they began to read when very young. Some began reading the "funny pages" when they were four years old, had graduated to top magazines by the time they were six, and were reading adult books by eight. Many were well-read by the time they were twelve years old. It is safe to say that most of them, before they finished college, had read hundreds if not thousands of books, as well as having developed a continuing and abiding interest in specific magazines, newspapers, and other forms of written effort.

Successful writers, in fact, seem to take more pride in their reading—judging by their conversation—than they do in their writing, if this is possible. They will regale you with stories about how much they read, and how diverse their reading tastes, if you have the time to listen. A lot liked fiction—the stories of *Tarzan and the Apes*, the *Tom Swift* series, Zane Grey's Westerns, *Gulliver's Travels, The Swiss Family Robinson*, and Kipling's stories.

Then, at a later stage in their reading, they started on magazines —*True Detective, Saturday Evening Post, Cosmopolitan*, among many others—and newspapers. Finally, by the time they were trying to sell their writings, the successful writers whom I interviewed mostly had developed quite eclectic reading tastes. They read "who-dun-its," popular novels, classical novels, and business newsletters, as well as popular magazines.

One writer who has become very successful realized when he was about 24 that he needed to know more fact material about the world in which he lives. So he set out on a program of daily reading the *Encyclopedia Britannica*. In several years, by a strict devotion to this duty, he found that he had read the encyclopedia through. Nothing daunted, he started on another publisher's encyclopedia.

Another writer went to the library every afternoon and would pick a book at random. He would stay there until he finished the book, or the library closed, whichever happened sooner. In case the library closed before he finished the book, he would get it the next day and finish it that day, if possible. Among other things, he read the 10,000 sermons of Charles Haddon Spurgeon, the great Baptist Divine, who was the Norman Vincent Peale of the late 19th Century in London.

With millions of children spending their spare time watching television, instead of reading, the question arises as to where the future supply of writers will come from. For the task of writing demands much reading and research in the early years to be well-grounded in both historical lore and in how writers in other generations developed their stories and ideas.

It may be that today's youngsters—nursed, as it were, on *Have Gun, Will Travel, Gunsmoke,* and *Tales of Wells Fargo,* as well as *Private Secretary* and *My Little Margie,* will have a better idea of the way the society operates today, and of its early beginnings, than many modern writers who grew up reading omnivorously about a variety of characters in early America and books ranging from theology to science fiction. On the other hand, the fact that most children are seeing the same thing, in all sections, may develop a uniformity of opinion that will make for more of the same TV fare twenty and thirty years from now—and all but a few grouches will think it is wonderful, for it will be what they are used to.

Why should reading be so essential to a person who wants to write? Several authors give their views:

"Well, if a boy is going to be an automobile mechanic, the sooner he starts tinkering, the quicker he learns what he can do—and can't do—with a motor," one of them said. "When a person starts reading early, he learns what he can do—and can't do—with words. He sees what others have written to express specific thoughts.

"The more motors on which a youngster works, the greater becomes his experience. He learns that there are many kinds of motors, but that there are certain fundamentals to all.

"In the same way, the would-be writer learns, by reading, that there are many words in the English language, and many ways of using these many words, for various effects. Yet, he learns the fundamentals of expression, so that, as his mind becomes more and more selective, he develops a power of discrimination among words and he understands why one word, or series of words, is more effective in a given writing situation than another would be."

Another writer pointed out:

"A lot of youngsters—and I was one of them—get buried in books at an early age. Their parents call them lazy, and the kids may well be, physically. But they are not lazy, mentally, for no one can read, and understand what he is reading, without keeping his mind alert all the time. You can't enjoy reading, for example, when you are half-asleep.

"As the child, or youngster, reads and reads and reads, somewhere along the line he is challenged to *write* something that is as good, or better, than anything he has seen on the printed pages he has read. The challenge comes not from outside—from his parents, or friends, or others—but *inside*. He quickly learns that there is a vast difference between *reading* and *writing*. One can be a pleasurable experience, but the other is work. He finds that writing demands more thought and attention than reading, for there is the added factor of *planning* that must be added to the concentration and attention involved in reading. The writer must know the beginning of what he is going to say, and also know where he is heading with the reader, and where he plans to end with the reader. The writing—whether it be a letter or a big book—must have unity and purpose and make sense, in every phrase.

"Once more, the reader is challenged—this time by his own inability to express himself as well as he thought he could. Millions of people live to be forty or fifty before they realize that it is easier to read than to write. But lots of people who are successful writers by the time they are forty or fifty found out, when they were in their teens or younger, that writing is infinitely more challenging than reading. Yet, writing must begin with reading. It is the same as the actors and actresses whom we consider to be successful. They started out by watching others perform. They were challenged to do as well, in their own minds. Then, they learned, very quickly, that long years of rigorous attention to detail might be involved in learning how to act as well as those whom they have watched. At this point, some give up. But those who really have what it takes are not discouraged by learning that work and sweat and effort are involved. They are determined to keep going, and they do.

"The writer's first faltering efforts convince him—more than anyone else, usually—that he has a lot to learn about expressing himself in writing. If he meets the challenge and sticks to it, he likely will succeed. If he tires easily, or discourages quickly, he is not likely to be a writer."

Is the reader—turned writer—working only for himself? This is a question lots of writers have asked themselves, and many people have asked writers. Why does a writer write?

"All good things are done for someone else, and then after a while a standard of excellence is formed, and the artist works to please himself," Elbert Hubbard pointed out. "But paradoxically, he still works for others. The singer sings for those who hear, the writer writes for those who understand, and the painter paints for those who would paint just such pictures as he, if they could."

But successful writers emphasize that they did more than simply read—or go to movies—when they were in their formative years. Every one I talked to admitted that he read more than the average boy or girl, but that he also led a full life in other respects—sandlot baseball and football, parties, and long hikes or explorations in the woods. However, very few of the men who became successful writers were those who would classify as BMOC (big men on the campus). The average writer, particularly in his early life, became an introvert, for one reason or another, and while with the passage of years and the gaining of experience, many of them develop a "platform manner," and can be hail-fellows-well-met when the occasion demands, writers never do become as glib and polished, in public give-and-take, as do those persons who go into business or those who get into politics. Perhaps the reader—turned writer— learns, by reading omnivorously early in life, that no one has a toe-hold on all knowledge. He learns not to be quite as positive, quite as dogmatic, and is not quite as sure of himself as is the less-well-read people with whom he is thrown into contact. So it may not be that the writer actually becomes more of an introvert, he just becomes more thoughtful than his glib friends. The reader-writer early learns the truth of the famous saying that "fools rush in where angels fear to tread." He also comes to appreciate the observation of Goldsmith, in *The Deserted Village,* about "the loud laugh that spoke the vacant mind."

Another prominent writer says:

"When a youngster starts reading, he gets the facts, so to speak, second hand, since they come to him through the writer of the book, or articles, he is reading. As he reads more and more, and is challenged to become a writer, he finds that he also is challenged to get out and learn for himself, rather than continually getting his information from other writers, living and dead, second hand. So the writer investigates for himself. He reads *all* that has been written—or all that he can find on the subject—and then he begins to go back to original documents. He finds that writers who have written about these documents, or old battles, or whatever, for one reason or another have left out facts and points that, to this new writer, are valid. Besides, he has read on other subjects and he has formed a standard of judgment as to what's interesting—today—that may not have been interesting when the other writers were writing last year, or a decade ago, or two decades ago. The writer, after a manner of speaking, is *not* rewriting what others have written, but he is making a fresh investigation of the old subject, after having seen all, or all that he could see, of what others have written on the subject.

"This is why a modern writer on some phase of the Civil War can write a more interesting article about it, perhaps, or a more interesting book about it, than writers of other decades. They were closer to it, but he has the advantage of their knowledge, plus an inquisitive mind and a body of general knowledge that they did not have.

"Thousands of books had been written about Abraham Lincoln before Carl Sandburg did his magnificent series of Lincoln books. And hundreds more books about Lincoln have been printed and will be printed. Yet, none of them will discourage the reader of all these books who feels discontented about the subject and is challenged, in his own mind, to do a better job on yet another Lincoln book."

The reader-writer, learning of modern developments—a revolution in Cuba, an economic development in Iraq, or a trade change in Burma—is stimulated to go there and do his own research, rather than to depend on the sketchy accounts of newsmen who may know how to get the running details, but are not skilled in presenting a tapestry of facts for those who want to understand developments in their context. The reader-writer's inquisitive instinct is whetted by his reading, in his early life. Later, as he reads more, and learns more facts, his mind winnows out the wheat from the chaff. The reader becomes more selective. Finally, if he can afford it, or can become a writer and gets the opportunity, he strives constantly to go to the original source for his information, rather than relying on other writers to bring it to him. This is the point at which he becomes a creator—of thoughts, and perhaps even of words—so that *he* can tell others, better than others have told him, about life and all its manifestations and developments.

How much time does a typical writer devote to reading? Some read one hour a day, some read two hours a day, and some read for five hours a day, or more.

What do writers read? A lot of writers read books regularly, a few magazines and one or two daily newspapers. Other writers read historical documents, or old newspapers, for several hours a day, while some read foreign newspapers. Many these days spend their time perusing state documents and releases—or "handouts"—from businesses, trade associations and private groups. Some of these special groups actually put out regular publications, and writers for popular magazines spend time going through these special interest publications striving both to increase their factual knowledge and to understand the viewpoint of the special interest, which may represent some millions of people, altogether.

I know a writer who reads an average of four hours a day. Because he is interested in government leaders, national and international developments, people in general, scientific developments, religious developments, legal developments, and a mass of other subjects, his reading is quite eclectic. Among other things, he reads:

The *Congressional Record* every day (during the time Congress is in session).

The full transcripts of all Presidential press conferences.

The press releases (and they are voluminous) from the Republican National Committee.

The press releases—including the *Democratic Digest*—issued by the Democratic National Committee.

The press releases, and regular monthly publication, of the organization known as Protestants and Other Americans United for Separation of Church and State.

The press releases, and some of the publications, of the National Catholic Welfare Conference.

The press releases, and regular publications, of all possible federal agencies. This writer is constantly looking for new federal agencies—since new ones are constantly coming into being—which issue releases.

The press releases—and the 200 or 300 regular newsletters—issued by our Senators and Representatives.

The *Federal Register,* which carries every executive order issued by the President and all the rule-changes and ukases issued by all federal departments. Before any rule is legal anymore, it must be published in the *Federal Register*.

In addition, this writer reads at least a book a week, two or three daily newspapers, about six different weekly magazines and perhaps thirty other monthly magazines. It is not difficult to believe that *he* reads four hours a day.

It is this constant reading and studying that makes some writers prolific, and the lack of reading and studying makes other writers "go dry." Writers, understand that, to write, they have to *know* something. Since most people have very little real knowledge, about anything but their own specialty, they find it extremely difficult to write anything, when faced with a blank page in their typewriter. The more a person *knows,* the less he is discouraged when he is faced with the task of writing an article, a series of articles, or even a book. That is why they say an article is like an iceberg—ninety per cent of it is underwater and cannot be seen. The writer of a fact article usually has studied so much about the subject, of which he is writing, and the various points that impinge upon that subject, he can write only ten per cent of what he knows. But the reader should never forget that the ten per cent which shows is based on a mass of material in the writer's mind, his notes, or in the reference works at hand.

To generalize, the biggest single reason writers fail is they will not pay the price to become knowledgeable enough on any one subject; they won't really "dig" for new slants, new angles, new material, to give their writing depth enough to make an impression on the editor.

The mental history of mankind is outlined in ten great books, recommended by Will Durant, the historian and philosopher. Anyone who wants to be a writer certainly should expose himself to them, as well as to thousands of other books. Durant's big ten were:

The Analects of Confucius
The Dialogues of Buddha
The Holy Bible
The Koran
Principles of Christian Religion, by John Calvin
Revolutions of the Celestial Orbs, by Copernicus
Encyclopedia, by Diderot
Social Contract, by Rousseau
Origin of Species, by Charles Darwin
Capital, by Karl Marx

If *I* were making up a list, for American writers, I'd put the *Republic of Plato* and *The Federalist* papers on the "must" reading list, and leave out two others. However, a writer, or a would-be writer, should not and cannot be satisfied with reading merely ten books, a hundred, or a thousand. Also, he cannot confine his reading just to books. A good writer reads newspapers, journals of opinion, magazines, blurbs on cereal boxes, poetry, news magazines, business magazines, unpublished manuscripts, and a wide variety of other editorial material. The average successful writer reads at least three hours a day, while some of them, at times, will read all during the day and far into the night, at least during the periods when they are getting ready to produce.

XXI

Writing

and the Future

We should all be concerned about the future because we will have to spend the rest of our lives there.
—CHARLES FRANCIS KETTERING

THIS is our last chapter together in this book. At this point, I would like to tell you why I undertook the project in the first place.

For one thing, I believed there were many Americans who might be interested in reading about how successful writers do their work. It was my thought—perhaps the wish was its father—that among the millions of students in high schools and colleges, there were thousands, if not tens of thousands, who are developing the desire to get into the field of communications and to help explore mental frontiers in some way to be of service to their fellowmen. If this book falls into the hands of any of these, and proves helpful to them in their thinking, it will have served its purpose.

The field of communications demands—and deserves—*courageous* men and women. If our nation—our world—is to make the progress we must make to take care of the constantly expanding population and to help unborn generations to understand the challenges facing them, and how to meet those challenges, it will be due to the fact that large numbers of young people are inspired to enter the field of communications—i.e., to become writers. In most cases, these persons will not find it to be the most lucrative field of endeavor, but they may find that in fighting the battles involved in it, they will become better men and women for having fought— better mentally, spiritually, socially, politically, yes, even better in the long run, physically. J. Petit Senn said: "True courage is like a kite; a contrary wind raises it higher." Even those of little courage who get into the writing field find they become enriched merely by the work and thought involved.

Another important reason I wrote this book, of course, was the money involved. I have a growing family and did not inherit a dime, so any time I can take on an editorial project, I do, as long as I feel it will be helpful to someone.

I thought I could do this book in my "spare" time. It helps an anxious, active mind to stay busy on a variety of literary projects. A book, by itself, is a number of projects—for each page, each chapter and each section represents a challenge to the writer. Besides, as I tell myself occasionally, if I were not busy on a book, I might be falling off horses, *à la* Faulkner, hunting big game, as Robert Ruark does, or going to too many cocktail parties, as many other writers do. Who can tell what a writer—with time on his hands—is likely to do?

The most important reason—perhaps—that I have worked on this book is that I, myself, wanted to find out what makes successful writers tick. I believe that a man who writes a book learns more by the research, the planning, and the actual framing of thoughts, than anyone who reads it.

But behind all those reasons for writing the book there was one other underlying purpose: I wanted, in every possible way, to contribute to the future.

Unlike many individuals—including some who write quite fluently—I feel that mankind now stands on only the threshold of knowledge. I believe that what man *must* learn is infinitely more than what he *has* learned—about the physical world, about his own marvelous mind, his potentialities, his body and his spirit, about every phase and facet of communications and existence.

Walt Whitman said: "None has begun to think how divine he himself is, and how certain the future is." Philip James Bailey asserted: "It is much less what we do than what we think, which fits us for the future."

In my view, all of us owe the future as much as we have received from the past. Or, as John Buchan, Lord Tweedsmuir, remarked: "We can only pay our debt to the past by putting the future in debt to ourselves."

Great men of the past have had much to say about the future.

Sir Arthur Wing Pinero said: "I believe the future is only the past again, entered through another gate." Maurice Maeterlinck wrote: "The future is a world limited by ourself; in it we discover only what concerns us, and, sometimes by chance, what interests those whom we love the most."

Patrick Henry declaimed: "I have but one lamp by which my feet are guided, and that is the lamp of experience. I know no way of judging of the future but by the past."

There is much speculation, among those in writing, about what the future holds for those in this field, and those who are to come into it in years to come. The advent of radio caused many persons to feel that the printed word was doomed. Television was considered another "threat" by those who thought in the same terms. Yet, as we know, the amount of printed material has continued to grow faster than the population for many years. Considering that our schools now have more than 42,000,000 pupils—from kindergarten through post-graduate courses—and the number increases yearly, it seems certain that the number of persons capable of reading will be increasing into the long future.

But it is important that we all realize that there is nothing inevitable about the spread of knowledge. There will be good communications in the future only if enough people are inspired, or encouraged, or dedicated enough to pay the price to become knowledgeable in various subjects and to write about these subjects in such a way as to interest and inform millions of readers, thus spreading knowledge and understanding.

As we know—from a study of nature, a study of history, and a study of man—there also is nothing inevitable about the fact that *truth* in all its various forms will be communicated by the writers of the future. The refinements of the means of communications can well mean that lies will be spread faster than facts, and that the people who think selfishly will be able to "sell" something faster than those who think unselfishly. There is no guarantee, in other words, that the knowledge to be spread in the future will be the *right* kind of knowledge. Tyranny historically has adopted many forms, and there is no reason to think that merely because we have some freedom left today we automatically will have it next year, or a decade from now. It will depend, in my view, on the writers who guide mankind, and how much thinking they do, how much courage they exercise, and how ingenious they may be in thwarting those who would tyrannize us.

There is no doubt that the *markets* for editorial work are changing. They will continue to change in the future, as they have changed greatly in the past. Certain types of magazines—the old pulps, for example—have come and gone, displaced by paperbacks. Farm magazines have gone down in number, while business magazines have soared in number and circulation. The market for movie material is not what it was, while the market for television material is greater than ever before.

Despite the shrinkage in demand for certain types of writing, there has been a regular increase (marked by interruptions and hesitations, of course) in demand for writing as a whole. Technical writing, with all its challenges, has come into its own. So has "house organ" writing, and "club writing," i. e., material for specific magazines put out by large industries or by service clubs of all kinds. The book market increased even during the recession year of 1958, while some other types of writing were temporarily falling in demand. All in all, those interested in getting into the writing field will find many opportunities in the future. The number of great writers who have died in recent years, and the number now approaching the end of the trail, indicates that there will be plenty of room at the top for those who will pay the price in work and study to achieve. We can be sure that those who view tomorrow as "today's greatest labor-saving device" will not take any of those vacant places at the top available as others pass from the scene or retire from the melee. The writing field is one in which a person must work regularly and learn without ceasing if he is to progress toward his dreams.

In the final few words of this book on successful writers, I want to express the hope that you have achieved some new angles, new slants, or new thoughts, on the profession of writing. I hope, too, that you will want to study further the works of the successful writers in this book for inspiration and for understanding about the many aspects of the lives of writers.

If you do get some new thoughts to help you in your daily work —whatever it is—then this book will have served its purpose. And I shall strive to do better in my next one, if I can learn enough to write another book.

THE AUTHOR AND HIS BOOK

LARSTON D. FARRAR *was born in Birmingham, Alabama, on February 25, 1915. He was educated at Birmingham-Southern College, Emory University and Millsaps College, from which he received his A.B. in 1940. He began his newspaper life as a copy boy on the old Birmingham Post (now Post-Herald). In 1942 he went to Washington as associate editor of Nation's Business, and has been in Washington ever since. In 1943 he became assistant to the publicity director of the Republican National Committee and in 1945 became Washington correspondent for the Gannett newspapers. In 1946 he opened his own agency to service business magazines, including Forbes. He has ghost-written for some of America's most noted political leaders. Through the years Mr. Farrar has contributed thousands of magazine articles to hundreds of different magazines, ranging in subject from religion to American business problems, and in media from the Restaurant Equipment Dealer to The Saturday Evening Post and is the author of* Washington Lowdown *(New American Library, 1956),* The Sins of Sandra Shaw *(Signet, 1958), and the extremely successful* How to Make $18,000 a year Free-lance Writing. *(Hawthorn, 1957).*

SUCCESSFUL WRITERS AND HOW THEY WORK *(Hawthorn, 1959) was designed by Ernst Reichl and completely manufactured by G. McKibbin & Son, Brooklyn, N. Y. The body type is Linotype Caledonia, designed by W. A. Dwiggins, one of America's best known typographers.*

A HAWTHORN BOOK